Chutzpah!

Chutzpah!

Hi-Diddle-Dee-Dee, An Actor's Life for Me

A Memoir by Allen Swift

Chutzpah! Hi-Diddle-Dee-Dee, An Actor's Life for Me

Cover art © AL HIRSCHFELD.
Reproduced by arrangement with Hirschfeld's exclusive representative, the MARGO FEIDEN GALLERIES LTD., NEW YORK. www.ALHIRSCHFELD.COM
Published in The New York Times 9/24/76 titled "Allen Swift in his play "Checking Out," accompanying John Corry's "Broadway" article.

HI-DIDDLE-DEE-DEE
Words By Ned Washington Music By Leigh Harline
© Copyright 1940 by Bourne Co.
Copyright Renewed
All Rights Reserved International Copyright Secured
ASCAP

iUniverse books may be ordered through booksellers or by contacting:

iUniverse
1663 Liberty Drive
Bloomington, IN 47403
www.iuniverse.com
1-800-Authors (1-800-288-4677)

ISBN: 978-1-4917-6919-5 (sc)
ISBN: 978-1-4917-6920-1 (e)

Print information available on the last page.

iUniverse rev. date: 10/27/2015

Contents

Preface

If you hear voices, it's me.

"How do you like that son of a bitch? He talks like a pencil." The producer jumped into the air and clicked his heels. The search was over. He and the copywriter were beside themselves with joy and relief. They had auditioned over a hundred actors the day before, to no avail. Allen Swift had not been available then. Today he was, and they knew this was probably their last chance. If Swift couldn't do it, they might have to scrap the whole concept.

I'm the son of a bitch they were talking about. I am an actor who has developed a reputation for being able to sound like anyone—or any*thing.* When I got off the elevator at the BBD&O Advertising Agency, both men were waiting to greet me. They were in their shirtsleeves, looking as if they were carrying the cares of the world on their shoulders.

"Swifty! Boy, are we glad to see you. We have one hell of a goddamned problem. We auditioned everyone in New York. I mean, who knows what the hell a pencil sounds like?"

"Fellows, please," I said in a manner calculated to allay their fears. "It's no problem. Is it a mechanical pencil or wood?"

"It's wood—a regular pencil," the copywriter answered.

"Is it round or hexagonal shaped?" I asked.

They looked at the storyboard, a series of panel drawings of the commercial in question. It was hexagonal.

I said, "In that case, it's not a problem. Is there an eraser on top?"

Both men said yes with notes of excitement and hope in their voices.

"That's it?" I asked. "That's the big problem? Give me the script."

The producer handed it to me. I headed toward the mike stand but paused to ask one more question: "I take it the softness or hardness of the lead is not in question?"

"No, no," the copywriter said, but the producer equivocated. "Well, I don't think it should be *too* hard; I mean, the pencil should be likable."

"Gotcha," I said. "Let's go for a number two."

This story might sound crazy, but this type of scenario has been part of my daily life for the past half century. During that time, I have racked up over fifty thousand voice-over commercials and become something of a legend in the industry. How much of this was due to my talent and how much to my chutzpah is something I, myself, have questioned.

Chutzpah is a Yiddish word that has worked its way into the English vernacular. Its meaning, according to the Free Online Dictionary is "utter nerve." That definition, however, can be misleading. A person with utter nerve might crash a party to which he was not invited. The person with chutzpah would, at the same time, convince the host he *was* invited. (As you can see, I have the chutzpah to improve on the dictionary's definition.)

As a child of the Great Depression, I had two goals. The first was to make a living; the second was to make that living as an actor. As a stand-up comedian, I ridiculed commercials in my act. So how did I become an actor who hawked soapsuds and foodstuffs for a living? It was a total accident.

Somehow I managed to get one voice-over commercial. It was for AT&T. Scale for actors at the time was thirty-five dollars per session. That was what I expected to receive, but a check arrived in the mail for $1,700. I was sure the check-printing machine had gone crazy, and I wrestled with the moral question of whether to cash the check or report the mistake. I reported it and was told the payment was not a mistake; it was for the session fee plus the residuals for the first thirteen weeks.

Well, if voice-over commercials were that lucrative, I decided I'd make myself the king of voice-overs. The result was that while I've earned close to a star's salary for forty years,

I'm probably the least-recognizable actor in show business. A small cadre of cartoon buffs know my name from the credits for hundreds of character voices I've created on records, animated films, and television shows, such as *Popeye*, *Mighty Mouse*, *Tom and Jerry*, *Diver Dan*, and many others. Or they know me from the thirty-five live and puppet characters I played on the legendary *Howdy Doody Show*, including Howdy, or from my run as the bearded Captain Allen Swift on *The Popeye Show*. But my face is unknown to the general public.

Now, obviously, there's more to the pencil story than my allegedly uncanny ability to sound like an inanimate object. I was using my reputation as "The Man of a Thousand Voices" to sell those admen security. The other actors auditioning could not compete with that. With all deference to them, the advertising business breeds insecurity. This might have been the first commercial they'd done that required a voice for an inanimate object, while I did them every day. I have talked for lamps, mailboxes, beer cans, sinks, and even a toilet bowl. I simply put a voice to the object that seemed right for it. If the object could talk, that was how it might sound.

And in the case of people, when sports figures, such as Mickey Mantle, appeared in commercials, it was often my voice emanating from their mouths. The sponsors wanted celebrities but were often unhappy with the way these icons delivered their messages. I duplicated their voices but gave them the kind of inflection and pizzazz the sponsor needed.

I can't say I'm proud of everything I did in order to survive and reach my goal as an actor, nor am I apologizing for any of it. I admit I'm a tricky guy. I used my magic—my cunning, talents, drive, *and* chutzpah—to make it. Together, it all worked, and I had many laughs along the way.

I came into this world as Ira Stadlen. How I became Allen Swift will be revealed later.

"The Man of 1000 Voices," photo by
Cal Stadlen, *Time Magazine*, Aug. 31, 1962

Chapter 1

The Great Depression: Street Smarts in Brooklyn

I grew up during The Great Depression. The experience contributed to my success. There's nothing like a childhood in poverty for developing drive – the drive to get out of it! If I came home from school and found our furniture out on the street, I knew we had been dispossessed again. That was the way things were. You rented an apartment and received three months free rent. They called it "concession." Maybe your family scraped together enough money to cover one or two more months, and then you were dispossessed again. They put your furniture out on the street and the cycle started all over.

It made sense. Why should my parents have to pay the moving men to bring down our furniture?

My mother was a great philosopher. She made us believe that anything that cost money was no good. "In restaurants, you get poison," she'd say. She would point to a man in the street and say, "See that poor man? Look how he looks. He eats all his meals in restaurants."

My brother, Cal, was nine years older than I and my childhood hero. He was wiry and muscular and strong. He was a short man but, of course, I didn't recognize that then. He was, after all, my big brother. He moved quickly and had a way of walking on his toes with the grace of a dancer, and in manner and looks he resembled James Cagney. He was pugnacious, too, like the characters Cagney often played, and he got himself into many fights, always with bigger men. The fact that he won those fights was not lost on me. I spread his fame around the neighborhood and charged my friends a marble or a trading card to come up and feel my brother's

1

biceps. No one had more influence on me or filled me with greater love. These feelings were to last a lifetime.

The Walt Disney cartoon film *Pinocchio* came out during my youth, and I was taken with the song "Hi-Diddle-Dee-Dee, An Actor's Life for Me." Who knew those words would become my mantra? As the years passed, my mother would refer to me as her "Playboy of the Western World." This was in sharp contrast to my brother and sister, who were a great deal older and bore the responsibility of working to help support the family.

We lived in many places, but our longest stay was in a four-story apartment house in Brooklyn, the basement of which was a maze of nooks and crannies, with hiding places that were both sinister and exciting. I was five years old before I had the courage to explore it thoroughly, but from then on, it was my secret world. One day, I tried to run down there to escape a group of older boys (probably no more than six months older) who were tormenting me. They caught me on the steps and held me captive. I was frightened, but suddenly a voice came out of me that sounded tough and angry. I said, "You guys are in a lot of trouble. I know where you live, and my father is a lawyer—he's going to put all your fathers in jail, and you'll never see them again!"

To my astonishment, they all started crying and begging me not to tell my father. Wow! This was some power I'd discovered—make up a scary story, act like those tough guys on radio, and they'd believe me. Hi-Diddle-Dee-Dee!

My mother was not a coddler. I've always joked that when I was born my mother threw me out in the backyard and said, "Grow!" Not quite, but she expected her children to do for themselves. I started to walk to school by myself long before the other kids my age. In fact, I picked up a few nickels by walking other kids to school. This was something I could not understand. "Mrs. Lerner, Burton is three months older than me. Why do you want me to walk him?" I couldn't convince her, so why look a gift nickel in the mouth?

Actually, my mother's tough facade paid off for me repeatedly. The first day she let me off the leash, she packed me a sandwich and gave me a penny to buy a piece of candy

2

from the pushcart outside the school. This was a big moment. It was not only the first time I was walking to school by myself but also the first money I'd ever had, and I was determined to spend it wisely.

After lunch, I made off to the candy cart and stood for a while, watching the owner dipping apples into a hot red sauce. They cost two cents and were over my budget. I perused his wares for quite a while, my fortune held tightly in my fist. A strange kid wearing a newsboy cap and knickers down to his ankles came up to me and asked what I was going to buy. "I don't know. I'm looking," I answered.

"Why don't you get Indian gum?"

"I don't like gum."

"It's bubblegum," he replied.

"I don't like gum."

"But you get a ticket."

"What's a ticket?"

"A card with a picture of an Indian on it. Then you can play toss with it. It's fun."

I was confused. The idea of getting something that I could play a game with was appealing. But before I could make up my mind, the kid told the candy man to give me an Indian gum, took my penny out of my hand, and paid the man. I opened the packet.

"You don't like gum, right?" Before I could answer, he popped the gum into his mouth and handed me the Indian card. I stood there looking at it dumbly. Then he produced a thick packet of cards and flipped one of them into the air. It turned over and over and landed on the sidewalk with the picture facedown. "There—you see how it's done? Now you toss yours."

I tossed the card. It didn't turn over and over like his. It just dropped flat down with the picture faceup.

"There. You lose. Mine was tails; yours was heads." He picked up both cards, his and mine, added them to his pile, pocketed them, and walked off.

My God, my fortune was gone. I hadn't gotten anything for my penny. I wanted to cry. Maybe I did, or maybe I held it in until I was home and reported the theft to my mother. If I was looking for pity, I didn't get it.

"So if that's the game they play, learn to flip cards," my mother said.

"How? I don't have any."

"Look in my sewing-machine drawer. There's a deck of playing cards. Practice on them."

And that was that. I did practice, day in and day out. I kept it up until I could flip fifty-two cards, either heads or tails, at will. *Ha-ha, another power!* I thought. I became the scourge of the neighborhood, the richest kid on the block. Sure, my fortune was all in trading cards, but that was the coin of the realm. I traded them for roller skates, baseball bats, comic books, and anything else that was up for barter. So I learned another lesson: practice makes perfect.

∞ ∞ ∞ ∞ ∞ ∞   ∞ ∞ ∞ ∞ ∞ ∞

My earliest memory has to do with a dog. I was lying on the floor over a heating vent in my aunt Ida's house, curled up with her little white poodle, Tootsie. I couldn't have been more than two or three, and the dog was as big as I was. I woke up hugging her to me. She didn't move, nor did I. The hot air was rising, warming us both, and the feeling was one of comfort. Dogs have brought me comfort all my life. I've been told that when my mom and aunt put me outside in my carriage, Tootsie would sit by me and growl at any stranger who came near. I can't remember that, but I have no reason not to believe it.

My mother wouldn't let me have a dog of my own. She maintained that dogs were dirty and messed up the house. My sister's friend Edith had a dog, and my mother would say things like "Can you believe it? She lets that dog *sleep* with her!"

Well, one afternoon when I came home from school, as I walked through the empty apartment to the kitchen, I passed the French doors of the living room and sensed something was wrong. The doors were closed, and as I reached the kitchen, it occurred to me that I'd seen, out of the corner of my eye, a great many things strewn around the living room. I quickly backed up and opened the doors. The room was in shambles. There were torn stockings and pillows on the floor, and ticking covered the chairs like snow. This was unbelievable. My mother was rigidly neat. Then, from behind the wing chair, a little white puppy's head poked out. I walked over and looked at it cowering there. He knew he'd done wrong, but how had he gotten there? Who'd brought him? My mother would have a fit. I set about cleaning up the room, and when my mother came home, I explained that there was a puppy in the living room.

"Yeah, isn't it cute?" she said.

"You know about it?"

"He followed me home."

She cut a piece of clothesline and tied it around the pup's neck. "Here—take it out for a walk, and here's a dime. Stop in the grocery and buy a can of dog food." It was a beautiful pup, but I knew my mother wouldn't keep it.

When I got outside, a kid told me the dog belonged to a lady in the redbrick house on the corner, so I decided not to buy the dog food. I rang the lady's doorbell. When she saw the dog, she said, "Oh gee, you brought him home? He's such a pain. Okay, thanks."

At home, my mother asked where the dog was, and when I told her I'd found the owner, she said, "Oh, too bad." I sensed her disappointment and asked if she'd like to have kept him.

"Sure," she said.

"But you saw what he did to the living room."

"So we'll train it."

"Wait right here. I think I can get him back!" I ran as if I were doing a hundred-yard dash straight to that lady's house. I rang the bell, and when she opened the door, I asked breathlessly, "Do you want to get rid of that pup?"

"*Do* I? You bet. He's messed up my whole house."

"My mother said we could keep him if you're willing."

"You're welcome to him, and good riddance. Here—take his leash and dish, and I have a few cans of dog food, if you want."

"Yeah, sure. Wow, thanks."

"You're welcome. Just don't bring him back."

"I won't! Thanks a million."

I had a dog of my own! Speedy was a spitz mix. I don't know what the other part was, but he was all white from head to toe and the cutest thing you ever saw. And he was mine. I fed him, I walked him, I trained him, and he slept with me every night. My mother never gave any indication that she felt it had been the wrong thing to do. From the day he followed her home, she was a dog lover.

∞ ∞ ∞ ∞ ∞ ∞   ∞ ∞ ∞ ∞ ∞ ∞

There was an art club in school that met every Wednesday afternoon after classes, and I was dying to get into it. The teacher, Mr. Santora, was a tall, good-looking man with a slim Edmund Lowe moustache. Everyone in his class loved him, but when I brought him a drawing as a sample of my work, he dismissed it, saying, "Sorry! We don't trace in this club." I was stunned and angry and adamantly denied that I'd traced it. He simply waved me away like an annoying fly. I felt a great sense of injustice. My drawing was of a horse, and I had not traced it. I didn't realize until a few years later why he thought I had. I'd drawn it with an indelible pencil, which looks like something traced using carbon paper. He didn't accept me into his club, but this was a minor injustice compared to some I would encounter later in life.

In the next grade, I had Mr. Santora as my official teacher, and true to his reputation, he was a good and likable one, even though he was hard on me. When Wednesday rolled around and the class came to an end, he asked those in his art club to remain behind. Deciding to stay, I scrunched down in my seat, hoping he wouldn't notice me. He passed out drawing paper to everyone, including me. I felt like a criminal, but I wanted desperately to be in that club. He took no notice of me, so I thought, *I'm home free.*

From then on, I was in the club. We all worked on drawings and paintings for a competition held each year for schoolchildren by the John Wanamaker department store. I was home in bed with the flu, and it looked as if I wouldn't be back in school in time for the submission. To my surprise, Mr. Santora sent a classmate to my home with a drawing board, a set of pastels, and a note saying that now I had no excuse not to do my assignment. Ha! I wasn't supposed to be in his club anyway! I'd sure fooled him!

I came home for lunch some months later to find a postcard informing me that I'd won first prize in the contest. Forgetting to eat anything, I grabbed the card and ran all the way back to school and up the three flights to the teachers' room. I burst in on him, out of breath, and with a so-much-for-you attitude, I shouted triumphantly, "Guess what?"

Without looking up he said, "You won first prize in the Wanamaker contest. I expected you to. Now get out of here—I'm having my lunch." He waved his hand in dismissal the same way he had when I'd shown him my drawing of the horse. The rat never withdrew his description of my drawing as a tracing. In retrospect, I don't think I ever put anything over on him. I'm sure he knew damn well I was not in his club. I certainly liked him, though. He challenged me and helped me put things in perspective.

∞ ∞ ∞ ∞ ∞ ∞   ∞ ∞ ∞ ∞ ∞ ∞

Responsible for the day-to-day survival of our family, Mom used her talents to create the appearance of a fine middle-class home. She did this on pennies. An excellent dressmaker, she made all our clothes, the curtains, and the drapes. She crocheted all the bedspreads on the beds and the doilies on the tables and living room chairs, and she knitted all our sweaters. We always had delicious, fresh-baked bread, cakes, and cookies, legendary among our extended family and friends. When visitors dropped in they never lacked either a meal or dessert. How she did this was magical.

She was an ingenious cook and an even more ingenious shopper. Shopping trips entailed walking to eight different stores to save a penny on an onion. I know because I was often pressed into shopping for her and walked miles from home to visit a store that had a special on some item she needed or to avoid a local merchant because we owed him too much money.

She also raised two additional young children, the orphaned daughters of her sister, my aunt Bella.

It is any wonder that she had high expectations of others and could be sharp and critical at times?

My father's temperament was the opposite. He was easygoing. He seemed to exude affection for everyone. He approached any family problem in a calm, kind way. It's important, though, to understand that he wasn't dealing with the day-to-day problems my mother had to face. Of course, he had his own struggles—chasing around with various deals to make a buck, being frustrated in his profession, and trying to write. I saw my father angry so few times in my life that I could count them on the fingers of one hand. The worst cuss word he ever uttered was "Sacramento!" The first time my teacher mentioned that city in class, I put my hand over my mouth and giggled. I thought she'd used a dirty word.

My father came to the United States from Romania at the age of sixteen. According to my mother, who also came from Romania, he could speak English like a native even before he got off the boat. It's possible. He had studied English in Europe and was able to go right into the University of Pennsylvania and come out with a law degree. He was not a happy lawyer. He should have become a professor or taken an MBA, because he spent most of his time as a businessman.

Dad was a soft touch. I must have heard my mother say that at least a hundred times as I was growing up. When he made money, he was Santa Claus—and not only to his own family. He made and lost money in cycles that did not necessarily have anything to do with the ups and downs of the economy. But since the Depression, it had all been downhill. My mother was constantly at him to collect the money he had loaned to others.

"Why don't you go see Dr. Sax and ask for your money?"

"Sallie, please—the man is not well."

"So what are you—the picture of health? It's your money. He wasn't too sick to borrow."

"He is not doing so well now financially either."

"He's rich enough to ride around in Cadillacs."

"It's an old car."

"Yeah, and he lives in an old mansion, too. It's your money. Why can't you ask for it?"

"Because he's an honorable man. When he has it, he'll pay me back."

"Yeah, in the grave. It's been twelve years already. Do you ever hear from him?"

"Yes."

"When?"

"I heard, Sallie, the man was in trouble. I helped him out."

"Well, you're in trouble now, Max. We need the money."

"Something will turn up."

"Yeah, a dispossess."

"Sallie, the man is a doctor."

"So what? You're a doctor too, a doctor of laws. Why does he impress you?"

"It's not that. The man was my friend."

"Yeah, everyone is your friend when they need money."

"Sallie, I will not beg!"

"Beg? Who's asking you to beg? It's your money. Demand it! God, you're such a patsy!"

One day, my father came home and announced that he was going to make dinner. My mother laughed, but he went right on by announcing the menu. Nothing he served us was possible to get at that time of year. The food consisted of fresh fruits and vegetables that were out of season, and it was all delicious. I especially remember the strawberries. My mother kept saying that it was impossible, but there she was, eating and enjoying the dinner cooked by her husband, who was unable to boil water.

After everyone in the family was satiated, he announced that we had been eating frozen food—something completely new that was bound to start a revolution in how people ate. He was going into business with his friend who had invented it. This, of course, meant my mother's wedding ring was going back to the hock shop, so she had some questions to ask, such as "How much will it cost for each of these items?" When he told her, she laughed at him.

"Oh Max, you are so impractical. No woman in her right mind is going to pay that kind of money for fruit and vegetables. They will wait until they're in season."

It's possible that my mother never bought frozen food, but she lived to see it in the market. When she had dinner at her children's homes and was served frozen food, she never neglected to say, "It was your father's idea, and they stole it from him."

This is how I see my parents now: My father was educated; my mother was not. My mother was streetwise; my father was not. My mother was frugal; my father was a spendthrift (if he had money). My father was intelligent; my mother was smart. My mother was crafty; my father didn't have a wily bone in his body. I know all this because I have genes from both of them, and I'm one hell of a confused man. I drive my wife and children crazy by giving them mixed messages. I refuse to take a cab because I don't want to spend the five dollars so I'll wait twenty minutes for a bus to take me to a dinner that costs $150. My mother's genes have me checking the prices on the menu before the offerings, and then my father's genes pick up the tab for everyone at the table.

There was a time when my father was in the chips. I have a vague recollection of riding in a chauffeured limousine as a young child. He had a few hits occasionally, and those must have been when he made all those bad loans to his friends.

There's a family story of my first birthday. My father was closing a sale at the Chanin Building on Forty-Second Street, near Lexington Avenue. He was the broker on the deal and expected to make a great deal of money. There was, at that moment, only twenty-five cents in the house, and my mother had spent it on the ingredients for a chocolate birthday cake. Everyone was sitting around the dining table, waiting for my father to enter with a huge check for the broker's commission on a million-dollar sale. As they heard my father's step on the stairs, they put a little birthday hat on my head and placed the birthday cake in front of me. My mother didn't like the sound of his steps. They were too slow and heavy. My brother, Cal, as he retold the story to me years later, recalled that her hand shot up and pinched her cheek, a mannerism that always foretold despair. When my father entered, his face was white, and his body sagged.

"What happened, Max?" she asked.

"We got up to the point of signing. The buyer had the check all ready."

"So?"

"The buyer said, 'Of course, you'll fix the violation on that basement door.' The seller said, 'No, you fix the violation.' The buyer said, 'I'm paying good money for a building free from violations. You fix it.' The seller said, 'You're getting a damn good buy—I will not fix it. You fix it!' The buyer stood up and said to his lawyer, 'Come.' Sallie, I swear to you, it would cost twenty-five dollars tops to fix it, so I said, 'Gentlemen, gentlemen, please—it's no problem. I'll take care of the violation.'"

"Good, so?"

"So he said, 'You will not take care of the violation! He'll take care of the violation.' Fifty thousand down the drain because of two egomaniacs."

Cal told me, "The room was so full of misery that you were forgotten until that moment. We looked over at you, and your face was buried in the chocolate cake. We all burst out laughing, even Mom and Dad."

∞ ∞ ∞ ∞ ∞ ∞ ∞   ∞ ∞ ∞ ∞ ∞ ∞ ∞

Summer was my time of year. We lived a short trolley ride from Coney Island. You could find me there every day. On weekends, when Cal and my sister, Esther, were off from work, our whole family was there. We stuck a flagpole in the sand so that all our friends could find us in this mass of humanity, and we sat around in a circle, singing and telling jokes. My brother and his friends would do gymnastic tricks. They built pyramids, standing on each other's shoulders. Everyone tried to outdo the others. Someone had a ukulele, and we clapped hands to the rhythm and made up funny lyrics to popular songs.

My mother would bring sandwiches and an aluminum container of coffee that stayed hot all day in the sun. By the time I got home, I was exhausted from fighting the waves, digging for clay, and running and playing physical games, such as Johnny on the Pony. I guess when one hears of Coney Island today, it conjures up pictures of hot dogs and amusement rides. That's not how it was then. Since money was not available for those things, we neither thought of them nor missed them.

I was ten years old when the magic bug bit me. I was walking along a street in Coney Island and came upon a crowd gathered before a sideshow. An Arabian magician named Gali Gali was standing on a platform before a tent, doing sleight-of-hand tricks with little live chicks and balls. This was a free show designed to entice you to part with ten cents to go into his tent and see the real stuff. I was enchanted by one trick in which good-sized balls kept coming out of his mouth. There seemed to be an endless supply of balls. No mouth could contain more than two balls at most, so how did he do it? I noticed that he always picked a boy in the audience to use as an assistant and then let the kid go inside for free. I hung around there all day, hoping he'd pick me, and after I'd watched about six shows, he chose me. To my great disappointment, he did exactly the same show inside that he'd done outside.

Nevertheless, that ball trick fascinated me. I couldn't get it out of my mind, and I told Cal about it. I said I thought he must have some sort of machine in his mouth that kept making balls. My brother, who was nineteen at the time, said, "No, they do it with palming."

"What's that?"

"It's a way of concealing things in the hand. It just *looks* like they come out of his mouth."

If my brother told me that was the way the magician did the trick, it had to be so, because my brother knew everything. Now the question was how I could duplicate that trick with the information I had. I thought about nothing else for days. Finally, I balled up Kleenex tissues with rubber bands and stood in front of a mirror, trying all sorts of maneuvers. This went on for about two weeks before, at last, it looked to me as if those balls were coming out of my mouth. I had to try my act out on someone, so I walked into the kitchen and, without announcing anything, started the manipulation. My mother looked up from stirring a pot on the stove and said, "Meshugana, why are you stuffing all that paper in your mouth?"

Aha! Fooled her! Now to do the same thing with rubber balls. I found some at Woolworth's, and using the same sleight-of-hand I'd learned with the tissues, I mastered my trick. I was a sensation. I mystified all the kids in school; I mystified adults; I mystified my own family, including my brother; and I was later to mystify magicians, too.

I was always doing something to earn money, and it always went into the family pot. When I was nine years old, I sold a product called CN, a household cleaner. My uncle Morris hired me to sell it door-to-door. It sold for ten cents, and I was supposed to earn a nickel a bottle, but my uncle cheated me out of most of my earnings. This did not surprise my mother, who always maintained that her brother was a shady character. She dried my tears at being shortchanged and proceeded to recite a litany of his offenses.

Like many boys, I also sold magazines: *Liberty*, *Collier's*, and the *Saturday Evening Post*. We sold them to earn prizes from a catalogue we were given, but there was no money in it, so I turned to newspapers. When I was eleven, I was hired as a candy butcher at a minor league baseball stadium, the Bay Ridge Oval. This was a fun job because of the camaraderie with the older boys. Before the game, we all sat around a huge bag of peanuts, filling the little bags we'd sell for ten cents apiece. Mike, the concession owner, taught us to push up the bottom of the bag so that it contained fewer peanuts even though it looked full.

As people started to arrive, we rented cushions. We'd yell, "Soft seats, soft seats—get your soft seats!" We were supposed to charge ten cents, but the boys put me wise to a scam. "Don't call out the price unless they ask. Usually they know and will give you a dime. If a man is there with a date and asks, say, 'Twenty-five cents,' but slur it and continue shouting, 'Soft seats, soft seats,' and look away from him like you're very busy and talking to someone else. Chances are, he'll pay you the two bits for each seat, and you can pocket the thirty cents for yourself. If he says, 'I thought it was a dime,' say, 'That's what I said, mister. Soft seats, soft seats.' See, if a guy is there with a girl, he won't argue, because he doesn't want to seem cheap."

We weren't allowed to sell beer, because we were underage. Anyone who wanted beer had to go to the concession stand for it, where they charged thirty-five cents. Sometimes a man would ask us if we could bring him a beer, and we never said we couldn't. One of us would run across the street to the saloon, buy one for twenty cents, and bring it to him. He'd give us at least a ten-cent tip, so we'd make a quarter for ourselves. I was learning all the hustles.

Given our shenanigans, it should not have come as a surprise to us that Mike, our boss, was ripping us off. As I came back to the stand for a refill of whatever I was selling, he would always complain that one or two of the boys were watching the game instead of hustling. This was important news, because we all pooled our earnings. At the end of the night, Mike would total the amount we'd earned and divide it among us. Sure enough, I always earned less from the pool than I'd have made if I'd sold the stuff myself. This went on for some time, until one of the boys angrily accused me of watching rather than working. His accusation tipped me off that something wasn't kosher. I spoke to the other boys, and they all had the same story.

I had a discussion with my mother about it, and she had a solution: "Tell everyone to make a mark on their cuff every time they check in for a new basket or a new pail of soda, and then you boys can do the arithmetic."

The other boys all agreed this was a great suggestion. We all wore white jackets, and we had pencils from selling score cards, so that was what we did. At the end of the night, we argued with Mike about the amount we'd earned. He was furious.

"Goddammit!" he said. "If you don't trust me, why don't you keep a record for yourselves?"

"We did," I said, and we all showed him our cuffs.

He looked me straight in the eye and asked accusingly, "Whose idea was this? Yours, Stadlen?"

I was afraid he was going to fire me, and this was a cash-cow job. "Mike, we all trust you, but you're so busy here at the stand with all the things you have to do besides keeping tabs on what we sell—we just wanted to help."

He grunted, "Uh-huh," and then mumbled under his breath, "Smart little bastard." I didn't lose my job, and he never cheated us again.

This was obviously a seasonal job, but it had many plusses. I got to see some of the greatest black baseball players of all time before any of them could play in the majors—men like Satchel Paige and Josh Gibson. I saw Gibson pull a man out of the stands for calling him a nigger and flatten him with one punch. The job also added to my knowledge of people and of wheeling and dealing. I was becoming streetwise at eleven years of age.

I wished I could have shared all this with my brother, but I hadn't seen him for a year. In 1934, he went off to California to seek his fortune—or at least find a job. Someone had offered to pay his bus fare to Detroit to pick up a car and cover his expenses to drive it out to California. His best friend was out there, so he'd have a place to stay. It was a terribly lonely year for me without him, and it would be another year before I'd see him again.

My next job was as a soda jerk in a drugstore located on the corner in our building. All the kids used to hang out in front of the store in hopes of getting a prescription to deliver or to call someone to the phone. It's hard to believe now, in an age when everyone walks around with a phone glued to his or her ear, that during my childhood, almost nobody in my neighborhood had a home telephone. People gave out the number of the nearest candy store or pharmacy, and whoever called would ask the proprietor to please get so-and-so to the phone. There were many calls but also many kids waiting to be messengers. Deliveries and phone runs were both good for a nickel tip.

I think the pharmacist, Doc Feder, was taken with me. I seemed more mature than the others, so he offered me the soda-fountain job. He paid me thirty-five cents an hour for five hours a day, from five in the afternoon to ten at night. The first day, I watched him so I'd learn to make all kinds of ice-cream sodas, sundaes, malteds, and so on. He then told me to help myself to anything I wanted at any time. This was clever on his part, because after the first week of gorging myself, I was so sick of sweets that I had no desire to even look at what I was serving customers. Even after I got over my initial revulsion, the most I ever allowed myself was a brief taste.

There was a beautiful gal who was often called to the phone. I thought she must have been a model, and when she came into the store, all eyes were on her. She no doubt was the object of many fantasies by those of the male persuasion—I know I developed a few of my own. One Sunday, no one was hanging around outside, so Dr. Feder sent me to her home with a prescription. All the way there, I fantasized that she would be half undressed, she would sweep me into her arms, and we'd make passionate love. I'd go all the way. It didn't happen quite like that. She came to the door wrapped in an old terrycloth robe, her hair in curlers, with no makeup, no eyebrows, and a nose red from a cold. I can't remember what her name was then, but in Hollywood, they changed it to Veronica Lake.

It was 1936. I was twelve and working in the back room of the pharmacy, filling capsules. My boss was handling the front. I heard someone greeting him. "Hey, whadda you say, Doc—whadda you say?" My God, it was my brother's voice! My heart felt as if it were exploding in my chest. I ran out of the back room, ready to jump into his arms. It wasn't possible, yet it was Cal all right. But I was a head taller than he was. We hugged and kissed, and I was crying with happiness.

"Wow, look at you, Butch," he said. "What's Mom feeding you?" We laughed and hit each other and hugged again. I must have grown several inches in the two years he'd been gone, but now he was back.

"Are you going to stay?" I asked.

"You betcha! I'm home for keeps. Let's go upstairs."

One day, after he'd been home awhile, we were finishing breakfast, when Cal, in his James Cagney mode, told me to knock off the dishes.

I answered in kind, "Knock 'em off yourself."

"Knock 'em off or I'll knock off your head."

I couldn't believe what I said next: "You think you're big enough?"

"Ho, ho, ho! Why don't you get down the boxing gloves and we'll see."

I went to the closet and brought them into the kitchen, feeling pretty sure of myself. There was a kid I hung out with, Angelo Bottazzi, who was in the Golden Gloves and had given me some pointers: "Always keep your side to your opponent; it gives him less of a target. Bury your chin behind your shoulder. Lead with your left. Keep your right up in front of your face, and keep jabbing, especially if you have the reach on him." This was the period of the great Joe Louis, and we kids were always sparring and talking boxing.

When we got out in the center of the room and started to spar, I realized how much of a reach I had on him, and I was really confident. The truth was, he could never come near me. I kept jabbing, and he kept ducking. I had him, and I knew it. Then, all of a sudden, he dropped his hands to his side, started dancing around, sticking his chin out at me, and taunting, "Hit me. Come on, tough guy—hit me." He was offering me his chin as a target.

Instantly, fear overcame me. *What am I doing?* I thought. *This is Cal, my big brother. He'll kill me.* And out of the blue, it was over. I was stretched out on the floor, and I didn't even remember being hit.

My poor brother was beside himself with fear that he'd hurt me. He bent over, picked me up, and hugged me. "I'm sorry. I'm sorry. Are you all right?" I was a little shaken but fine. And in a way, I was glad he'd won, and our relationship remained as before. To his credit, he admitted that he couldn't hit me, and it was only thanks to a psychological ploy that he'd beaten me.

∞ ∞ ∞ ∞ ∞ ∞   ∞ ∞ ∞ ∞ ∞ ∞ ∞

The first motion picture I saw was *Whoopee*, starring Eddie Cantor. I was four years old, and I was walking past a theater in the evening with my father. There was a cardboard cutout of a man with big eyes that kept rolling around. I asked my father what that was, and he said, "That is Eddie Cantor, a very funny man." I begged my father to go in. I believe we were due home at the time, but he found it hard to deny me anything. I also trust he wanted to see the movie himself. I was fascinated. I remember little other than the color moving pictures in a darkened room with Indians and the funny man who rolled his eyes and sang. I must have fallen asleep, because I remember being carried home and awakened by hearing my mother berating my father for keeping me out so late.

I was to become a great fan of that funny man. I always had my ear glued to the radio when he was on the air, and the worst punishment was not to be allowed to see the latest Eddie Cantor film.

As a child, I was not interested in reading. My father tried many ways to awaken my interest, and finally, he hit pay dirt. He bought me an autobiography by Eddie Cantor: *My Life Is in Your Hands*. I couldn't put it down. I reread it recently to see how I would like the first book I had ever read. I loved it. I couldn't put it down again, seventy years later. Those were two firsts: my first movie and my first book.

I was taken by the sweetness of the man, which was evident in the book, and his drive and chutzpah in climbing out of poverty and making it in the toughest business of all, show business. I was determined to do the same. So you can imagine what a thrill it was for me in later years to meet and work with the great comedian.

I was twenty-four at the time. An agent sent me to an audition for *The Four Star Review*, a television show starring Eddie Cantor. He was looking for an actor to impersonate the great Jimmy Durante. Well, as far as I was concerned, I was the greatest living unknown impersonator. When I arrived at the audition, a mob of actors filled the room, waiting. The audition process hadn't started yet, and I was determined to get the part. Finally, Eddie Cantor walked in. There he was, in the flesh, slim and wiry, with those big dark eyes, wearing a little porkpie hat.

"Hello, boys," he said in that musical voice. "I'll be right with you." And before he could turn to go into the audition room, I stood up in front of him, slapped my hands at my sides in a typical Durante gesture, and, in my Durante voice, said, "Send everyone home—I'm here!"

He looked at me with a smile and said, "That's good. That's very good. Come with me, please."

That was it. I followed him into the adjoining room, and he hired me. All the other actors must have hated me, but hey, that's show business. I don't know what happened after I left. I didn't wait to find out. I was going to work with my idol. Also, I needed the money.

You might wonder how I had the nerve to do what I did. It was simple: I had read his book. I utilized the same daring chutzpah with him that he had used with others.

The Four Star Review was on each week and alternated its stars. One week it was Jimmy Durante; one week it was Ed Wynn; one week it was Martin and Lewis; and of course, this week, it was Eddie Cantor. The show was to air on New Year's Eve. It was live.

There was no tape-recording at the time, and this was the plot: Mr. Cantor wanted to fool the audience into believing that this was Jimmy Durante's show. I opened the show as Durante did, fully made up to look like him, schnoz and all, singing one of his songs. After a while, Eddie Cantor came on and joined me. He too was wearing a Durante nose, and after him, the other cast members came on, followed by the chorus girls— all wearing Durante noses. Finally, a little trained dog walked across the stage, also wearing a Durante nose, and the music segued from my song to a song everyone sang, with the lyrics "If the world was full of Durantes, what a wonderful world it would be." At the end of the song, the real Jimmy Durante came on and hugged Eddie Cantor, and the show was off to a great start.

I found him to be just as sweet as he came across in the book and on his radio programs. I've worked with many comedians and found most of them to be nasty people. I have a theory about why these nasty personalities are so prevalent, having been a stand-up comic myself. Until a comedian is well known, he has an uphill battle with an audience. This is especially true in nightclubs, where people come for many reasons other than to see an unknown comedian. They come to drink, to entertain a business associate, or to make a girl, and the performer, unless he's well known, is an annoyance. He or she has to fight for the audience's attention. Most comedians become bitter and angry at the very people they must please. After years of the uphill battle, the negativity seeps into their personalities. The comedian stands before the audience naked, not like the actor in a play, who has a script and others to back him up. It is the toughest job in show business.

Chapter 2

The Castle on the Hill

Everything in life seems to be a question of timing, of being in the right place at the right time. New York City's High School of Music and Art opened only a year or two before I graduated from grammar school, and it was the first public school of its kind. Each public grade school in the city could recommend four students: two for music and two for art. We had to take an exam and, in my case, as a prospective art student, bring a portfolio of my work. My father stayed up all night before the test, making my portfolio case out of cardboard covered with blue oilcloth. It was a very professional job.

The following morning, I set out early from my home in Brooklyn. I had to take a streetcar and then the subway to 135th Street in Manhattan. I remember exiting the subway and looking up to see what appeared to be a castle on a hill. I climbed at least seven flights of stairs in Morningside Park, but when I reached the top, there, indeed, was a beautiful Gothic building.

The school had everything any aspiring artist could want: gifted teachers, brushes and canvases, art supplies for every medium. There were classes in sculpture, painting, printmaking, decorative design, metal crafts, and ceramics. Music and Art was the right place for me, and I was there at the right time, when the school was in its prime. I spent four years, from my fourteenth to my eighteenth birthdays, in the castle on the hill.

Aside from its great art courses, M&A also had a full academic program. I managed to get through the academics using my writing and acting talent, my conjuring and sense of humor, my cunning, and an inordinate amount of chutzpah. I loved history and creative writing, but my favorite subject was girls. I believe there were more beautiful girls in the High School of Music and Art than anywhere else in the world.

And that wasn't all—they were also bright, and they did my homework for me. We were all members of the American Student Union (ASU). As president of the M&A chapter, I was always working like crazy for it, so maybe they felt this was good for the cause. At any rate, I never did homework.

Miss Allen was my French teacher. I know she liked me, but since I never did my assignments, she was losing face with the other students. Finally, she said to me before the entire class, "Monsieur Stadlen, your assignment is to do a report on Marseilles. You may do it in English." She was making it easy for me. "However," she added, "if you do not do this assignment and bring it in tomorrow, I will flunk you for the term."

I believed her. There were no ifs, ands, or buts in her statement. The following day, in the middle of the class, Miss Allen said, "We will now hear a report on Marseilles from Monsieur Stadlen."

Oh my God, that's right! Now I remembered. It was a terrible catastrophe. What was I going to do? My mind was racing. Slowly and carefully, I removed my assignment book, stood up, and searched through the pages for the assignment I knew was not there. Finally, I stopped on a blank page and, pretending to read from it, intoned, "This is Marseilles, Port of Seven Seas, a city that contains a little of everything, of rich and of poor, with fishmongers hawking their wares along the riverbanks—a city that never sleeps, for the pushcarts clang along the cobblestone streets day and night. The mornings find the merchants sweeping up before their shops and the housewives carrying home fresh bread for the morning meal. It is a city in some ways like any other city yet different, very different, for this is Marseilles, Port of Seven Seas." I closed the notebook and solemnly sat down.

Miss Allen had tears in her eyes. "Ira, that is beautiful. You see, class, Monsieur Stadlen didn't just go and copy something verbatim from the encyclopedia. He creatively captured the feeling of Marseilles." She then asked me for it, so she could read it to her next class. I, of course, demurred.

"You'll never be able to read it. I knew I was going to read it out loud, so it's scribbled. I'll have it typed and give it to you." She accepted that answer, and one of my girlfriends typed it as I dictated. I'm not sure the final product was exactly as I had improvised it, but if I couldn't remember it word for word, Miss Allen certainly wouldn't. The crazy thing was how I was able to come up with the fake report. It had practically nothing to do with Marseilles; I had never read anything about that city. But I had once seen a movie with Wallace Beery called *The Port of Seven Seas*, and I remembered the opening narration. I combined it with the spiel for the City of Light from the GE exhibit at the New York World's Fair, along with a little improvisation of my own. I did not flunk French that year.

Most of my teachers were aware of my shortcomings, but they didn't care. They found me charming and entertaining. Even teachers who were appalled by my radical politics liked me and went out of their way to see that I got through their subjects.

Miss Ridgeway and I were always battling about politics. She was the finest, most progressive art teacher I had and the most reactionary individual in other ways. She had the look of an old-fashioned schoolmarm, with pince-nez glasses and a voice that sounded exactly the way she looked. Interestingly, though, she was always dressed in the most beautiful materials imaginable. She made her own clothes, and her secret, she told me, was that she used upholstery fabrics.

My friend Eddie Slotkoff was in her art class with me, and we became inseparable buddies. One time, Eddie was working in clay on a bust of one of the students, Wilford, who was black. Miss Ridgeway was giving pointers to Eddie on the shape of his forehead. "You see the way the slope goes?" she said, pointing to Wilfred. "This is the reason for the inferiority of the Negro."

I was painting Wilford at an easel nearby, and I was shocked. "You Fascist!" I blurted out, and an argument ensued in which I claimed that she was still living in the dark ages of racial misinformation.

She accused me of being one of those out-and-out radicals. "Well, it's perfectly natural for you to be a radical, Stadlen. You're young. You'll change."

"If you're so sure I'll change, why are you always trying to change me?"

"Because, Stadlen, you're a very intelligent young man, so as you get older, you'll change. But in the meantime, you have a lot of little hangers-on who follow you, and they're not smart enough to change."

"And you're too old to change," I blurted out. "I mean, how many years do you have left?"

She gave me a little slap across the face, clapped her hands a few times in typical schoolmarm fashion, and said, "Back to work, everyone, back to work."

I think of her often and the paradox is that I think of her with affection.

I also had a wonderful creative-writing teacher, and in his class, I flourished as a poet. I had a piece of luck that made my reputation with the entire faculty and wiped out any negative feelings they might have had about me for my poor academic record. Mark Van Doren, who later won a Pulitzer Prize for poetry, wrote to the school to say, "Ira Stadlen's poem 'My Street,' which I read in your school magazine, is one of the finest pieces of folk poetry I have ever read."

If you're wondering how such an illustrious figure came to be reading the M&A magazine, the answer is simple: he had two children in the school. If you'd like a copy of this poem suitable for framing, simply tear out this page and mail it along with $4.95 to my publisher. You will receive, as a bonus, a copy of the complete, unexpurgated poetry of Ira Stadlen, a.k.a. Allen Swift. As an alternative, you can Xerox the following):

> My Street
> By Ira Stadlen
>
> Kids play ball 'neath the rumbling El
> Play where the pushcart peddlers sell
> Knick-knock pollywack jinga saw
> My old man can't play no more
> Forty-nine, fifty who's round my base
> Come on, Joey, I seen your face

Chosen sides, ah gimme a game
We don't play with any dame
Kids playing potsy, kids playing jacks
Kids hitching trolleys, kids scaling tracks
El train's gone with its thundering sound
Street hasn't changed for the kids on the ground

Knick-knock pollywack jinga saw
My old man can't play no more.

∞ ∞ ∞ ∞ ∞ ∞   ∞ ∞ ∞ ∞ ∞ ∞ ∞

Sam Scheiner was one of my dearest friends all through high school. One day, I took him swimming at Coney Island. When we were ready to go home, I suggested we go into the restroom and change out of our bathing suits. This was against the law; there was a big sign saying so. I knew it, but I felt it was a stupid law. What difference did it make if you went into the stall to sit on the toilet or to change your bathing suit? Although Sam was nervous, I felt we could get away with it. We didn't! No sooner had we removed our trunks than a policeman grabbed them and told us we had committed a crime. Sam was terrified, but I whispered, "Be quiet. I'll do the talking." The policeman asked Sam for his name and address, and I said quickly, "We're brothers. We both live in the same place. It's my fault, Officer. He didn't want to do it."

"All right, what's your name?"

"It's Stadlen."

He was writing. "What was that? Stanton?"

"Yeah." I had to poke Sam to keep him from correcting the cop. I was using the same technique I used selling soft seats in the ballpark, slurring my words. "Don't worry," I assured Sam. "I'll tell Mom and Dad it was my fault."

"Where do you live?"

"At 230 Clinton Road," I said. I actually lived at 230 Quentin Road.

The policeman finished writing, closed his book, and told us to beat it.

Sam was in a state of anguish. "You gave him the wrong information!"

"No, I didn't. He heard me wrong. That's his problem."

"But what if he checks and—"

"Relax, Sam. We didn't rob a bank. He doesn't have your name. This is the end of it, believe me."[1]

∞ ∞ ∞ ∞ ∞ ∞   ∞ ∞ ∞ ∞ ∞ ∞

There was a young, pretty girl in school whose father was a famous magician, Theo Doré. Ruth Doré was also a magician and had performed in the school auditorium with a stage show full of wonderful illusions. The kids, however, were less impressed than I and would brag to her that there was a kid in their class who could make balls come out of his mouth. She came up to me in the lunchroom one day and said, "I hear you're a magician. How would you like to join a magic club?" I was thrilled.

The club was run by the Parks Department and met in the Puppet House in Central Park. Dr. Horowitz, a fine magician known professionally as Peter Pan, the Magic Man, was a kind of patron saint of the club and much beloved by everyone. After I was introduced to all the members, Dr. Horowitz said, "All right, Ira, show us your act." I then realized that in order to be admitted, I had to perform for them. These people were all advanced in the art of magic. I was dazzled by the tricks they did and felt I was there under false pretenses. Shades of Mr. Santora's art club! I wasn't really a magician; I had only one trick. Nevertheless, I decided to bull my way through it. I

---

[1] Max Stack, who later became my boss at Town & Cruise Sportswear, helped Sam's father, his brother-in-law Max Scheiner, with a loan so he could start a restaurant. He turned out to be a great restaurateur. Scheiner's, on Seventh Avenue and Thirty-Fifth Street, was a smash success. He followed it up with the Jolly Fisherman in Roslyn, Long Island, which has been a landmark for more than forty years. Sam's brother, Freddie, ran it after Max retired, and today Freddie's son runs it.

stretched my trick to the limit, and in the end, I received a round of applause. I was in the club!

Dr. Horowitz didn't teach magic. He would simply help members who asked for guidance about where to find information on magic or for a critique on what they were doing. How they were coming along and what they were learning was up to them. This frustrated me. I'd been in the club for about a month without learning anything when I said to him, "Dr. Horowitz, I'm going to quit the club."

"Why, Ira?"

"I'm not learning anything."

"Well, don't you swap tricks with the other fellows?"

"I have nothing to swap."

"What about your ball routine?"

"Oh, they must all know that."

"The hell they do. *I* don't know what you're doing."

"Really?"

"You have moves there I've never seen. Who taught them to you?"

"No one. I sort of worked it out myself."

"Ira, those sleights are new. I don't know them, and neither do they. Let me tell you something: magicians are a selfish lot. They don't give anything unless they get something in return. You see, you're not going by the book, so those are sleights you've created. Don't give them away for free. Trade them for what you want to learn."

The first member who came up to me after those helpful words was a young German refugee named Jerry Bergin. As far as I was concerned, he was the best magician in the club. It seemed to me he could do anything. He had a tremendous arsenal of tricks. Casually, he said to me, "That's nice handling in that ball routine. What sleights are you using?"

I tried to be as casual as he was: "Oh, they're probably the same as yours."

"What do you want to swap for them?"

"Okay. You teach me your card production, cigarette production, thimble moves, and coin production, the color-changing silk, and the egg bag"—in other words, everything

I'd ever seen him do. And over time, he taught them all to me, and I taught him my balls-from-the-mouth routine. On the face of it, it looked as if I'd made a good deal, but it was a good one for both of us.

Many years later, I ran into my old mentor, Dr. Horowitz, and he said, "Ira, I just came from the international magic competition in Holland, and Jerry Bergin won the championship with your ball routine."

Jerry died a few years ago. He was a wonderful magician, and whenever I came backstage after seeing his act and people congratulated him on the ball routine, he never failed to introduce me as the man who'd taught it to him. Most magicians take credit not only for their own tricks but also for everyone else's. So Jerry was not only a great magician but also a gentleman.

∞ ∞ ∞ ∞ ∞ ∞   ∞ ∞ ∞ ∞ ∞ ∞

In 1940, at age sixteen, I cut school religiously every Friday to see the latest stage show at the Paramount, the Capitol, or the Loew's State. I had to see every comedian, and I would come away with their entire acts in my head. At every party, I was the entertainment, and my friends thought I was a sensation. Why not? I was doing Red Skelton's Guzzler's Gin act. Every gag Milton Berle stole from every other comedian, I stole from him. At one of those parties, a friend of the parents who worked at a hotel in the Catskills asked if I'd like a job for the summer. I was hired by the Swan Lake Inn and became a professional entertainer.

It turned out that I was more than that. I was the entire social staff, except for the three-piece band that played for dancing. I was the social director, the comedian, and the one who swept out the casino; I was the athletic director, and I also took care of the boats. For all this, I was paid the grand sum of thirty-five dollars for the season. I loved it.

Obviously, this was a small hotel. It accommodated only two hundred people, but for the first time in my life, I was in the country. For a few days before the first guests arrived, I had nothing to do, so I luxuriated in a rowboat on the lake, daydreaming and communing with nature.

The owner, Mr. Shinderman, was an elderly gentleman with a strong Yiddish accent and a set of false teeth that rattled so badly that they heralded his arrival. He took great pride in the fact that everything he served was wholesome and pure, including fresh milk and heavy cream in abundance to fatten up all the guests' children (the guests themselves didn't lose weight either). As social director, I dined with the patrons, and every time I heard the rattle, I'd say something like "Would you pass the evaporated milk, please?"

"*Crim, crim!*" he'd shout. "It's *crim!*" This always broke up everyone at the table. I don't know if he was the straight man or I was, but it worked with every new batch of guests. During the dances, he would rattle up to me and whisper, "Sprinkle mit da guests." That was his euphemism for "Dance with the ugly ones."

I was probably the youngest social director in the mountains. Nobody had any idea I was only sixteen years old—not Mr. Shinderman, not the ugly girls I "sprinkled" with, and certainly not the pretty ones I romanced. As part of my duties, I did a show every Saturday night; on Sunday, I would *tummel*[2] with the new arrivals, playing silly games to introduce them to each other; Monday night was horse racing; Tuesday was bingo; on Wednesday, I did a dramatic reading; on Thursday night, our guests were pressed into putting on a show of their own, with my help; and Friday night was for worship, which most of the young people skipped in favor of making out with the partners they had teamed up with during the week.

Believe it or not, on my salary, I was able to treat my mother to a weekend at the hotel. She really crimped my style, though. While sitting on the porch, she overheard a woman saying

---

2   tummel: noise, commotion, noisy disorder. A tummler is one who creates a lot of noise (tummel), a fun maker, a live wire, a clown, a prankster, the life of the party, and the paid social director and entertainer in the Catskill resorts that constitute the Borscht Belt.

she would like to make a *shiddach*[3] with that handsome social director, and my mother laughed hysterically. When the woman asked why she was laughing, she said, "He's a baby!" and she added that she knew because he was *her* baby. Word got around, and it broke up my hot romance with a twenty-two-year-old girl, who told me she had never been so humiliated in her entire life. It was two weeks before I could get back into action.

∞ ∞ ∞ ∞ ∞ ∞   ∞ ∞ ∞ ∞ ∞ ∞

When my brother came home from California in 1936, he was all fired up about the goings-on in Spain. He was passionately on the side of the Loyalists and talking about the dangers of Fascism. This was my introduction to politics and world events. Cal joined the Communist Party, and at fourteen, I joined the Young Communist League (YCL). It was the start of my radical phase, which would last through high school.

I don't remember who said of those times, "If you were not a Communist at twenty you had no heart, and if you were still a Communist at forty you had no brains," but it is quite apt. Let's face it, capitalism failed during the Depression. It failed as much as Communism failed in the Soviet Union. One-third of our nation was living in poverty (today that would mean one hundred million people). Although this is terrible to contemplate, it was the reality then. Is it any wonder that so many young people who were looking for a solution found it in a different system of government? Of course, there were things we didn't know at the time. We didn't know that Communism lacked something important to any system: democracy. Only in a democratic society can things be changed if they aren't working. It might take time to find the answers and put them in place, as was accomplished by the economic reforms during the Great Depression, but it can be done in a free society. It

---

[3]   shiddach: an arranged marriage, a match. Leo Rosten, *The Joys of Yiddish* (New York: McGraw-Hill, 1968).

took us ten years but the Soviets never solved their depression in over sixty years. So much for hindsight.

The fact is, I had a great time in my radical youth. The American Student Union (ASU) was accused of being a Communist front organization; that may or may not have been true. Certainly, some of the students in the ASU were Communists, and some of us were in the YCL as well as the ASU. But the ASU was more like a giant social club of young people with heart who only wanted to do good for society. None of us were interested in trying to overthrow the government. We wanted blacks in major-league baseball. We wanted to end racism and the poll tax. We wanted to protect civil rights and the Bill of Rights. Most of all, we belonged to a community of like-minded friends. We ran dances and entertainments. There were discussions and romances. All of my friends from that period are still my friends, and those of us who embraced Communism at that time now believe we were wrong but for the right reasons.

One of my pals in the ASU was Flora Manoff. We both lived in Brooklyn, about twenty-five minutes apart. We had a purely platonic relationship but a close one. She was a year ahead of me in school, and we discussed everything. We could talk about our love affairs, real and imagined. We gave each other advice and argued about what we knew of Marxism, which wasn't much. Flora was smart and a bright student. She was also a good writer and poet, and since she was a year ahead of me, I used her book reports, and no one was the wiser. Sometimes I would roller-skate to her house, and we'd yak and yak, and then I'd ask her to walk me back to my house or skate back. We'd have such a good time telling stories and laughing that we wouldn't want it to end, so I'd turn around and walk her back home.

I remember her telling me a great line her mother once delivered. She was always fighting with her mother, as teenage daughters are apt to do. Her mother, who knew her daughter was a Red, said to her, "Flora, if I'm not asking too much of you, do me a favor: just treat me like a colored person."

Flora's brother, Arnold Manoff, was becoming fairly well known as a dramatist in radio. Since I was writing a full-length play, I thought, why not get him to look at it? True, I'd never seen a full-length play; I'd only seen second or third acts, because I'd sneak in during intermission. Nevertheless, I brought him each scene as I finished it.

He was always effusive in his praise, so I decided that when it was complete, I'd produce my play as a fund-raising vehicle for the national drive of the American Student Union. When I finished the play and Arnold read it, he said, "Okay, now when you rewrite it, these are the things you should try to do."

"Rewrite it?" I asked, shocked. "Why should I rewrite it? You kept saying it was terrific."

"It is. For a first draft, it's wonderful, but there are a number of things you must do to make it into a play," he said.

I was crushed. *Make it into a play? What is it now?*

It had taken me so long to write; I felt he had lied to me all along. What a bummer. But Arnold was kind. He tried to explain to me that rewriting was part of the process. "Ninety-nine percent of plays are rewritten," he said. When he finally critiqued my play, there were so many things wrong that I abandoned it, and I didn't attempt to write another one for seven years. It took me thirty-seven years to get one produced on Broadway.

∞ ∞ ∞ ∞ ∞ ∞   ∞ ∞ ∞ ∞ ∞ ∞

Boys normally go through a girl-hating period, yet I was immune to this. I always had a girlfriend. At eight or nine years of age, it was Lilly London. She lived across the hall from me; we used to sit on the marble steps of our apartment house, and I'd tell her a movie. This was a big deal for my male friends as well. Whenever we had nothing to do, they'd say, "Ira, tell us a movie." I never had to be coaxed. I was always telling someone a movie, and believe me, when I told a movie, I left nothing out. I did all the dialogue, including all the voices of the actors. I set up every scene, including the fade-ins and fade-outs. With Lilly, this pastime was especially enjoyable; I'd sit on a lower stair so that I could see her petticoat.

Going to a movie was always an important experience for me. Afterward, I'd be moody. I didn't want to talk to anyone. My friends would come out of the theater raring to play games; they'd say, "Let's play ring-a-levio," or "Get some of the other guys, and we'll choose up a game." Most of the time, I didn't know how to get out of what they wanted to do, so I'd start an argument and walk sullenly away. I had to be alone, to play the movie over in my head. I couldn't believe they could simply walk out of a movie without it reverberating and act as though nothing wonderful had happened.

I don't want you to think that it was only a matter of sexual attraction with my girlfriends. I was hopelessly in love with all of them. Helen Plavner lived across the street in the elevator building, and that was where we first kissed—in the elevator. It was electric. Beautiful and a wonderful musician, she eventually followed me into M&A. Our romance was forbidden—which made it even more exciting. Her father didn't want her to see me, because I was too old (I think I was a year older), so we devised all kinds of codes to elude him. I would stand in the street under her window and sing a particular song—I think it was "South of the Border"—and she would find some excuse to come down and join me. We always walked hand in hand. Shakespeare knew what he was doing when he wrote about young people like Romeo and Juliet. I don't think we would have killed ourselves over our love, but nevertheless, we were in love. I had many babysitting jobs, and she would often come with me. Those were the best of times, when we could be together and smooch. We'd come up for air in time to listen to Arch Oboler on the radio at midnight.

My next girlfriend (though I'm not sure she was ever really mine) was Kay Steiner. She led me a merry chase and apparently did the same with many other boys. She was extremely sexy and knew it. My pal Eddie and I hung around her like a couple of dogs in heat. She was also secretive— or, I should say, semisecretive—about her other boyfriends, dropping hints about her affairs. *Did she or didn't she?* I wondered. Kay was the most mature and sophisticated girl I knew. She was also imaginative and highly intelligent. We would sit on a bench on Riverside Drive and pet (my, what an old-fashioned word!). Across the Hudson River on the New Jersey shore stood the huge Spry sign. It's gone now. Does anyone still use Spry today?

I took Kay to an ASU party at a member's home, and this was to become an extraordinary night for me. I always felt special when Kay accompanied me and people thought she was my gal. In a sense, I was letting them believe something I was not sure of at all. I don't remember much about the party other than that we were playing records. At one point, a Russian song was playing. When I identified it and said it was one of my favorites, a girl claimed it was a different song by a different composer. In typical macho fashion, I retorted, "What do you want to bet?"

She thought for a moment and answered, "All right. If I win, you have to take me home tonight." I was sure I was right, but for the first time, I took a good look at her. She was unbelievably beautiful. Kay was pretty and flashy; this kid was simply beautiful. She looked like a young version of Louise Rainer. I couldn't take my eyes off her. Who was she? Where had she been? How come I had never seen her before? I really wished I had been wrong about the title, but I was sure I was right. When the record stopped, we turned it over and read the label. She had won. *How about that?* I thought to myself with glee. *I'll make the sacrifice.*

Her name was Zora—an exotic name, too! Kay was standing within earshot, and I wondered how I could manage this. I couldn't welch on a bet, but at the same time, Kay was my date, and I had to take her home. Then it came to me: I'd take Kay home and then come back for Zora. I explained my plan to Zora, and she was perfectly willing to wait. Kay acted as though she was unaware of these goings-on, but when we reached her home, she insisted I come in. She said her parents were out and wouldn't be back until late. Oh God, was I in a bind. This was just what I'd been waiting for, but at that moment, I knew Kay was in my past. I dragged myself away, knowing full well that I was leaving a sack of goodies that finally might have been mine for the taking.

I was about to be exposed to a new way of living. Zora inhabited what seemed to me a bohemian enclave: two high-ceilinged rooms on West Fifty-Seventh Street. Her parents were Bolsheviks. Her mother, Nastia, had sung with the Russian opera, and to me, she seemed a freewheeling gypsy. Her father—a handsome man—gave piano lessons and accompanied singers in the room that was fixed up as a studio. There was a kitchen so small that occupancy by more than three people would have been dangerous, if not unlawful. That was where the sparks flew between my exotic Russian lover and me. It's amazing how much passion can be generated standing up in a kitchen—that is, when you're sixteen years of age.

The first time we were alone in her home and fooling around on a bed, suddenly the light turned on and her father walked in. Never have I felt such panic. Runia excused himself, turned off the light, and walked out. I was devastated. My fifteen-year-old lover was unfazed. I didn't know what to do. I jumped up and started pulling myself together.

"What's the matter?" Zora asked.

"What's the *matter*?" I couldn't believe her. She hadn't moved. She gave me that superior little smile, the same one she'd given me when the record label had proven she was right. It was the smile I'd see many times in our relationship as I came to realize she knew things way beyond my ken. She stood up and suggested we have some tea.

"Your parents are in the kitchen."

"So what?"

"I can't go out there. How can I face them?"

"Don't be silly. Come on—we'll join them."

I had to steel myself for the occasion. *Be casual now—be casual*, I told myself over and over. The casual ones were her parents. They had just seen a play and immediately started telling us about it. We all had tea, and in short order, I was able to relax. I guess I was wrong: occupancy in that kitchen must have been possible for four, because I don't remember standing. This was a different life than I knew in Brooklyn.

I was madly in love with this girl. I know because I felt things I'd never felt before. I was also in love with a new way of life and with her parents, especially her mother. This was a family steeped in generations of theater. Zora's uncle David was an actor on Broadway and a director. Theater, politics, and music were always topics in that home. Zora played the cello, and her sister, Leah, played the piano. Runia, aside from his music, was also a painter. There were aunts and uncles with exotic names; one, a chess master, had been an officer in the tsar's cavalry. And here I was, a romantic idealist, in the midst of it all.

My love for Zora brought a mixture of joy and pain. I couldn't get enough of her. In the mornings, I found a way to go to school by changing trains at Fifty-Seventh Street in the hope of meeting her on the platform. If I was lucky, we'd ride to school together. Whenever I had a chance during the day, I'd pass her room so that I could see her through the window. I'd sit in class and write her notes. At home at night, I'd write her letters and poetry. She never wrote me back. She never actually acknowledged any of it. Worst of all, she never said, "I love you."

∞ ∞ ∞ ∞ ∞ ∞　　∞ ∞ ∞ ∞ ∞ ∞

I had announced to my ASU chapter that I intended to produce a play in order to make money for the union's national fund drive. Now that I had given up on my own play, I had to find another. This became a great excuse to do what I really wanted to do: act. I went to the New Theatre League, a left-leaning group, and read the plays on their list. My requirements were that the play had to be dramatic, have a social message, and offer good parts for Zora and me. The only one that seemed to fit the bill was a one act, *Rehearsal,* by Albert Maltz. Since a one act wouldn't be long enough to fill a whole evening, I decided we could combine it with a dance.

As I look back on this evening I produced, I find it difficult to believe I pulled it off. Never in my professional career could I have accomplished the things I did at that time. The first thing I needed, after deciding on the play, was to find a theater. It had to be a hall large enough for dancing, and it had to have a stage. Scouting around led me to the Transport Workers Union hall. I went to see the man in charge of renting the hall and talked him into renting it for a night, with an agreement that we'd pay him on the night of its use. We signed contracts and set the date.

The next problem was to hire a band—and not just any band, but one with enough of a name to help ticket sales. Zora's cousin Nicky Kornakoff, who was about my age, was a jazz aficionado, and he suggested we go down to Café Society and try to hire Frankie Newton and his band. We walked into Mr. Newton's dressing room between shows and found him sitting on the edge of his bed without any clothes on, smoking a joint. (I didn't know it was a joint at the time, but my jazz aficionado informed me later.) His eyes were glazed and red, and throughout my pitch, I wasn't sure he understood me. I kept talking, and he kept saying, "Yeah, man!" In the end, I signed a piece of paper agreeing to pay him $200 the night of the gig.

With all this activity, I wasn't getting home before two or three in the morning. One day, at breakfast, my father asked why I was staying out so late.

"I'm producing a show, Dad."

"That's nice. In school?"

"No, not in school. I'm doing it to raise money for the ASU fund drive. I've hired the Transport Workers' hall and Frankie Newton's Café Society band. It's going to be a show and a dance."

"Uh-huh. Where are you getting the money?"

"Oh, you don't need money. We pay them the night of the show."

"They agreed to this without a contract?"

"Oh, I signed contracts."

"You signed *contracts*?" I could hear a bit of panic in my father's voice. "You're not old enough to sign contracts."

"Well, nobody said anything."

37

"Oh my. They could hold me responsible."

"No, Dad, it has nothing to do with you. We're selling tickets. We'll have the money."

"What if you don't?"

"Dad, the hall holds five hundred people. We'll make more than the costs."

I really couldn't understand my father's concern. Five hundred tickets at $1.25 a ticket—we'd make over $200 profit—that was simple arithmetic. I figured my mother must have been right; he wasn't a good businessman.

A few days later, I was summoned to the national office of the ASU. The national secretary wished to speak to me. "What is this rumor I hear about your chapter doing a play?"

"Oh yeah, we are. We're running a play and a dance."

"What do you mean? Where?" she asked.

I told her where and when and filled her in on the particulars.

"Who gave you authorization?"

"What do you mean?"

"I take it you're using the ASU name."

"Sure: the High School of Music and Art chapter of the ASU presents."

"Who authorized this?"

"I did. I'm the president. It's for the fund drive."

"But you can't do this. Oh my God. Let me tell you something. Every year, the National Organization of the American Student Union puts on a show with college students called *Pens and Pencils*."

"I know. I was in it last year."

"Yes. Okay. We put this on using material from professional composers and writers. We have our members all over the country selling tickets, and we never break even—and you think you're going to make money? Who's going to sell these tickets? Don't you understand? All right, I have an idea. The date of your play happens to coincide with the first day of the national convention. You'll decorate the hall with banners saying 'Welcome, Delegates,' and we'll cover the tickets. That will get you off the hook and save the ASU's name. But you must never do a thing like this again."

Well, that was easy, right? No, wrong! Four days before the performance, I got a call telling me that since Congressman Vito Marcantonio could only address the convention that night, they'd have to hold conference sessions, so the delegates would not be taking the tickets after all. How nice—they left me to swing in the breeze.

It was time to rally the troops. I called an emergency meeting and gave every member of our chapter a batch of tickets and a pep talk, and then I dispersed them all over the city to sell, sell, sell. I placed an ad in the *Daily Worker* newspaper, again on the cuff. Everybody who gave trusted me. Frankie Newton's band became Frankie Newton's Café Society Orchestra.

I then heard that the Teachers' Union was holding its convention at the Hotel New Yorker on Thirty-Fourth Street, which had a huge theater with about fifteen hundred seats. I took a slew of our members down there and scattered them throughout the auditorium with tickets. Then I went to the stage wings and told someone there that I was with a delegation from the American Student Union and that we wanted to voice our support for the assembled members of the Teachers' Union. I was immediately whisked to the podium and introduced. I made such a rabble-rousing speech in favor of teachers that Vito Marcantonio, with all his bombast, couldn't equal it. There was tremendous applause, and when it died down, I told the audience about *Rehearsal* by Albert Maltz and the dance we were running. I explained that there were students all over the auditorium with tickets for sale and said I hoped they would all come in a show of solidarity between students and teachers. We sold a lot of tickets, but there were still a great many left.

Meanwhile, back at the ranch—or, rather, at the rehearsal for *Rehearsal*—things were not going so well either. My cast didn't know how to act, and I didn't know how to direct. It seemed to me that they couldn't even walk without looking awkward. I couldn't understand it. I tried to show them. I gave them line readings. Nothing helped. Finally, my leading lady said, "My uncle is a director. Should I call him in?"

David Pressman is a wonderful director, and he was a godsend to our production. At the time, he was also assistant director to Sanford Meisner at the Neighborhood Playhouse. In no time, he had those amateurs acting like professionals. I watched him, and I could see what he was doing. He didn't give anyone line readings or show them what to do, yet he got them to do what he wanted. It was a good lesson for me. He only had to work with the cast one afternoon, and I was able to take it from there.

We rehearsed right up to curtain time. I could no longer be bothered about sales. I'd done everything I could, and now I had to concentrate on my performance. If we didn't cover our expenses, I'd deal with it later. I had my sister, Esther, in the box office. Our members were ushers. Everything was covered, and now—hi-diddle-dee-dee.

Everything seemed to go well. Nobody tripped over his or her feet or dropped lines, and the curtain came down to tremendous applause. I felt a great rush. When we took our curtain call and I was facing the audience, it looked as if many people were out there. I was heading back to the dressing room to change, when I heard Frankie Newton's orchestra start to play as chairs were being folded up to make room for dancing. I was anxious to get to the box office, but people kept stopping me to congratulate me. Strangers and adults were telling me how much they'd enjoyed the play. The crowd seemed awfully big as I pushed my way through to the box office. Esther was counting the money and motioned to me not to interrupt her. When she'd finished, she said, "There were a few people who wanted to come in, but we were out of tickets. I let them in. Is that all right?"

Like a good, honest producer, I paid off all our debts, and the next day, I walked into the national office, laid a big fat envelope labeled "High School of Music & Art Chapter's Contribution" on the desk, and walked out. Now, what ensued would be funny if it weren't so stupid. The following day, I was informed that I had been elected national cultural director at the convention, and I had to be presented to the assembly and chair a session. I wondered whether this kind of dimwitted behavior went on only in left-oriented organizations. I was just a kid, and these were college people. Harpo Marx might as well have chaired that session. At least he'd have had a horn to use every time someone yelled, "Call the question!" or "Point of order!" I had no idea what people were talking about. No one had told me to read *Robert's Rules of Order*. If they had, I'd have left the club long ago.

What I couldn't comprehend was how they could have elected me to anything. They didn't know me. Who'd nominated me, and why? Was it because I'd run a successful show and dance or because my production had made money, while theirs never had? Whatever the reason, I never heard anything more about my directorship after the convention ended. It probably was an honorary title for bringing in all that dough. It's all about money. Isn't that why rich kids who were as lackluster as I as students get honorary degrees from colleges?

That summer, Zora and I were part of the social staff at Camp Beacon, which was really a Communist camp. I know this because they had what amounted to a commissar. I wrote a comic song for one of our shows. Everyone on staff loved it, but word came down from the commissar that it was politically incorrect. The director fought with him to no avail. It was just a silly piece of comedy. These were the lyrics:

> Oh, the Nazis can take Bensonhurst,
> The Nazis can take Borough Park,
> But they'll never get to Brownsville,
> They'll never get to East New York.
>
> Oh, the Nazis may take Brooklyn Heights,
> The Nazis may take Seagate too,
> But they'll never get to Brownsville,
> They'll never get to East New York.
>
> Lay your peg pants down,
> Stop your jiving around.
> The Nazis and the Fascists
> Think they're coming to town.

We got the BMT blocked
And the IRT the same.
And if they try to get to Brownsville
They'll miss the train.

I never got to perform it. If that didn't teach me a lesson about the stupidity of their system, I don't know what would have. Another unhappy thing happened that summer. Zora broke up with me. She left me for some hunk by the name of Gino. Did I say "unhappy"? That's like saying Romeo was annoyed at finding Juliet dead. I was devastated. I was maudlin. I wrote the sappiest songs, the likes of which I would be embarrassed to print here. She came back to me after the summer, but it wasn't the same. She had betrayed me.

At the time she broke up with me, we were doing a play in which I was a Nazi SS officer who was supposed to beat her. The day before our breakup, the rehearsal had gone well. I'd tilted up her face admiringly and said, "You have a very beautiful face, my dear—the face of a Jewess," and then slapped the hand that was holding her chin. She'd duly snapped her head back as though she'd been slapped and then brought her hand up to her face as if it were hurt. I'd then slapped her hand with the back of my hand, and again she'd snapped her head back, bringing her other hand up to her face. Then I'd delivered a punch that hit her hand, and she was to fall down. That was the way it worked in rehearsal.

In the actual play, I missed my hand the first time and really slapped her face. I apologized under my breath. She brought her hand up to her face not because she remembered it was going to be slapped but because it had hurt her. And just as I came across with my backhand, she dropped her hand, so I ended up smacking her face again. The entire sequence we'd rehearsed went out the window, and before I knew it, I'd decked her. The audience gasped because it looked so real—and of course, it was. I felt terrible and believed it was all just a mistake. Was it?

Okay, I thought, *how about I buy Zora a ring?* (See? A dishrag never learns.) There was this wonderful craftsman in the Village by the name of Rebaches. All the art students loved his work. I needed three dollars, and the way I got it was insane. In those days, each subway line cost a nickel, so for me to get to school cost ten cents one way, but I figured out how to get to and from school for one fare. It meant an additional half hour each way, but as the song in *A Chorus Line* goes, "What I did for love." I did this for thirty days, saved three bucks, and bought her this knockout, handcrafted ring. She never wore it, claiming it was too heavy. I felt like strangling her. You know the calypso song "If you want to be happy and live a king's life / Never make a pretty woman your wife"? I felt that if I were to lead a nice life, I had to start weaning myself away from her. Looking back, I can say, "All right, so she wasn't a very demonstrative person, but she could have loved me just as much as I loved her." Ah, but that requires maturity, and that I didn't have.

∞ ∞ ∞ ∞ ∞ ∞   ∞ ∞ ∞ ∞ ∞ ∞

The bane of my existence, from childhood on, has been my inability to spell, and this was the one subject I worked at. I have to conclude that it is some form of dyslexia, because no matter how often I make a mistake and try to remember the correct spelling, I repeat the same error again and again. My shrink put it to me this way: "Well, Ira, just think—if you could spell, you could be a secretary." If he'd told me that on my first visit, think of the thousands of dollars I could have saved.

As a senior in high school, I had a momentous task ahead of me: how to graduate. I was so concerned that I might not make it that I didn't put my picture in the yearbook—I just drew my caricature in my friends' books and signed my name. This was probably the last time I avoided publicity of any kind.

French was my downfall. There was no way I could pass the Regents Exam in that subject. There was, however, one long shot. It required great delicacy. I went to see the head of the French department, Dr. Stock, a solidly built Englishman with a quiet, dry sense of humor who hardly moved his lips when he spoke. I always imagined that when he was not at school, he smoked a pipe.

"Dr. Stock, may I ask you a question?"

"If it's not too difficult, my boy."

"What happens if someone flunks the French Regents, but for some reason, by an error, his paper is given a passing grade?"

"That would be a very rare occurrence."

"I realize that, but what if that rare occurrence happened?"

"Why then, no doubt the Regents test would be sent back from Albany."

"But by that time, the person would have graduated, wouldn't they?"

"Interesting. Yes. He or she probably would have."

"Dr. Stock, I'm not going to be a Frenchman when I graduate. I'm going to be an actor."

"Are you suggesting—"

"No, no, no. I was just curious."

"Uh-huh. Run along, my boy. Run along."

I passed my French Regents with a 65. There is no way in hell I could have earned 65 on that test. *Look out, Broadway; I'm coming your way!*

∞ ∞ ∞ ∞ ∞ ∞   ∞ ∞ ∞ ∞ ∞ ∞

David Pressman had recommended me to Sanford Meisner for a scholarship at the Neighborhood Playhouse. When I met with Meisner, he asked if I could do a scene for him. I didn't see how I could do a scene alone, and besides, I didn't have a scene prepared even if I'd had another actor to work with. So I said no.

"Well, what can you do for me?" he wanted to know.

"I can do some impersonations."

"All right, go ahead."

So I did an impersonation of Lionel Barrymore.

"Who's that supposed to be?"

"Lionel Barrymore."

"All right, do another."

I did James Stewart.

"Who's that supposed to be?"

"Jimmy Stewart."

This went on for Jimmy Durante, Ronald Colman, and Charles Laughton.

Finally, he asked, "What makes you think you have an ear for mimicry?"

I laughed. "Because people pay me to do it, and I never tell them beforehand who I'm doing. I can tell by the applause they know who it is. You must have a tin ear."

I couldn't believe that this man was reputed to be one of the best drama teachers in the country. Needless to say, I never received the scholarship. I did learn subsequently that he was also renowned for his cruelty to students who declined to sit at his knee in homage. I probably wouldn't have fared well in his class anyway.

∞ ∞ ∞ ∞ ∞ ∞   ∞ ∞ ∞ ∞ ∞ ∞ ∞

After high school, I got a job as a shipping clerk for Town and Cruise Sportswear, but I was also moonlighting, playing occasional club dates. Every year, members of the Lawyers Guild put on their *Follies*. They played it on Friday, Saturday, and Sunday nights at the Heckshire Foundation, and wanting a little insurance, they hired a pro—me—to do a single in both the first and second acts. They paid me fifteen dollars for the three shows, or one dollar less than I made in a week at Town and Cruise. I figured that was a pretty good deal. Since I was the only pro (or semipro) in the cast, I was a standout, or, as the saying goes, a showstopper.

As I was getting my things from the dressing room after the second performance, the lawyers were all kidding me, calling me a star. One of them said, "Hey, Barney Josephson wants you to call him at Café Society."

I took the kidding and said, "Yeah, sure," and went home.

After the Sunday night show, they were kidding me even more, and I was told, "William J. Fadiman of MGM wants you to call him." I took the ribbing and my salary and ran.

The next day at work, I was called to the phone. The man on the other end excused himself for calling me at my job. He had called my home, and my mother had given him my number. He introduced himself as William J. Fadiman and said he was the national movie editor at MGM. "Are you the young man who did the two singles in the Lawyers Guild show last night?"

"Yeah."

"How would you like to go to Hollywood?"

"That'd be nice." I thought, *How long are these guys going to keep kidding me?*

"Can you have lunch with me today?"

"I already had lunch."

Another voice came on the line. My boss was listening on the extension in his office. "He can go—he can go; it's all right."

We had lunch at the Gladstone. I don't remember where it was, but it looked posh, with tablecloths and lots of silverware. I felt like a schlump, the way I was dressed, with everybody else in suits and ties. I knew who Clifton Fadiman was, because I listened to him on the radio. It turned out this guy was his brother. He was nice and kept telling me how much he'd enjoyed my performance. He said he believed I could be successful in movies and wanted to set up a date with a man named Jack Maylor, who was the head of the talent department of MGM in New York. He wrote his name, the MGM address, and his phone number on his business card and told me someone at MGM would be in touch with me for an appointment. That was all. He shook my hand and wished me luck, and oh yes, he paid for lunch. I'd been a little worried because my lunch alone cost over two dollars.

Well, you can imagine how everyone in the shop carried on when I came back from lunch. They all stopped working—the cutters, the salesmen, and even my boss, Mr. Stack. They were all over me, wanting to know what he'd said, what I'd said, when I was going to Hollywood, and whether I would remember them when I was a big star.

The call about an appointment came the following day. The waiting room at MGM was plastered with photographs of all their stars. I really didn't believe this had anything to do with me; I just couldn't get it into my head that this was real. A line by Clifford Odets kept going through my head: "This is not for the dogs, which is us." After about five minutes, I was shown into Maylor's office, an ordinary-looking space with an ordinary-looking man mouthing a big cigar behind a desk. He wasn't standing, but I could see he was short.

"Bill says you got sumtin'," he said in a dees-dem-dose accent. "Where ya been woiken? It's not important. Lemme see your stuff. I won't laugh; I seen everyting. I'll stiff ya, but don't worry. I can tell if you got sumtin'. Bill says you have, an' Bill's pretty good. We'll see."

I just looked at him incredulously. "You mean here?"

"Yeah, ya gotta routine or sumtin', right? Let's see it."

My routine took place in the subway and featured all the different characters you'd see there. The first was a pitchman selling a variety of crazy things. Then I was a kid who had just taken his girl home to the ass end of the Bronx and had to go back to the far end of Brooklyn; he told his troubles to anyone who'd listen. Next, I impersonated the way different people slept on the subway. Maylor listened for a few minutes and then flipped a switch on his intercom and spoke quietly into it. The room suddenly filled up with people, mostly women, and they began laughing. Now I had an audience, and did I go to town! At the end, they applauded, and he dismissed them.

"Bill's right—yer okay. Dere's ony one trouble wit ya. Yer a mockey" (meaning a Jew). I bristled at that, and he quickly added, "Relax, so am I, but I'm not gonna be in front of da camera—you are. Okay. We got classes on da lot. Dey'll have ya torkin' like Churchill before ya know it. Look at yer fingernails—dere filty!"

"What do you want from me? I'm a shipping clerk."

"So waddaya wan? Ya gonna be satisfied to make two hunnit a week fer da rest of ya life?"

Did he say two hundred a week? I would have signed a contract with the devil for that. At that time, my rich cousin worked for the post office and had a job for life. He made thirty-five dollars a week, and everybody said he had it made.

Maylor set up a meeting for the following week with the contract department. "Ya got a lawyer?"

"My dad's a lawyer."

"Bring 'im!"

There were a number of people at that meeting. Everyone was introduced, but I don't think I attempted to learn anyone's name. I was in a sort of haze. They handed both my father and me a contract, and one of the men explained it to me.

"This is a seven-year contract. You'll receive one hundred twenty-five dollars a week for the first year, two hundred twenty-five the second year, and three hundred twenty-five the third year. Each year, you'll receive an additional hundred a week, so in the seventh year, you'll be earning seven hundred twenty-five dollars a week. Do you understand that?"

"Yes." I understood it, but I didn't believe it.

"This all depends on whether your option is picked up. MGM has the option of continuing your employment each year or discontinuing it."

My father cut in at that point. "Does Ira have a similar option to void his own employment?"

"No, he does not."

One of the other men laughed and said, "He's an indentured servant, but hell, the pay isn't bad." They all laughed, and the other man continued, "You're 4F, right?"

"No."

"What are you—1A?"

"No, I'm nothing."

"What do you mean you're nothing?"

"I'm too young for the draft."

"Too young? How old are you?"

"Eighteen."

"Oh shit, you'll be drafted."

"No, they haven't passed the eighteen-year-old draft yet."

"They will."

"Maybe they won't."

"They will, sonny—believe me, they will. We know." He turned to the other men and said, "This'll have to go back for a war clause." Then he turned to my father and said, "I'm sorry, gentlemen—we'll have to postpone this meeting. Nobody realized he was so young. You'll get a call."

They were right. The eighteen-year-old draft law passed. I did get a call from Jack Maylor, who was shocked that I was so young and asked if there was any way I could get out of being drafted. I said no, of course, and that was the end of that.

You might think I was terribly disappointed, but I wasn't. I really didn't believe any of it. Hollywood seemed so far away, and the money—that wasn't real. That was Monopoly money, and besides, I had a great summer job coming up. I'd been hired as a staff member at Chester's Zunbarg, one of the best hotels in the Catskills. By "best," I mean the best place for performers. The staff produced original shows each year, and out of each season came the future big names in directing, acting, and comedy. This was a Catskills resort unlike any other Catskills resort. Most places were gauche or ostentatious; Chester's had taste because its owners, Ann and Herman Chester, had taste. It was a resort that drew intellectuals, writers, composers, and all manner of interesting people. No Catskills resort staff was treated as well as the one at Chester's—and I don't mean just the social staff. It was the same for the waiters and everyone else who worked there. A guest once complained to Herman Chester that the staff members were everywhere: "If I go into the pool, it's crowded with staff. If I want to play Ping-Pong, I have to wait because two staff people are playing. I think this is disgraceful."

Herman answered, "Look at it this way: In order for you to come here and enjoy our resort, you have to pay us. The staff, who make this place what it is, are so important we have to pay them."

The heart of the place was the music room, a large, beautiful space with comfortable window seats all around and casual pillows where you could lounge about on the floor and listen to music or lectures or improvised entertainment. There was always something of interest going on in the music room, even into the wee hours of the morning, when a few of us would listen to, say, Josh White, who'd dropped in after a gig somewhere else. The Chesters always welcomed performers.

They might have been playing at Grossinger's, the Concord, or elsewhere, but the Chesters would put them up for the night. In the years after that summer, when I played anywhere near there, that was where I'd head. Performers such as Jack Gilford, Bernie West, and a host of others would do the same.

We put on a weekly revue in the theater. Stanley Prager, who directed, went on to a seven-year Hollywood contract and then to a fine career as a director on Broadway. Unlike me, Stanley was 4F. He had a heart murmur and died too young, at fifty-two. Stanley was the greatest porch comic I ever knew. He had a quick mind for improvised humor and kept the guests and me in stitches. We both handled the comedy in the shows.

Billy Korff was our dancer, choreographer, and set designer. Adele Jerome worked in sketches and sang. She was married to Martin Ritt, the fine actor-director formerly with the Group Theatre. Our overall social and musical director was Lou Kleinman, a fine, gifted gentleman who was probably the soul of Chester's, having been a fixture there for many summers. The music wasn't confined to the music room. Throughout the grounds, hidden in the trees, were loudspeakers sending out soft classical music.

Chester's was made for me. I was in my element. Every so often, I'd put on a magic show. I used all of my abilities and then some. I wish that resort still existed; I'd go there as a guest. The resort ended when Ann Chester died after outliving Herman by many years. She was as beautiful on the outside as she was on the inside.

Along with everything else, I found love at Chester's. Sitting at my table one day were two newcomers. One was a plain-looking girl wearing a pair of red-framed glasses. You might wonder, in this age of designer glasses in every shape and color, what was so different about red-framed glasses. Believe me, they were startling back then, when all glasses looked pretty much the same. It was an era when Hollywood movies loved the cliché wherein the plain girl takes off her glasses and turns into a beauty. Actually, this girl's glasses attracted attention to her deep-set and beautiful eyes. Her name was Vivienne, and the words that came out of her mouth were peppered with wit and humor the likes of which I have never heard from any woman—that is to say, any woman I knew personally. Dorothy Parker comes to mind. Vivienne had that same gift—the ability to turn a phrase that was memorable. There was no doubt about it: I was in love. The summer came to an end, but our relationship went on.

I did a number of shows that fall for Russian War Relief, doing my comedy routine and acting as master of ceremonies. One production I'll never forget, because of the fantastic array of talent I worked with. Here was our lineup: Sammy Mostel (soon to be called Zero); the Reviewers, a group consisting of Judy Holliday, Betty Comden, and Adolph Green; a tall, gangling young man by the name of Pete Seeger; Woody Guthrie; and the legendary Lead Belly. Everyone on that bill was not just good but great, and if they weren't well known then, they've since taken their places in the hall of fame in each of their specialties.

In between my occasional club dates, I was seeing Vivienne. One day, I went over to her house early to pick her up, and her father was there. He was a handsome man with dark, wavy hair, and we got into a discussion. He was funny, and he was kidding me about being a comedian. Actually, he was baiting me, or attempting to. I detected a hint of cruelty in the humor he aimed at me, so I gave it back to him in spades. I was used to handling hecklers in my line of work, and that was how I treated him. There was no question as to who won the battle of words. I didn't know it at the time, but this man had never come out on the short end in such an encounter. As Vivienne and I left the house, she grabbed my arm and said in the most passionate way, "I love you!" That seemed kind of strange, because unlike me, she'd never said this before. It would be years before I understood the reason for that sudden declaration.

You might be wondering what happened to Zora. Zora, no doubt, was wondering what happened to me. I never broke off with her. Coward that I was, I simply stole away in the night, letting Vivienne wean me away from her. At the time, I believed that Vivienne was unaware of the part she was playing in this process, but as I got to know her better, I realized that little escaped her.

Chapter 3

"This Is the Army, Stay-ud-lin"

Eddie and I decided that since we were going to be drafted, we might as well enlist and choose the branch of service we wanted. We were inducted on November 9, 1942. Remember that date. It was the date my name changed from Ira Stadlen to 12183023. I will dispense with the mustering-in routine; if you didn't go through it, you've certainly seen it in the movies. I shall only report the highlights and lowlights of my life as one of the fighting men in uniform.

First of all, my father came down to see me off. As we were marched away, I looked back at him and was embarrassed to see he was crying. I couldn't understand what there was to cry about. I am a father and a grandfather now, and believe me, I know what there is to cry about.

We were at Camp Upton. One of the first procedures I remember was an interview by a personnel officer. Among his questions was "What is your occupation?"

"Entertainer. I'm a comedian."

"How long have you been in that line of work?"

"Three years."

He wrote down "semiskilled."

"What, you caught my act?"

"You have to be in a profession ten years to be skilled."

Well, that made a lot of sense. What was I going to do, argue with the guy?

I met a number of people I knew who were inducted the same day. One of them was Zero Mostel, but he didn't stay in for more than a few weeks. He happened to pass by a general without saluting. The general stopped him and asked him if he knew what the stars on his uniform were, and Zero answered, "Yeah, you have a good job. Don't fuck it up."

He was discharged at the convenience of the government. Zero was a genius actor and comedian but an irrepressible personality. It was probably for the best that he was discharged early on. I hate to think of the trouble he was capable of wreaking on the armed services and on himself. He was a definite individual in a place that brooks no individuality.

The following day, we were all given aptitude tests. We were warned again and again that anyone who flunked the math test would be sent to Cooks and Bakers School. This was not something that was said only once or twice—it was drummed into us with such force that we all tried to get math books to study. It turned out that if you knew two plus two and four minus two, you passed the test. I was happy I passed until it dawned on me: *What is so frightening about Cooks and Bakers School? I love to cook, and I love to bake.* They gave us a mechanical aptitude test on which I scored a 40 out of a possible 150. But then—ta-da!—the radio code test. Now I was in my element. They played various combinations of Morse code, and we had to identify two sets at a time and tell if they were the same or different. To me, it was as simple as the math test.

Fortunately, Eddie passed too, so eventually, we would both be sent to radio tech school. But first, we were shipped to basic training in Atlantic City. Eddie and I were assigned to room 407 in the Ambassador Hotel. The rooms were stripped of their luxury, but who was complaining? We marched and did close-order drill on the boardwalk. On our day off, my parents came to visit with my sister, Esther; her husband, Gideon; and my girlfriend, Vivienne. *Hey, this is the army, Mr. Jones?*

Our drill sergeant was from Alabama, and none of us could understand him. His commands for close-order drill sounded like a foreign language. Since nobody understood him, we were all bumping into each other. He would get angry, come up to me, stick his face into mine, and shout, "Ga daim you, Staden, you dun know yow ass fum a bushel o' wheat!"

In desperation, I answered, "Sergeant, if you could speak English, this wouldn't happen. We don't understand you."

"You thank youal can do a batter jaab. You ge-out fronncenteer anchuoudrill 'em."

If you can't understand him better than me, I'll translate. He said, "If you think you can do a better job than me, you get out there front and center, and you drill them."

I did just that. I used my actor's voice and diction, and—voilà!—they drilled like the Radio City Rockettes. Apparently, my drilling was not missed by the brass, because that night, I was called to the captain's office.

"Private, how would you like to become a drill sergeant? Before you answer, let me tell you the advantages. You'll spend the whole war right here in Atlantic City. You live in New York?"

"Brooklyn."

"You'll have a class-A pass. You will be able to go home every weekend."

"I don't know, sir."

"You can't get a better deal in this man's army."

"I don't know, sir. It sort of seems like I'd be wasted."

"All right, but why don't you think it over?"

"Yes, sir, I will." There was really nothing to think over. Why would I join up to spend the war there? It didn't make any sense. I might just as well have gone to Hollywood.

∞ ∞ ∞ ∞ ∞ ∞   ∞ ∞ ∞ ∞ ∞ ∞

I have never been as cold as I was in Truax Field, Madison, Wisconsin, where we ended up at radio tech school. Let me set the scene for you: it was twenty degrees below zero. We were put up in summer barracks that were no more than tarpaper shacks with one potbelly stove in the middle of two parallel lines of double-decker cots. I slept on the bottom cot, and Eddie was topside. We shivered all night. It was so cold that from time to time, there was a rumor that someone in another squadron had a way of making his bed so that he stayed warm at night. We'd all hike over to his shack to see how he did it. Nothing worked. In fact, my aunt Ida knitted me a woolen scarf so long that I wrapped it around me three times when I went to bed. I was still cold. I wrote my father about it, and he wrote back, "Yes, twenty below is cold, but it's a dry cold, and you don't mind it so much."

It turned out that Truax Field was a huge pork barrel for some congressional representatives from Wisconsin and their buddies, who bought up a large tract of marshland, threw up these supposed barracks, and cheated the government even on the slop they served us for food. On our way to the mess hall, we knew what was being served by the vomit in the snow from those who had already eaten. Eddie and I lived on mayonnaise and ketchup sandwiches. We dumped the rest.

We had been in Wisconsin only a few weeks when we learned that Atlantic City had been converted into a giant base hospital for the returning wounded and that all the permanent party personnel were being transferred into the infantry and shipped overseas into combat. That was where I'd have been, had I taken the drill-sergeant job; everything in this man's army was a matter of the luck of the draw.

While I was a whiz at receiving Morse code, there was something else expected of me: I had to learn to fix the radio if anything went wrong. This called on my mechanical ability, which, as you might recall from my aptitude test, was nonexistent. I sweated over this in class to no avail. I had recurring dreams that I was up in a plane, and the radio went dead. The other men shouted, "Well, fix it. You're the radio operator." And I answered, "But I only know how to turn the dials."

The classes in tech school were divided into three shifts. Mine was on the day shift, but during the night, instead of sleeping, I would also go to the graveyard class in the hope of getting the mechanical theory into my head. I would plead with the instructor to help me. He would say, "Oh, this is easy. You are an intelligent guy. I'll show you. You'll pick it up in a minute." I couldn't understand a thing he was talking about. I was terribly afraid they would graduate me because of my coding ability, which was phenomenal. I took code so quickly that they had to use a special sending device called a bug that could send it as quickly as I could receive it. There was only one way out of this. I applied to take the test for aviation cadets. If I passed, I figured I had good eyes, so I'd become a bombardier.

I passed. Thank God I would not be called on to fix a radio in flight. The only drawback was that I would be separated from Eddie, but we had already been together long enough to defy the law of averages. It couldn't go on forever. We did have a three-day pass coming to us, so we opted to spend it together for what might be our last time for the duration of the war. We went to Chicago. There were two things we wanted above everything else: a pizza and a Turkish bath. In those days, there was no such thing as a slice of pizza. In fact, pizza was unknown other than in Italian neighborhoods, and you had to order the whole pie. We got out at Union Station, jumped in a cab, and told the driver to take us to the Italian section. We drove around looking in the windows of Italian restaurants for a little white plaster statue of a chef holding a pizza. If that statue was in the window, they had pizza.

We found one after blowing a great deal of money on the cab. We didn't blow any money on the pizza. In fact, the mom-and-pop owners insisted on making us a banquet. They wouldn't hear of taking a penny from these two soldiers from New York. That might seem unbelievable today, but that situation occurred again and again all over the country during the war. The feeling of togetherness and support for the soldiers was heartwarming. We then found a Turkish bath of sorts and luxuriated in the warmth of the steam room to heal our frozen Truax Field bones.

The first day back at the base, I woke up feeling sick. I was coughing and had an awful headache. We were due to have a cross-country run that day, and I just didn't feel up to it, so I went on sick call. The medical officer stuck a thermometer in my mouth, informed me that my temperature was only one hundred, and sent me back to duty. I asked him, "Isn't a hundred a fever?"

"You have to have a hundred and one to be admitted."

"Well, can I at least be excused from the cross-country?"

"Get back to duty, goldbrick!"

I ran the cross-country while feeling sicker and sicker and continued running at the end, all the way to the hospital. I came before the same doctor who had dismissed me before, saluted, and said, "PFC Stadlen reporting, sir; I believe I have the necessary points now, sir."

I had a fever of 104. I was given a bed in a ward and was examined by a nice doctor who prescribed medication and bed rest. Unfortunately, he went on furlough the next day and was replaced by a doctor who must have been a Christian Scientist. Each day, he walked down the ward with a nurse at his side, asking each man how he felt. It didn't matter how the men answered—some said they were fine, some said they were terrible, and some groaned as if they were dying. At each bed, he would turn to the nurse and say, "Stop all medication and put him on fruit juice."

He repeated this every day for ten days until the original doctor returned. He took one look at me and whispered something to the nurse, and the next thing I knew, I was being moved onto a stretcher. I woke up in an oxygen tent in a private room with a nurse sitting by my side. "Well," she said sweetly, "we thought we were going to lose you." I had a bad case of double pneumonia. Come to think of it, I've never heard of a good case.

While I was recuperating, Eddie was shipped out—to where, I didn't know. He graduated while I was in la-la land. I was worried that I'd missed my chance for cadets, but they assured me I'd go out with the first batch as soon as I was well enough.

I was no longer bedridden and was free to walk around the hospital, so I was immediately whisked into a patients' show. Interestingly, the hospitals were the only places in the armed services that did not practice Jim Crow. I made friends with a Negro soldier in our ward who had been in show business. Roger was a singer, and he was also in the show. You cannot imagine what hostility Roger and I were subjected to in that ward. Every time I entered the ward, the other patients would yell, "Here comes Stadlen, the nigger lover." It seemed as if everyone was from Texas or somewhere in the south. After

Roger was discharged from the hospital, they didn't let up on me.

I remember a Sunday in the ward when they were particularly cruel. I, in my naïveté, tried to reason with them. I said, "Hey, fellers, you're all Americans. We're fighting for freedom. We stand for all men being equal. Don't we?"

"'Cept fo' niggers and nigger lovers."

"Come on, guys—we're all on the same side. What are you fighting for?"

"I ain't fightin' fo' shit, man. They fuckin' drafted me."

"Okay. You were drafted, but don't you realize your anger at Negroes is just a case of color blindness? If you couldn't see, you would judge a person for what he is, not for the color of his skin."

"Hey, nigger lover, you come to my town, talk like dat, we gonna string you up by da balls."

The loudspeaker, announcing that it was time for Sunday services, interrupted us. All of these God-fearing men went to their footlockers, collected their Bibles, and headed for the auditorium for prayers. I remained in the ward, alone except for a nurse who was privy to all that went on between the other men and me.

"Aren't you going to services?"

"No."

"It's nondenominational, you know."

"Yes, I know."

"And you're not going?"

"No. I'm not."

"Don't you think it might do you some good?"

"Well, what do you think? You've been listening to all that hate spewing out of those men. They all went to services with their Bibles. Is that where they're learning all that hate? I think I'll just sit here and read." I doubt that I got through to her any more than I did to them.

I was feeling homesick at that point. I wished I could be with Vivienne. I reread her letters, which were all full of humor, insightful commentaries, and, most important, love. If ever I felt like going AWOL, it was at that moment. I was fed up with the bigotry in the ward. I just wanted to be with nice, intelligent people. I wanted to be home, so what did I do? I took out a pad and wrote a radio script on the importance of not going AWOL. I went into the recreation hall and recorded it on a number of Red Cross discs, which were made of some sort of paper to enable the servicemen to mail them home so that Mom and Pop could hear the voices of their offspring in faraway places. I did all the voices, and it turned out well. The chaplain happened to be there at the time and asked me if I would record it again for him. I said he could have the set I had already recorded, since I really had no use for them. "They don't last, you know. You can only get a few plays out of them."

I was finally discharged from the hospital and sent back to radio class until my orders came through for the cadets. It was just a question of marking time. I had missed the graduation, so I was sent back to a beginner's class. Two days after I returned to class, an officer came in asking for me. He said that Colonel Dies, the commander of the base, wanted to see me. His staff car was out front to take me. For the life of me, I couldn't understand why the colonel would want to see me, and I was a bit nervous. He cleared that up quickly. The chaplain had given him my Red Cross discs, and he wanted me to go to the radio station in town to make a professional recording of it for training purposes. He had already made arrangements with the radio station, and I was to be taken there immediately.

Wow! This was great. I actually recorded in a real radio station in front of a real microphone. Not only that, but the colonel's driver and the engineer thought I was terrific. They couldn't believe how I did the whole script from start to finish, doing all the voices, without stopping.

After the recording session, the driver, who was a master sergeant, asked me if he could buy me a drink. I agreed, and he drove us to a bar that he said was his favorite watering hole. I confess that I am not a drinker. My specialty is egg creams. Of course, I would never have let on to him—I was a soldier, for heaven's sake. I didn't know what to order, so whatever he ordered, I said, "Make it two." I felt that was pretty good drinker talk. He asked many questions about my career in civilian life, and as the alcohol started taking effect, I told him one lie after another. I told him I was a big radio actor, which, of course, was my dream of what I wanted to be. He was impressed and ordered two more, so I told him the names of all the radio shows I was never in. We became bosom buddies, and when we got back in the car, he asked me where I wanted to go. "Don't we have to go back to the base?"

"I do. You don't. I have to get this back to the motor pool. You want to hang around town for a while? You can take the bus back."

"Yeah, thanks. I think I'll do that." I went to a movie, something with Irene Dunne. Then I had a steak dinner. After that, I went over to the Wisconsin Union, which was the hangout of the kids at the University of Wisconsin. Eddie and I had hung out there when we'd had a day off, and we had dated a couple of the girls. One of them, Lillian, was playing Joan in *Joan of Arc* that night at the university, so I went to see her. There were a couple of Music and Arters there, so I had no trouble bunking with them. All in all, I stayed AWOL for three days and filled my time with people as different from my fellow soldiers as could be. I even found myself thinking it could be fun to go to college.

When I got back to the base, there were three notes on my bunk: "Report to the barracks chief," "Report to Corporal Proski," and "Report to the first sergeant." I skipped the first two and went straight to the first sergeant.

"Yeah, what is it?" he said.

"I was told you wanted to see me."

"Who are you?"

"PFC Stadlen."

"Stadlen!" he screamed. "Where the hell were you yesterday?" That was a piece of luck—I was only missing one day.

"With Colonel Dies, Sergeant. Didn't they tell you?"

"Colonel Dies? What the fuck you doing with Colonel Dies?"

"Gee, nobody told you? See, I'm a writer and actor, and I was working with the colonel on a script for an orientation-training program. He called me out of school, sent his staff car for me. I thought you knew."

"I don't know diddly shit."

"Well, call the colonel. He'll tell you."

"No, no, that's all right. Shit, lemme know next time."

"I certainly will, Sergeant. I'm sorry."

"Forget it. Not your fault. Fuckin' army's run by feather merchants."

I was streetwise. Now I was getting armywise. I knew he would never call the colonel. You know why? Back in the hospital, I had written a letter to President Roosevelt. I was pissed off about something I'd read in the newspaper. We had shot down some Nazi flyers and had given them a burial with a ten-gun salute. I wrote to him to say I was outraged that we would waste ammunition on saluting the enemy. I reminded him that everyone at home was turning in pots and pans for the war effort; kids were collecting silver foil to be melted down for bullets. The next day, I received a visit from the provost marshal with my letter. He bawled the hell out of me.

"Where do you come off writing to the president? I could throw you in the guardhouse for that!"

"What do you mean? He is my president, and this is a free country."

"He is not your president, soldier. He is your commander in chief. You want to write to him, you go through channels!"

That was how I knew he would never call the colonel. He'd have to go through the lieutenant, who'd have to go through the captain, who'd have to go through the major, and who would like to go through all that and possibly come out of it looking like an asshole?

This ploy has been used many times in motion pictures about the German army. It's fun to laugh at them, but it is true of all armies and, to a lesser extent, in the corporate world. You can fool some of the people some of the time, and that's enough to make a good living.

∞ ∞ ∞ ∞ ∞ ∞   ∞ ∞ ∞ ∞ ∞ ∞

It was two in the morning when I was awakened to be told I was moving out. My orders for the cadets had come through. I have no idea why this kind of thing always happened at some godforsaken hour. I never did get shipped anywhere when the sun was shining. Maybe it was to foil the enemy so that they wouldn't attack our troop train. Did anyone ever attack our troop trains on this side of the Atlantic—or the Pacific, for that matter?

It was all hush-hush where we were being shipped. We traveled on a troop train that zigzagged across America. Where could we be going that took fourteen days? Nobody knew except Vivienne. She wrote me that she thought I'd be shipped to Jamestown, North Dakota. How did she know such secret information? She said she had figured it out because she knew of someone who had recently been sent there as a new cadet. If she could figure it out, you'd think the enemy would be able to, also. In that case, couldn't we just have gone there in a straight line? Sleeping on a cold, hard railroad train floor for two weeks was no fun. It had a point, however—the brass was getting us accustomed to the hardships that awaited us.

"All right, drive out of those cars on the double. Move your ass. You're not a goddamned GI any more. You are fuckin' cadets. Move it. Line up on that platform at attention. You, mister, suck in that gut. Reach for those suitcases. Look alive."

We weren't even awake yet. It was still dark out. Who was yelling at us? Where were we? There was a great deal of grumbling, but some sergeant would stick his face right into our faces and scream, "Are you deaf, mister? Stand at attention! Suck in that gut, get a couple of wrinkles in that chin, and reach for those suitcases!" He was so close to me that he was spitting in my face. I had no idea what he was taking about. What wrinkles? What suitcases? We had duffel bags.

Someone had the nerve to shout out, "Where are we, Sergeant?"

"In hell! Unless you stop acting like a bunch of piss-assed fairies and shape up."

I think I was awake by then. I wanted to look around to see if there was a sign on the platform that would give me some inkling as to where we were, but we were standing at attention, and if we moved, he shouted, "You're at attention, mister! You know what *attention* means? You face front. Your eyeballs face front. You don't breathe unless I give you the order to breathe."

A lieutenant walked over to him and whispered something. He nodded and backed up a few feet. The lieutenant left. He looked us all over for a few minutes and then went into the following spiel:

"Now hear this, and listen like you never listened before. Your lives depend on it. My name is Sergeant Joiner, but as far as you're concerned, I might as well be God. For your information, you are in Jamestown, North Dakota. You are going to be stationed at Jamestown College. The college is coed, but as far as you're concerned, there are no girls there. You don't fraternize with them. You don't talk to them. You don't look at them. You see them on the campus, you look straight ahead and walk past them. You understand? Now you gotta get it through your heads that you ain't stupid GIs anymore. You're future officers. According to what they tell me, you are supposed to be in the top sixty-percent of the men, and that is why you are here. Well, by God, you're going to be in the top twenty percent when I get through with you, or you're going to be dead."

At that point, one of the men asked, "Can we stand at ease, Sergeant?"

I thought the sergeant was going to burst a blood vessel. He charged over to that man and, nose to nose, screamed, "Who gave you permission to talk? Did I give you permission to talk? Did anyone hear me give this man permission to talk? Identify yourself, mister."

"I am Master Sergeant Kimble, Arthur." Some of the men snickered because Joiner was a staff sergeant. He was outranked.

"No. You're not a master sergeant here, mister. Here you are a mister. You're a cadet, a future commissioned officer unless you keep fucking up like you just did. Get back in line and stand at attention like everyone else, and by tomorrow, I want to see those stripes off your arm," he ordered.

"Now hear this! All of you," he continued, "forget what you were. You were stupid GIs. Your past rank means nothing here, unless you don't want to be flyboys and go back to what you were. Things are different here, and the difference starts right now. From now on, you don't walk. You double-time. You double-time to your classes. You double-time to the mess hall. Your walking days are over. Company, right face! Double-time, march!"

We ran up the hill from the train station to the college with all our worldly possessions in our barracks bags over our shoulders. We were tired. We were breathing hard, but we were no longer cold. What we were was angry and full of uncertainty about our choice. This didn't look as if it were going to be a happy experience. Then again, as the sun was coming up, the campus looked beautiful and was a big improvement over Truax Field.

There was something about Jamestown, North Dakota, that we learned concerning Sergeant Joiner's admonishment about the coeds on the campus. Every man of eligible age in the town had been killed in combat at the beginning of the war in the Pacific. It made no difference what we did. Every coed on the campus and every woman in town would not leave us alone.

That said, a perilous incident almost befell me. On my first open post privilege, I was walking down the hill into town, when I heard the sound of high heels clacking along behind me in an apparent rush to catch up with me. When the woman did catch up, she breathlessly asked me if there was a dance in town. I said no but I was available to dance even if there was no dance. It was early evening, and there were no streetlights, but I could see she was well built, and what I could see of her face when the moonlight shone through the trees was pleasing. It took about ten minutes to walk into town, and by then, we had already agreed I'd get us a room in the hotel. We stopped at a combination drugstore and ice-cream parlor. She wanted to call her mother to tell her she'd be late.

While she was on the phone, I had a good look at her. She was pretty; she wore maybe a little too much makeup, but she was nice looking. At that moment, one of the cadets left his date at the table and came up to me to say that his date had told him to tell me that the kid I was with was twelve years old!

I couldn't believe it so when she came out of the phone booth I asked her. She gave me an imperious look and said, "I'm old enough. I'm fifteen." I sent her on her way without even buying her a lollipop.

∞ ∞ ∞ ∞ ∞ ∞   ∞ ∞ ∞ ∞ ∞ ∞

Our quarters were on the top bay of the main building. The room was about fifty feet long but narrow. There was a single line of double-decker beds. I had the lower one again. It was first come, first take. I was sitting on my bed, showing Harold, who had the upper, some card tricks. After being mystified for a while, he asked me if I could do hypnotism. From my vast store of ignorance, I answered, "I don't believe in it."

"Oh, it has nothing to do with believing or not. It's a fact. I was hypnotized."

"You were?" I was suddenly interested. "Do you remember how they did it?"

He certainly did, and he went through it for me, word for word, with all the movements, including falling forward and backward with his eyes closed and the hypnotist catching him each time. He told me everything he remembered until he was under, answering all my questions, even about how he was brought out of it.

He could see I was fascinated, so he asked me if I'd like to try it on him. I jumped at the chance. We went to the middle of the room, and I started. All the men on the bay gathered around. "I want you to close your eyes and listen to the sound of my voice. I am going to ask you to trust me. I will ask you to let yourself fall forward. Don't worry—I'll catch you. I will never allow you to be hurt. Now, fall forward. There—you see? I caught you."

I did everything he had told me, and I began to understand what it was all about and why it worked. Then, at that moment, we heard the lieutenant on the floor below coming up for bed check. Someone turned off the lights, and we all jumped into our beds. They were terribly strict about everything. If they caught you up after lights-out, you could be walking tours while everyone else was off the post.

I was under the covers when the lieutenant came up to the bay, shining his flashlight over the bunks from the far end of the room. I was at the other end. When he got to the middle, he started swearing at someone. "What the hell are you doing out of bed, mister? I asked you a question, mister. Okay, what is your name, goddammit? Are you fuckin' with me?"

Suddenly, it dawned on me—Harold. He was yelling at Harold. Oh my God, he was hypnotized. *Wow, it works.* I got out of bed. "He is hypnotized, Lieutenant. He can't hear you."

"What the fuck you talking about?"

"I'm sorry, sir—I hypnotized him. He's in a trance."

"No shit, lemme see. You did that?"

"Yes, sir. He will only react to my voice."

"What are you—some fuckin' wizard or something?"

"No, sir. Hypnotism is a scientific fact." After ten minutes, I was an expert already. I did a little demonstration for the lieutenant. All the men got out of bed and watched. I said, "Harold, your left hand is getting very light. It's so light you can't keep it down. It is rising up, up." And of course, it did just that.

I had Harold do similar things; I became inventive with what I was asking of him, and he responded. I was excited at the prospect of being able to add hypnotism to my magic routines. "Harold," I said, "I am going to wake you up now. You are going to come awake slowly. I am going to count to ten. On each number, you will come more awake. On the count of ten, you will be wide awake. You will feel wonderful. You will see the lieutenant here, and you will shake his hand and tell him how happy you are to meet him."

I started counting, and he did as I asked him to do. He awoke with a smile, walked right over to the lieutenant, shook his hand, and told him what a pleasure it was to meet him. I asked him how he felt, and he said, "Fine. Did it work? Was I out?"

The lieutenant said, "I never saw anything so amazing in my life. Okay, men, hit the sack. You're going to have to show that to the major."

I was like a kid with a new toy. I would hypnotize anyone and everyone. I hypnotized the bugler to come and wake me up every morning before he went out to blow the wake-up call. It gave me more time to get out and answer roll call. I read everything I could find on hypnotism. I sent away to Max Holden's Magic Shop in New York for all the books he had on the subject.

The big thing—the most important thing—was the respect the skill brought me. In this college training detachment, where they treated us as if we were the enemy, where my life could have been a holy hell, I escaped a great deal of the chickenshit.

The reason we were assigned to the college was because aviation cadets were supposed to have at least two years of college. Since none of us had gone to college or completed a full two years, we were given an expedited course that was supposed to compress two years of college into six months. "Hey, Mom, believe it or not, your dumbbell son went to college!"

What further seemed about to save my life from being a holy hell was an offer from the local brass to become a cadet officer. As a cadet officer, I would be representing the wishes of the brass. I would be in charge of my squadron—drilling them, seeing that they stayed on the ball, and doling out punishments in the form of demerits.

The rule was this: when someone received more than ten demerits, he walked an hour's tour for each additional demerit. That meant instead of the eight hours of open post time that cadets were permitted each week—when cadets could go into town—the cadet had to spend the allotted time marching around the campus at 120 steps per minute. If you had eighteen demerits, you walked for eight hours while your buddies were whooping it up in town. In other words, I was to be given a chance to be a capo—a shit to my own fellow cadets.

I asked for time to think it over. It would make my life easier, and I figured I'd be in a position to make the lives of everyone in my squadron easier. I called them all together and told them, "I'm going to put this to a vote, guys, so listen to what I have to say. The only reason I would take this job is to get out of all the chickenshit. I think as your cadet officer, I can do the same for you. We are eventually going to fly together. I want us all to be friends. I don't want power over you, but I'm an actor. Out on that field, I can sound as full of shit as Joiner. I can sound like Simon Legree. You are the only ones who will know it's an act. You know how you will know? Because I'll never give out a fuckin' demerit. No one will ever walk tours because of me. If you pick them up from someone else, that's your problem. When we are in front of the brass, I'll sound like I'm kicking ass. You will have to do a little acting yourself and act like you believe me. When we're alone, though, up here in the bay, you can call me shithead or whatever you want. You will all have to vote on whether you want me as your cadet officer or not. If it's no, fine; I'll turn the job down, and we'll get who they assign us."

They voted unanimously to go with me, so I accepted. The next day, I was called to an orientation meeting with all the other cadet officers and the real ones. Major Young, the CO, was there. He was a southerner, so of course he was a CO. Up to this point, I had never met one who wasn't.

We were given a quick course on how to hate the men. The major said, "A good officer is a feared officer. That is the only way you can lead men into combat."

I was about to open my mouth and say that sounded like the infantry. We weren't going to lead anyone into combat. We were going to fly with each other as a team. But I kept my mouth shut; I would have enough time to get into trouble with the major in the future. He then asked if there were any questions. I raised my hand.

"Yeah, what is it?" he asked.

"I don't have any questions, sir. I believe you were quite explicit. I would like to make a suggestion, though."

"Yeah?"

"I thought it might be a good idea to have squadron competitions. We could drill our asses off during the week and, at the parade, show our stuff to you and the other officers. You could pick the best squadron, and maybe that one could be given extra post privileges or something."

"We ah not in summah cayemp, Stadlen. These men ah caidetds, an' we doan' mollycoddle dem."

"Yes, sir. I'm sorry. I just thought it would get everyone to do their best."

We were dismissed, and two days later, the major announced on the loudspeaker that there was going to be an intersquadron competition that would be judged by reviewing officers each Saturday at the weekly parade. The winning squadron would receive four extra hours of open post time. My squadron had all heard my suggestion as well as the major's reply, so there were many laughs.

"Okay, men, we are going to win this competition every week," I instructed them, "and I'll tell you how we're going to do it. We're not going to bust our ass. Each week, we are going to work on one thing and one thing only, which, viewed from the reviewing stand, will be so perfect that their eyes will be drawn to us. That is going to be the only thing they will remember, because it will stand out from every other squadron. Now, in order to do this, I will be using theater techniques like they use on the Radio City chorus line. It means I will give you certain rhythms to get into your heads each week. We will practice that way on the drill field whenever the officers are not around."

That is what we did—and we won the competition every week for ten weeks. As an example, one week, we focused on "eyes right" as we passed the reviewing stand. Every head turned as one, and from the officers' vantage point, that had to grab them. It stood out, and we won.

I was then called on the carpet by the major, but not for that; nobody knew what we did or how we did it. He was pissed off at me because the records indicated that I had never given out a demerit. I asked if there was any indication that my men were goofing off.

"Shit no, Stadlen, but you can't tell me you got a bunch of angels there."

"No, sir, I don't think they are angels, but you said something at our meeting that stuck in my head: 'A good officer is a feared officer.' Now maybe they fuck up with somebody else but they are too damn afraid to do it in front of me. The moment they do, I'll throw the book at them."

What could he say? He mumbled about never having seen a group without a fuckup. He made it a point to come out on the drill field to watch us one day. I acted like the sergeant in *Beau Geste*. God, I was mean! When I went over to one of the men, I must have been so convincing that he said, "Fuck you, Stadlen."

I didn't think the major was in earshot, so without losing a beat, I said under my breath, "Schmuck, the major is watching." Fortunately, the major didn't hear him, or I would have had to give Mr. Russo my first demerit.

We were all being taught to fly at a small airfield in Jamestown. We weren't flying anything big, of course—light planes, such as Piper Cubs. They were two-seaters. The instructor sat in the front, and the student in back; there was a dual set of controls. A rumor started circulating that before we could graduate, we would each have to make two practice parachute jumps. This caused much consternation among the men. There was a great deal of talk of quitting. "We didn't join that branch of the service," people said.

I must say that I was frightened myself. Somehow, when you're in a plane, there's a sense of safety and comfort in being surrounded by the walls of the fuselage. I figured I'd never have the guts to jump out at eight thousand feet. Major Young was always terribly upset by the rumors, which he called "latrine-a-grams." Four or five times a week, he'd get on the loudspeaker and warn that he would not tolerate latrine-a-grams and that anyone spreading them would be severely punished.

The parachuting rumor turned out to be false. My flying instructor set us straight when he asked, "Why practice something that has to be perfect the first time?" We all breathed sighs of relief.

I found being up in a plane exhilarating. My training took place before most people flew on commercial airlines, and I enjoyed the power of flying the plane myself. I'm not sure my instructor felt the same way with me at the controls. My big problem was that I never knew what direction I was flying, but other than that, I practiced takeoffs and landings without killing either of us.

Finally, I was on my solo flight, flying with the instructor in the plane—he was not to do anything other than just sit there. It was early in the morning, and the weather was sunny and beautiful; the air was clean and crisp. I climbed into the rear seat. My instructor looked at me through the rearview mirror and asked, "All set, Smiling Jack?"

I gave him a thumbs-up and answered, "Roger." I don't know if the cartoon strip *Smiling Jack* is still in newspapers, but it was big in those days.

"Take her up to seven thousand feet, do two and a half spins to the left, level off, bring it out of the dive, and we'll go from there."

I went down the field and did a perfect takeoff. I climbed to seven thousand feet; raised the nose up till it stalled into a dive; gave it left aileron, making it spin to the left; counted two and a half spins; leveled out into the dive; and started to pull back the stick to take it out of the dive. But the stick was stuck. I pulled hard, but there was no give. I pounded on the instructor's back and indicated I couldn't get the stick back and shouted over the sound of the engine. I could see that he was trying to pull his stick back. He turned his head to me and shouted, "It's jammed. We'll have to jump."

Remember my feeling of comfort at having the plane's walls about me? I wouldn't let him beat me out of the plane. I sprang up from my seat, but at that moment, he put his hand up, holding me back from the door as he leveled off. "You'll find it awfully hard on your feet without a chute," he advised.

I looked down at my seat, and there was my chute. I'd never buckled it on me. He obviously had noticed when I'd gotten in and decided to teach me a lesson. It worked. To this day, when I am in a commercial airliner, I always feel my backside as if something is missing.

∞ ∞ ∞ ∞ ∞ ∞   ∞ ∞ ∞ ∞ ∞ ∞

One night, up in the bay, I was showing Harold some card tricks. In this case, I was exposing various gamblers' cons that were really not gamblers' cons at all. They were magicians' tricks, but I was talking as though I were an expert on gambling. I would make up stories that enhanced the tricks and my reputation at the same time. In one particular trick, I showed an ace of hearts, and as I placed it facedown, I let flash that it was not an ace of hearts but, in reality, the three of hearts. I did this in such a way as to make Harold think he had seen something he wasn't supposed to see. Then I said, "What will you bet that I can change that ace of hearts into a three of hearts?"

This is a sucker trick. Since he had seen what he believed was a three of hearts already down there, he would call me on it and say, "It's already the three of hearts." I would act hurt that he disbelieved me and ask him to pick up the card to see it was the ace of hearts. That basically is the way the trick is supposed to work. However, unbeknownst to me, a stranger who had wandered up to our bay was standing behind me and was privy to the same thing as Harold. Just as I asked Harold, "What will you bet I couldn't change that ace of hearts into a three of hearts?" the stranger leaped forward and angrily said, "I bet you fifty dollars it is already a three of hearts."

"Excuse me—I'm just showing my friend some card tricks."

"Bullshit, I'm calling your bet. Fifty bucks says you can't change the three of hearts into the ace of hearts."

This, of course, is the way it is supposed to happen in my gambling story, only I was not gambling and couldn't convince this fellow of that. He became more and more belligerent, insisting I take his bet. I decided to milk it for what it was worth.

"Look, my friend, I don't want to take your money. I'm a magician. I can make any two cards change places."

"Horseshit. Fifty dollars."

"Look, fella, you're pissing your money away. I can do it."

"Fifty dollars. You made the bet. I'm calling."

"Yeah, but you don't know me. You didn't know I was a magician. I can't take your money."

"You're not takin' mine, buddy—I'm takin' yours. Come on—fifty dollars!"

"I'll give you one more chance to get out of this."

"Fuck you!" He kept waving his fifty dollars in my face. Finally, I took my money out. We had all been paid that day, and I guess he was burning for some action.

"This is going to hurt me more than it hurts you, because I am not a gambler. You're on!"

By this time, all the men in the bay were gathered around, drawn by the stranger's loud and vitriolic behavior. I put my money down and told him to pick up the card. I wish I could convey the smug look on his face as he turned over the card and then the instant shock as he threw his money down and ran out of the bay and down the stairs, cursing all the way.

Now, you might think I would never have heard from that fellow again, but I did. About half an hour later, he arrived with about six or seven men from another squadron, pointed me out, and said, "This is the guy."

One of his buddies took a deck of cards out of his pocket and went through them, removing the three of hearts and the ace of hearts. He put them on the floor and said, "You can make these cards change places?"

"He can do it," said the stranger. "That's what he did to me. Cost me fifty bucks."

Now everybody was standing around to see the show. I said, "Pick up the ace and put it in your pocket, and turn the three facedown and step on it. I have a hundred dollars that says the card in your pocket is the ace. Look in your pocket. Make sure it's the ace." He did. "Now look at the card under your foot. Make sure it's the three."

"It is," he said without looking.

"Look at it. I want everybody to see that the three is under your foot and the ace is in your pocket. I don't want any misunderstanding. Now I have a hundred dollars that says these cards will change places. The ace is going to be under your foot and the three is going to be in your pocket."

"He can do it. That is exactly what he did to me," the stranger said.

Now, of course, that wasn't at all what I had done to him. But the psychology here was that he had a choice. He was a fool, or I was a miracle worker. Obviously, I was a miracle worker. His buddy with the ace in his pocket said, "You can do that?"

"I have a hundred dollars that says I can."

"Don't bet him. He can do it. That's what he did to me."

"If you can make the card in my pocket change places with the card under my foot, I'm getting out of this outfit."

"Well, that is your choice. You can see it for a hundred dollars." He picked up the card on the floor, took another look at the card in his pocket, and then placed them back in the card case and left with the entire entourage.

I am quite sure that those men never forgot that evening and have probably told the story, which grew in its telling and in their minds as fact. I know this because people have told me stories of impossible feats of magic they claim to have seen that I know did not happen as they told them. In magic, the effect (what the audience thinks they have seen) in most cases differs completely from what was actually done.

There is one exception: accidents. Magicians do have accidents. Some are happy accidents, in which case someone might have seen a miracle that probably could not be duplicated. I remember an accident that I had some years after World War II. I was never a magic act per se. I acted and did voice-overs but only occasionally did a full magic show, and then it was mostly for magicians. On this occasion, I planned to open my show with a cigarette routine where I produced a lit match from my pocket to light the cigarette in my mouth. Throughout the act, I would put the lit match back in my pocket and repeatedly take it out and put it back, always lit. In order to accomplish this feat, I had a piece of sandpaper in my pocket, along with a number of matches. What I did not know was that I had four eight-by-ten sheets of flash paper in my pocket. I had forgotten they were there, because I hadn't worn that suit for some time. When I pulled the lit match from my pocket, I went up in a sheet of flames. The fire lasted no more than a second, but it enveloped my entire body. It shot out from my pants legs, my sleeves—everywhere—and though I felt a moment of heat, miraculously, I was not burned. I received tremendous applause from my peers, and those who were there always refer to that great opening in my act. They all would love to see it again but "Leave them wanting more," I always say.

∞ ∞ ∞ ∞ ∞ ∞   ∞ ∞ ∞ ∞ ∞ ∞

Ira and his dad, Max Stadlen 1943.
Home on leave during World War II.

I received a letter from home saying my mother was ill so I was given a 10-day furlough. My mother didn't look very sick; in fact, she looked damned good for a woman with blood pressure of 200. Perhaps she was simply HOMEsick for her baby. It was seven months since I was home and being back with my family was rejuvenating but I couldn't wait for another rejuvenating experience.

Vivienne! Holding her in my arms reminded me of all I'd been missing and I didn't want to miss it any more. I asked her to marry me. She agreed but we had to work fast. There were blood tests to get and we had to tell our folks. Train travel took up four days of my furlough so it was all rush-rush.

It's interesting, now that I look back on it, that nobody tried to dissuade us from rushing into marriage. After all, I was nineteen and Viv was four years older. Not that I thought about it then. I guess they didn't for the same reason we didn't. We were in love and a war was going on. Everything was speeded up. Hurry up and live.

On June 22, 1943 we had a traditional Jewish ceremony where the bride circles around the groom a number of times. Vivienne's grandmother was very old and religious so it was really for her. We were a very small group, maybe ten of us. Viv's father took us all to a wedding breakfast at Horn & Hardart's Automat.

At nineteen I didn't really have any insight. Had I, I would have wondered what kind of relationship my new wife had with the father of the bride. Here was a wealthy man whose only daughter was getting married and this was his way of sending her off? It didn't have to be breakfast at Tiffany's, but the Automat?!!

Our honeymoon night was spent in the Hotel Brevoort on Fifth Avenue down in the Village, a lovely old historic hotel. Of course, it no longer exists. I was ecstatic. I hoped Viv was, too, but what was most memorable, unfortunately, was the morning after. I've always been an easy riser. As I've mentioned, at home we always had the radio on in the morning and there was the smell of homemade bread or something wonderful cooking on the stove. I woke up joyously on my first married morning, turned on the radio, got back into bed, kissed my wife and said, "Rise and shine, sweetheart. It's a beautiful day." She whipped her head around to look at me. Her face was contorted like someone responding to Dracula, ready to put his fangs in her neck.

"You must be CRAZY!" she shrieked.

OK, so she is not an easy riser, I thought. I'll have to remember that.

∞ ∞ ∞ ∞ ∞ ∞   ∞ ∞ ∞ ∞ ∞ ∞

Jamestown was extremely hot during July and August. This provided a wonderful opportunity for the brass to practice their cruelty. Out on the parade ground, they would keep the men standing in exaggerated positions of attention until they keeled over. By God, they were going to make men of us! I hated them. There was no reason for it except to feed their sadistic lust for power. I remember poor Harold fainting, and I was powerless to do anything but stand there. Anyone who went to help suffered so many demerits that he would never get off the campus. I remember we would come off the parade field and drink bottle after bottle of Coca-Cola. Some men would pour it over their heads.

As our schooling was coming to an end, the proverbial shit hit the fan. I was attending a meeting of the combined cadet officers and the real ones. A lieutenant was giving a report on his problem getting special shoulder patches made in town. He said, "I went to the damn Jew in town and showed him the design. At first, the damn Jew didn't want to do it unless we came up with how much we'd pay. I tried to Jew the damn Jew down but—"

At that point, I was smoldering, so I said, "Do you use the words 'damn Jew' like they are one word, Lieutenant?"

"Yes, I do. What's it to you?"

"Plenty. I happen to be Jewish."

"Well, that's too fuckin' bad; that's how I feel about them."

"Then you're fighting on the wrong side. You should be in Hitler's army."

At that point, the major entered the fray. "For that matter, Stadlen, Hitler is the worst damn Jew I know of."

"Hitler is a Jew, Major?"

"It's been rumored to that effect."

"Oh, we're spreading rumors now, eh, Major? We are spreading latrine-a-grams, are we?"

"Don't you talk to me like that!"

"Fuck you, Major!" And I started to walk out.

"You come back here, Stadlen. I can call Western Command for someone and have you court-martialed."

"Why don't you do that, Major? Maybe they'll teach you that anti-Semitism is against the law for officers in the United States Armed Forces. And fuck you too, Lieutenant!" And I was out the door.

I was totally out of control. After I calmed down, I wondered if there really was an order against officers using anti-Semitic language. I had made it up because it seemed only right. Either there was such a law or the major thought it was the better part of valor not to try to find out. That was the last of it. There wasn't any punishment or even a demerit. I finished pre-preflight, as our studies at our college training detachment were called, and I was on my way to preflight.

Once again, we were on a troop train in a circuitous route to our secret destination. Again it took quite a few days, and we spent a great deal of the time playing cards. This was no doubt a stupid thing to do, considering my reputation as a finger flicker. I was tolerated in the game as long as I lost, which was most of the time. When my luck started changing, everyone suddenly felt tired and decided to call it a night.

There was a different capo or cadet officer selected for the train ride. He came in at one point and chewed us out for making too much noise. He happened to be my old friend, the bugler, so I simply looked at him and said, "Sleep." That was it. He was out on his feet to the laughter and amazement of the noisemakers. Of course, I couldn't do that to everyone, but I had been giving him posthypnotic suggestions all through our pre- preflight time at Jamestown, and "Sleep" was one of them.

We finally were to arrive at the real thing, the big enchilada: Santa Ana Army Air Base. The real training would take place there. No more schooling. No more Piper Cubs. There I would learn to drop those bombs directly on the Reichstag. It was an exciting moment.

Chapter 4

Wising Up and Beating the Odds

The Santa Ana base had twenty-seven thousand men and barracks stretching as far as the eye could see. We were lined up in front of the barracks we were to occupy, and a captain from below the Mason-Dixon Line addressed us.

"I want to take this opportunity to welcome each and every one of you all to the Twenty-Third Squadron of the Santa Ana Army Air Base, Santa Ana, California. You men are to be congratulated. You are future officers. You are not ordinary GIs. You are the top twenty percent of the forty percent of the sixty percent of the men. You are intelligent! Now, I want you to know that if you play ball with me, I'll play ball with you and we are gonna be a couple of good ball players, but if you fuck with me, I'm gonna fuck with you and we gonna fuck each other. I expect you guys to keep these grounds policed. There are butt cans here, and you are to use them. I want this place to be kept in a number-one apple-pie order.

"You see these buses going by here?" he continued. "They are to transport the permanent party around the field. The buses are off limits to you. You understand that? Don't you be caught getting on one of them buses! Now you go inside. Pick your bunks, make them, and stow your gear, and when I say make 'em, I mean make 'em right. Make 'em tight. I come around an' drop a half dollah on your bed, it don't bounce, you in trouble. All right, dismissed!"

Our first payday in Santa Ana was an interesting experience. I reported to the paymaster in an exaggerated position of attention and was kept that way until I was out the door.

"Mr. Stadlen, Ira, 12183023, reporting for pay, sir." I received my money and then walked down a line of tables with the following signs: "Post Bus: $2," "Laundry: $2," and "Grass Seed: $2."

Of course, being in an exaggerated position of attention, you were not supposed to talk. Someone said, "I thought we were not allowed to ride the postbus."

Immediately, an officer charged up to him and said, "Pop to, mister. You're at attention. Suck in that gut. Reach for those suitcases. Get a couple of wrinkles in that chin, and march out that door."

Hey, thought I, the streetwise kid, *you have to shell out money for the postbus, which you are not permitted to ride, for the laundry which you have to do yourself and for grass seed? Twenty-seven thousand men spending two dollars each equals fifty-four thousand a month for grass seed? Give me a break.*

I saw the scam, but what could I do about it? This is how it was finally brought to light: a young cadet reporting for pay broke the rules and spoke. "I respectfully request an itemized bill, sir," he said.

"Pop to, mister. Suck in that gut. Reach for those suitcases—"

"I respectfully request an itemized bill, sir."

"You're at attention, mister. Don't you know there's a war going on?"

"Yes, sir, but I'm told I am entitled to an itemized account."

"You are, are you?"

"Yes, sir, my father told me that was my right."

"Yeah? Who the fuck is your father?"

"Senator Hickenlooper, sir." The senator's name was not Hickenlooper; I forget his real name. Nevertheless, that exchange led to a full investigation that charged Colonel Cannela, the CO of the base, with having stolen $80 million. I believe that after a military trial, he was given a scolding and transferred to another base. There was a great deal of publicity at the time. Obviously, he spent a quite a bit of his ill-gotten gains on public relations, because *Time* magazine did a story about him that claimed the boys (that was us) called him Pops and that he played basketball with his men. I know this because my brother-in-law, Sey Chassler, Vivienne's twin, worked for *TIME*, and he wrote to me, asking if this colonel was really such a nice guy. The moral of this story is this: if you're going to steal, steal big enough so that you can pass some of the money around in an emergency.

Next on the agenda were the physical tests to see if we had the right stuff. None of the tests were a problem for me, even the one in which I had to keep something that looked like an ice pick at arm's length in a minuscule hole that would register a buzz every time it touched the sides. I had to do that while the tester was badgering me to try to make me lose my concentration.

After all the physical testing came the ARMA. To this day, I do not know what those letters stood for, but it was a visit with the psychiatrist. We were all lined up and would go in three or four at a time for about ten minutes. Imagine my surprise when I was taken in alone. The psychiatrist was talking to someone at the door and asked me to go in and sit down, promising he'd be right with me. He ended his conversation with the other man by saying, "Yeah, they're funny, these colored boys."

He came in and shut the door. He looked down on some papers on his desk and said, "Ira Stadlen. Hi, I'm Captain Lewis." He shook my hand. "I noticed when you were coming in and I said something to the other gentleman at the door about colored boys, you shot me a look."

"I did? I wasn't aware of it, but it's possible."

"I didn't say anything derogatory about them."

"No. I was probably wondering why the colored boys as opposed to anyone else."

"Because they fit into a pattern—that's all. Okay? Let's get to know you. Are you married?"

"Yes, I am," I answered.

"How many times did you have intercourse with your wife the first night?

"Huh? Once, I think."

"Really? I went at it about three times."

"Yeah, but my wife wasn't used to it."

"That's funny."

"I'm sorry, sir—you gave me such a perfect straight man's line."

"That's all right. You consider yourself a comedian?"

"Yes, sir, I've worked in clubs as a civilian."

"Tell me about your hobbies. Do you like to make model planes?" he asked.

"No, sir, I paint."

"How about cars—do you like to drive hot-rod cars?"

"I don't know how to drive."

"Uh-huh. I noticed on the choice sheet where you were to select, in order of your preference, pilot, bombardier, or navigator, you chose bombardier. Was that a mistake?"

"No, sir."

"Wouldn't you like to be a pilot and fly commercially after the war?"

"No, sir, I'm an actor. I will act after the war."

"I see. Why do you want to be a bombardier?"

"Because I'm going to study hard and drop those eggs right on the Reichstag, and I don't want to be a chauffeur for some clown who will goof off and drop them in the Rhine River."

"You feel pretty emotional about this war, don't you?"

"Yes, I do."

He was quiet for a few moments and then said, "Ira, I'm going to recommend that you be washed out of this program."

"Why?"

"Well, actually, you are a very emotional guy. You are the kind of guy who, instead of being able to sack out before a flight, would lie awake thinking about home."

I grew angry and sarcastic and started talking like James Stewart. "Isn't that what we're supposed to do? Lie there and think of Ma's apple pie?"

"Ira, it is a known fact that actors do not make good flying personnel."

"Yeah, well, somebody better tell Jimmy Stewart. The schmuck keeps knocking them out of the air every day."

"There are exceptions. Look, son, I'm going to level with you. You are an intelligent young man."

"Sure, I'm the twenty percent of the forty percent of the sixty percent of the men."

"You're angry. I know that, but believe me, you don't fit the profile."

"What does that mean?" A profile, to me, was the side of a face.

"We have a profile of the type of person who makes good flying personnel. We want kids who are looking for excitement. They're not political. They're not emotional. They are the kind of kids who made model airplanes, drove hot-rod cars—the kind who can't wait to get in a plane and buzz the field."

"But that's against the law."

"That's right, but that is exactly what they want to do. They really don't care who they are fighting against or why. They want excitement."

"And that's the kind of men you want, huh?"

"It is not who I want. It is the type of person we have found can do this job best. You are not right for it. Believe me. You're angry and disappointed now, but someday you'll thank me."

That was it. I was not going to be a radio operator. I was not going to be a bombardier. What the hell was I there for? Almost an entire year had gone by—a wasted year. *What am I going to tell them back home? The psychiatrist washed me out!*

My darling Vivienne,

Your husband is psychologically unfit to drop bombs on the Nazis. My problem is I know who I'm fighting and why I'm fighting.

Why hadn't they asked me these questions when I'd enlisted? They could have given me a 4F rating and sent me off to Hollywood. I would have been doing as much for the war effort and earning $125 a week instead of $22 a month. Not only that, but I could have saved the war effort from wasting all that money on my training. I was angry and bitter as all the washouts were herded into a huge amphitheater to learn what was to become of us. We were a group of about five hundred. We were called to attention as a major entered the front of the room. I do not feel it is necessary to say what part of the United States he was from—by now, you know.

"At ease! Be seated. Now, you mayen have washed out! There are a number of opportunities open to you. You can become armament gunners, radio gunners, waist gunners, or tail gunners. If you wanted to help your country as pilots, bombardiers, or navigators, I want to tell you that there is a much greater need for you as gunners. The average life of a gunner in combat is eight seconds. Even when the planes manage to get back, we usually have to hose out the gunners. So if you wanted to help your country as pilots, bombardiers, or navigators, I want to tell you there is a much greater need for you as gunners."

I turned to my classmate Nelson at my side and whispered, "This guy is going to make a great salesman after the war." *This is beautiful,* I was thinking. *I am psychologically unfit to be a bombardier, but I am fit to be hosed out of the plane as a gunner.* One of the men in the room raised his hand.

"Yes, soldier?"

"Isn't there anything else open?"

"What's the matter soldier—yer scayred?"

The fellow sheepishly sat down.

"There is one other thang open—the pressure chambers. It's experimental, and it's purely voluntary. You can volunteer for that if you want it."

I thought about this for about a tenth of a second and stood up.

"Yes, soldier?"

"I'd like to volunteer for the pressure chambers, sir."

Nelson grabbed me at the seat of my pants and said in a frightened voice, "Didn't you hear? It's experimental."

"I know. With the other thing, they have the odds all worked out."

I was the only one in that entire room who volunteered. I was directed to the front of the room and was given some papers to fill out. A warrant officer cut my orders and told me to take them to the Thirty-Third Altitude Training Unit. It was connected to the base hospital, and I was to look for the building that had a big sign with the letters *ATU.*

I set off a bit nervously to find the place. Was I having second thoughts? No! There was no question in my mind that nothing could be worse than the picture the major had painted of the eight-second life of a gunner. What a dumbbell he was. Weren't there any intelligent officers in this man's army? For a moment, I thought of taking the post bus. After all, I was not a cadet anymore. But then I thought, *What's my hurry?* There was no order to be there by any certain time, just to report there. I wandered around and stopped in the PX for a bottle of 3.2 beer, trying to imagine what I was getting into, but I had no frame of reference.

I finally found the base hospital, and sure enough, there was the building with the big ATU sign. There was a master sergeant standing outside, so I said, "Excuse me, Sergeant, is this the pressure chambers?"

"That's right."

"Do you work here?"

"Uh-huh."

"What's it like?"

"Why do you want to know?"

"Well, I just volunteered for it."

"You have your orders?"

"Yes, sir."

"May I see them?"

I handed him my orders, which he looked at for what seemed to me to be a long time. He pocketed them and shook my hand.

"Welcome to the biggest fuck-off outfit in the United States Army. You married? Send for your wife. You'll live off the post. You'll have a Class-A pass. You'll be in LA every weekend."

This sergeant was a much better salesman than the major who was trying to sell us on being aerial gunners. This made me think of the offer to be a drill sergeant in Atlantic City. Look what happened to those guys. Of course, things had changed since then—or more to the point, I had changed. I had become a little jaded. I was not so gung ho any more. I realized that it made no difference what I wanted. The military works in its own peculiar way. Maybe he was overselling me. He never did answer my question of what the pressure chambers were like. Maybe I was being fattened up for the kill. Why was this a great fuck-off outfit if you had to be some kind of an experimental guinea pig to get in? The answer would come soon enough.

The pressure chamber was a thick iron room with glass portholes. Inside, it resembled an Air Corps plane—that is, there were seats in two facing rows with oxygen masks at each seat. It held about thirty men, with a seat at the end for the instructor. This was a low-pressure chamber that simulated the pressure one would feel at high altitudes—actually, the lack of pressure, as opposed to divers, who experience high pressure. It was experimental because we would experience higher altitudes than man had ever flown. We flew to thirty-eight thousand feet, and we did it a number of times a week as we instructed flying personnel how to live at high altitudes. They only had to go through this training once. No one knew at that time what harm might come to us over longer exposures. In a sense, it was similar to how astronauts are treated today. We were constantly checked by doctors and physiologists.

Each job in the armed service is given an MOS number. Ours was 617, and it was considered to be the most important MOS in the service. Again, we were treated as astronauts are treated today. It might seem silly now, when we travel routinely at thirty-five thousand feet, but then, our airmen had no comfortable pressurized cabins.

Attached to the pressure chamber was a small chamber called a lock. This was used only in an emergency. One of us was in charge of the main chamber, and one would be on duty on the lock. If someone got the bends or the chokes (nitrogen bubbles forming in the bloodstream, which were painful), we would take the lock up to the altitude of the chamber, open the connecting door, bring the fellow out into the lock, close the door, and bring him down to ground level. If we thought it was an emergency of great importance, we could drop from thirty-eight thousand feet in as little as ten seconds flat. I have felt at times in recent years that this affected my hearing. I can't really blame my hearing loss on that, though, as my father, brother, and two sisters were also hard of hearing.

At last, I had intelligent officers. In the ATU, everything was different. My officers were medical doctors, physiologists, psychiatrists, or scientists of various stripes. It was a pleasure to be able to carry on a conversation with them. Gone were the permanent army men. There was an occasional chickenshit lieutenant assigned to the outfit for a short while, but it was rare. Major Lombard, the CO, was a physiologist. In civilian life, he was a professor at UCLA. He was also the inventor of a special oxygen mask that delivered oxygen when needed as opposed to the constant-flow mask. Captain Palmary was a medical doctor, as was Lieutenant Sugar, who was also a surgeon and who, after the war, became famous for separating Siamese twins joined at the head. There were Captain Toth, who was mainly an administrator but no doubt had at least a PhD after his name, and a terrific psychiatrist, Captain Lewis— no relation to the one who washed me out of cadets. Also, I really must not forget Captain McMichaels, who was a book publisher from Philadelphia.

My first job in the morning was to take the temperatures of the flying personnel who were scheduled for the flight, eliminating anyone who was feverish. Then I would lead them into the chamber, demonstrate the use of the oxygen masks, and explain the workings of the chamber.

"First of all, there will be no smoking or the use of lighters or matches of any kind due to the danger of fire in the presence of oxygen. Also, we will all be passing a great deal of gas as we climb. Believe it or not, that gas is highly combustible." This always brought a laugh. "Don't worry—you will all be breathing oxygen, so you won't smell anything." Again, my words received a laugh.

"You will not be getting oxygen in your masks until we reach ten thousand feet."

The heavy iron doors were then closed with a solid clang, and the noise of the air being withdrawn was unnerving to almost everyone. I know it was to me my first time up. As a matter of fact, on one flight, my friend Nelson went through the chamber with his gunnery class. He looked at me and asked nervously, "What's it like, Stadlen?"

I felt so bad for him and so full of guilt that I answered, "It's hell."

The job I liked best was lecturing from the outside of the chamber. I did all kinds of routines after giving them the necessary lecture. One day, I told them I was going to turn on the radio for them. Then I did a phony radio announcer interrupting the program to bring them a special announcement. I impersonated Winston Churchill, telling them that the war was over. Did I fool them? You're damn right, but I quickly gave the ruse away, or they would have killed me when the flight came down. On one flight, at the end, when everyone had removed his mask, a colonel took out a cigarette, put it in his mouth, and was about to light it. I happened to look up at that moment and quickly smacked it out of his hand. He looked at me, shocked, and started to say the oxygen was off.

"The gas, Colonel. There is enough gas here to blow us all up."

∞ ∞ ∞ ∞ ∞ ∞   ∞ ∞ ∞ ∞ ∞ ∞

Captain McMichaels was a rich man who rented a house in Lido Beach for $1,700 a month. Think of that in 1944! He hired me to do a magic show and hypnotism at one of his parties. I had never seen such an opulent house. I tasted caviar for the first time and all sorts of other goodies. They also plied me with liquor, which I was not used to. When it came to doing my act, I not only was not feeling any pain, but I was feeling omnipotent. One of the captain's guests was, I was told, a famous writer who had just returned from living among various jungle tribes, where he was studying the magic of shamans. He had developed some illness there and walked with the aid of crutches. He had written a book, *Black Magic and White Wine*. I don't remember his name, but he was complimentary of my performance. I did a number of mental tricks that resembled mind reading. This prompted him to tell us about a shaman who had absolutely stunned him with his ability to find hidden objects. He intimated that he knew of no one else who was able to accomplish such a feat.

I was drunk enough to say, "Oh, I can do that." I realized, in my fogged brain, that the people in the audience were probably giving the shaman clues without realizing it. I'm afraid I'm a cynic. There were two lovely young ladies sitting at my feet who gasped at everything I did. They unquestioningly believed I was psychic, so I decided they would be my aces in the hole. If I couldn't get clues from anyone else in the audience, they would clue me, and indeed, they did. I wandered about the room in almost a trancelike state with my eyes partly closed, but I was able to see clearly where the young ladies were looking.

The item that was hidden was a silver cigarette case. As I neared where the girls were looking, I noticed a man who was doing his best to look away from me. I closed in on him and heard an audible gasp from one of the girls. I knew that as far as she was concerned, I had found the person who held the case. So I wandered away from my quarry to the other side of the room and made a few feints at someone else, and then, looking completely away from the man, with my eyes tightly closed, I described him and what he was wearing. Everyone broke out laughing and applauding. Over the din, I said, "Sir, may I have the cigarette case from your inside jacket pocket?" The last was a happy guess, but I figured if I were mistaken, the laughter and applause would cover. It so happened that that was exactly where he had it. It was a fine case. What would he do—sit on it?

I had a great deal of fun with my fellow soldiers with a particular game, the one where you place your hands on top of your opponent's and he tries to slap your hands before you can pull them away. I once saw two men playing this game for money, and they asked me to gamble on it. I said I wouldn't play for money, because they would never be able to hit me. They laughed at first, but just before we started, when my hands were on top of my opponent's, I looked him in the eyes and said, "You will never hit me!" Neither ever did. Of course, I had the advantage that they had seen me do hypnosis, and I knew it. Word got around that I was invincible at the game, and then they claimed I was hypnotizing them. It wasn't that. It was the power of suggestion.

Since I was by now a full-fledged altitude training technician, I was permitted to live off the post with my wife. I wasted no time in sending for Vivienne and searched for a place for us to live. Our first domicile was a rented room in Mrs. Lang's house. The address was RFD 4, Costa Mesa, California. You walked out of the base, across a golf course, and up a dirt road to Mrs. Lang's. It was a long walk but doable. However, I decided to look for an inexpensive car.

While we were at Mrs. Lang's, Vivienne's mother came out to California to visit us. I always had great affection for my mother-in-law. Her name was Henrietta, and I mention it because it figures in a funny story. Train travel was difficult during the war. Civilians had to wait a long time to get reservations. While she was with us, she wished to stay longer but realized it would be impossible to change her ticket. I had an idea: I would take her tickets to the train station and tell them I was on furlough, my furlough had been extended, and I had to change my tickets so that I could get back to New York. As I was a soldier, they would have to honor it. Off I went with the tickets and told my fake story to the ticket seller. "No problem," he said, but while he was making out the new reservation, he noticed something and said, "Wait a minute. These tickets are made out to Henrietta."

I looked him in the eyes and said, "Yeah, couldn't you die with a name like that?"

He shrugged and gave me the new reservations.

So now the New York kid shopped for a car. The first thing I did was to check the company bulletin board. Sergeant Munt came over and was looking over my shoulder. Sergeant Munt was a wispy, milk-toasty sort of a guy who talked through his nose. He once pissed me off, and I told him to go fuck himself. His reply was "I don't like your initiative, Stadlen." This time, he simply asked me, "What are you looking for?"

"I want to buy a car."

"How much money have you got?"

"A hundred and fifty."

"I have a car I'll sell you for a hundred and fifty."

"Where is it?"

"Over near the parade ground. Come with me." He took me over to the car.

"What kind of car is this?"

"A Chevrolet coupe, 1930. See? It has a rumble seat in the back." He opened it.

"Okay. It runs right?" I knew the question to ask.

"Sure."

"Okay, show me how to use it."

"What do you mean?"

"What do I do? How do I drive it?"

"You mean you don't know how to drive?"

"No. I never had a car before. You show me how to drive it, and I'll buy it." I drive a hard bargain. Nobody puts anything over on me. Maybe you'd buy a car without the seller showing you how to drive it, but not me! Sergeant Munt looked at me as if I were a little crazy, but we both got into the car, and he quickly pointed out what everything was: the stick shift and the clutch, which you step on whenever you move the stick shift. It was a rudimentary lesson. I never even got to drive it with him in the car. He spent most of the time telling me how to care for it. "Every time you put water in the radiator, you put in a can of this sealer."

"Where do I get it?"

"In a gas station. The same thing for the oil. You put this stuff in for the oil. Don't mix them up. It says on the cans what they are for, and never run out of oil. Every time you buy gas, you buy oil."

The lesson was over, and I gave him the $150. He took off like a thief, and I was left to start and stall, buck like a bronco, and strip gears. After a few hours, I tamed the wild beast and believed I was a driver. Fortunately, there was a great deal of space on the parade ground, with no other moving traffic.

The big laughs came each morning as I rode onto the base while the men were doing their exercises. I didn't know why they were laughing until a few of them put me wise. They could hear me coming from a mile away because of a noisy piston slap. I didn't know. I thought, *Cars make noise.* I was brought up in subway cars. Then they showed me that I was driving on four oversized tires that were completely bald. Also, I had no spare tire. Got the picture?

I drove this car for a year. Vivienne and I went into LA every weekend, usually with another couple in the rumble seat. We never broke down. We never had a flat, and when I sold it, I got exactly $150 for it. I became more and more knowledgeable about cars as time moved on, but I never had such good luck with one again.

∞ ∞ ∞ ∞ ∞ ∞   ∞ ∞ ∞ ∞ ∞ ∞ ∞

While in the barracks, before Vivienne arrived, I heard the men taunting a Chinese-American soldier—that is, before seeing him, I was made aware by the taunts that he was Chinese.

"Hey, Lew, I have some laundry for you."

"Yeah, I have some shirts too."

"No starch. How many time I have to tell you no starch?"

"No ticky, no shirty, right, Lew?"

"No. No ticky, no shitty. Ha-ha."

He was on the other end of the barracks, so I couldn't see the man who was getting the business. I had been sitting on my bed, sketching. I walked along the bunks, looking for a Chinese-looking person, and I found him. James Lew was the saddest of sad sacks I'd ever seen. He could have been the model for the cartoon character in *Star & Stripes.* None of his clothes fit him. Clearly, he was not a military man. He didn't belong.

I introduced myself and asked him if he would mind posing for me. I told him I would like to do a portrait of him.

"Why?"

"What do you mean? I just want to do a sketch of you. That's all."

"But why me? For what reason?"

"Oh, well, I'm an artist, and you have an interesting face. I never did a portrait of anyone with Oriental features. It would be good practice for me."

"All right."

That was the way Jimmy tested me about everything between us. He was always suspicious of my motives, and he probably had good cause to be. The type of ridicule he suffered at the hands of the US Army would make any sane person root for the enemy. Who could blame him if he distrusted any overture of friendship? It took me quite awhile to get through to him that I was not the same as the other men in the barracks. We eventually became great friends, but at the time, it was difficult. Jimmy was so miserable in the army that he asked to be assigned to the Chinese detachment from China that was being trained in Santa Ana. My major pulled enough strings to make it happen for him. Of course, this was only temporary. It was a sad commentary that an American soldier born and bred in our country could feel comfortable only in a foreign army.

There is an interesting follow-up to my story of Jimmy Lew. Santa Ana was eventually turned into a base hospital, and we were all shipped to different airfields. Jimmy was sent to a field in Texas, and I went to Arizona. I received a letter from Jimmy telling me that while he was in the service club, a group of WACS (Women's Army Corps) were having a discussion about prejudice. He wrote, "One of the girls spoke just like you, so I asked her if she knew you. She got all excited and said yes, she was in your class in high school. Her name is Mitzy Silver." I felt sad about his story because he must have believed there were only a few people in this country who were not racist and that they were all connected. I'm sure he knows differently now.

We lost track of each other after the war, but in 1954, I came out to California with the crew from *The Howdy Doody Show*. We broadcast from Burbank for two weeks in order to hype the ratings on the West Coast. I knew Jimmy lived somewhere in Los Angeles; at least, he'd said he was going to live there after the war. The LA phone book had a few pages of James Lew, J. Lew, James J., James R., etc. Undaunted, I went to LA's Chinatown and started asking people how I might find my friend. I asked some people who turned out to be Japanese. After a hurried apology, I went on to the next Oriental person and the next.

Finally, I stopped a pretty young lady, thinking that even if she were of no help, something might develop between us. "Excuse me, young lady. I'm looking for a Chinese friend of mine who was in the army with me, and I'm simply asking people if they might know him. His name is Jimmy Lew or James Lew."

"That is a very common Chinese name. It is like Jones."

"Yes, I know. I've been searching the telephone directory."

"Have you any idea what part of LA he might live in?"

"None. He used to live in Arizona. He's small, very shy, always reading—I mean the classics. He has a wide interest in and knowledge of literature."

"Is he a teacher?"

"Could be—it's been ten years."

"He's about thirty?"

"Yeah. Just about."

"You are describing a very good friend of mine, a fellow teacher. Here, let me find his phone number for you." She looked through a little book and wrote it out for me. "It's a long shot, but maybe my friend is your friend. If he is, tell him Suzi gave you his number."

I lost no time in getting to a phone booth and calling. It was him all right. I knew his voice as if it were yesterday. "Jimmy," I said, "it's Ira Stadlen. What is it with you? You don't call. You don't write."

"Wow, Ira, how are you? Where are you? How did you get my number?"

"Suzi gave it to me—your gorgeous fellow teacher."

"Suzi? How do you know Suzi?"

"Ho-ho, if you knew Suzi like I know Suzi. It was simple. It's all over the LA papers that you two are a duo."

"Come on—cut it out. She's a married woman. Where are you?"

"Jimmy, you're carrying on with a married woman? I'm in Chinatown."

"Where? I'll pick you up."

"No, give me your address—I'll grab a cab."

"No, Ira, it's too expensive. They cost a fortune out here. Are you anywhere near the big red arch?"

"About twelve feet."

"Stay there. I'll pick you up in about fifteen minutes. You will have dinner with us. My wife, Chabela, is a great cook. She has heard so much about you. Now you two will finally meet."

"Don't worry; I won't say a word about Suzi."

"Just stay there. Good-bye."

That was how I found him. It seemed like a miracle. Really, what are the chances? It reminds me of one of my mother's stories of the greenhorn who came over to the United States looking for a relative whose address was Number 1, America. Jimmy and I had a wonderful reunion and never lost touch again.

∞ ∞ ∞ ∞ ∞ ∞   ∞ ∞ ∞ ∞ ∞ ∞

I don't know who suggested that since I had already been driving for six months, I ought to get a driver's license. I thought that was a pretty good idea, so I drove to city hall, where they gave me a driving test. It was rudimentary. In fact, the tester only asked me to drive around the block before he said, "Well, you're a driver, right? All you need is a California license!" He assumed that I already had a license from somewhere else, but he never even asked me for it. Since I had never driven before, I had no idea that this procedure was out of the ordinary. So I walked out of there a licensed driver.

∞ ∞ ∞ ∞ ∞ ∞   ∞ ∞ ∞ ∞ ∞ ∞

Lieutenant Sugar asked me if I would agree to participate in some experiments. He was working with something called a brain encephalograph. It might be a common piece of medical equipment today, but it was completely new at the time. While I was lying in a cot in one room, he attached various electrodes to my head that were connected to a machine in another room. He asked me to think erotic thoughts while the pen on the machine made various markings on paper. Then, after a while, he asked me to do a mathematical problem in my head, along with other tasks, such as thinking of a frightening experience. Then, after getting all that down, he asked me to think again of any of those things, and on each occasion, he would tell me what category my mind was on. He'd say from the other room, "You're doing a math problem" or "You are thinking erotic thoughts," and each time, he was correct.

I found it particularly exciting because of my fake mind reading. I asked him if he thought someday we would actually be able to read minds with such a machine. We discussed extrasensory perception. He had a scientist's attitude. He never believed or didn't unless he saw proof either way. I suggested that finding proof would be almost impossible. Most people are easily deceived because they want so desperately to believe. I mentioned Dunninger, who was, at that time, on radio and fooling the world with his tricks. Lieutenant Sugar felt hypnosis could be proven under test conditions.

"Yes, but who is to set up those test conditions?" I asked. "Scientists are not immune from being fooled." I pointed out that Dunninger had accepted the challenge from Dr. Rhine of Duke University to submit to their test conditions. He had fooled them all. "Does that prove that Dunninger has ESP?" I said.

Captain Lewis asked me to do hypnosis on some of his patients. He said he was never able to do it himself and felt it might speed up their recovery. I was not only flattered but also eager to do this experiment; in a sense, I would be doing it under his guidance. I would be an assistant to a psychiatrist—PFC Ira Stadlen 12183023!

He was treating a GI who woke up one morning with the left side of his face paralyzed. The doctors could find no medical explanation for his problem and referred him to Captain Lewis. He discussed the patient with me before his appointment. Captain Lewis had told him on his last visit that if he agreed, he would bring in a hypnotist. He knew that his patient had awakened with the problem on the morning after returning from furlough. He had driven for two full days without sleep, staying awake on Benzedrine. We used Benzedrine during the war as if it were aspirin, including to stay awake and to lose weight. Captain Lewis suspected the man's issue had something to do with the drive back. His patient—let's call him Joe—felt there had been nothing out of the ordinary on the trip. He said he often drove on Bennies to stay awake. Captain Lewis asked me if I thought we could find out anything under hypnosis that might help.

I suggested I put him under and re-create the drive to see if we could find out what his thought processes were at that time. He thought that was a good idea, if it could work. I assured him it could. A short time ago, I had done a show in a convent where I'd brought a girl back to her childhood and had her write her name for the first time in her life. After the show, the mother superior got excited. She had in her files the girl's first writing and ran upstairs to get it. When we compared them, they were identical.

"Let's do it!" He was keen to get started. He brought Joe in and introduced me as the hypnotist.

We shook hands and chatted awhile. I asked him if he knew anything about hypnotism. He didn't. I explained certain things about it. I told him I would need his cooperation and assured him that he could not be hypnotized against his will. I also told him I was certain that this would help Captain Lewis to treat his paralysis and that under any circumstances, when he awoke, he would feel wonderful. I then began to put him under.

I told him he was in his car, driving back from his furlough. I asked him to tell me what he was seeing as he drove. His description was amazing. He was calling out road signs, other cars, trucks, and motels. Captain Lewis wrote down questions he wanted him to answer, and as I asked them, he answered. I asked what was uppermost in his mind. "Tell me what you are thinking, Joe," I said.

"My watch. It's broken. I can't tell the damn time."

"How did it break?"

"I don't know. Damn thing just stopped running."

Captain Lewis passed me a note that read, "Ask him why that's important."

"Why is that so important, Joe?"

"I'm not going to make it."

"Make what?"

"Reveille. I'm not going to make reveille."

Again, the captain showed me a note: "Ask him what of it?"

"Well, what of it? Suppose you miss it?"

"He'll nail me to the cross, that chickenshit bastard."

Captain Lewis signaled me to end the hypnosis. He apparently had learned enough in that session. I spoke reassuringly to Joe and, before I brought him out of it, gave him a posthypnotic suggestion that to hypnotize him in the future, I would simply say, "Sleep." That would get us into it quickly.

After Joe left, Captain Lewis asked, "What do you think?"

I said, "I think I think what you think."

"What is that?"

"He fucked himself up with worry about getting back on time for reveille."

"Well, that's not exactly the way we'd phrase it in medical jargon, but that's it. Ira, this is wonderful! I don't know how to thank you. This is a great time-saver. I had seen that young man four times before and never got that out of him."

"Because he didn't know it himself."

"Exactly. Now let's think how to use what we have just learned."

"Oh, that's simple. He'll be cured next shot." What chutzpah I had. "Let's give him an extension to his furlough. Make him forget the real trip and give him a relaxed one."

"After the war, Ira, maybe you should go back to school and become a psychiatrist."

"Not me. You go back to school and become a hypnotist. It will serve you better in your field. Being a psychiatrist won't help my comedy."

"I don't think I could do that."

"Sure you could. Just do what I did. Anyone can do it. Believe me—it will be easier for you. You're a doctor. You already have the authority. I have to act like I have the authority. I'll lend you a few books on the subject."

At our next meeting with Joe, we did exactly as I'd suggested. We had him stop at a phone booth and call home. His wife told him he had an extension of three days on his furlough. We told him he stopped at a motel for a good night's sleep and arrived at the base relaxed and refreshed and much earlier than he was expected. That was it. When I brought him out of it, the paralysis was gone. Wow, was that a great feeling!

I learned a great deal from Captain Lewis, mostly about what not to do. He saw nothing wrong in my using hypnosis as entertainment but cautioned me not to play around with someone's subconscious.

"You have a great deal of natural insight, but leave the healing to the trained professionals. Keep it simple. Keep it fun."

In the service and afterward, I continued to do hypnosis without harming anyone, and I must have hypnotized hundreds of people. It was always for sheer entertainment. Nothing, however, was more exciting than doing it under the guidance of Captain Lewis and seeing what a fabulous tool it could be for diagnosis and treatment. Just think: if I had not been such a lousy student, I could have become a shrink on the GI Bill.

Just as I was having a wonderful time playing psychiatrist, the Santa Ana Air Base was to be closed and turned into a major hospital. Some of the men, my friend Charlie included, were sent to Las Vegas. I was being shipped to Kingman, Arizona, where I would report to the Kingman Air Base ATU. Vivienne and I decided that she would stay in our little green shack until I could find a place for us to live. If that were not possible, she would go back home to Brooklyn.

Kingman lived up to its lousy reputation. The town was one grimy cowboy street and a hotel whose sign read "The Hotel Beal (Your Home away from Home)"—they should live so long! A Bowery flophouse would look like the Waldorf-Astoria in comparison. I rented it for the night, figuring I'd look around for a decent place the next day. I couldn't find a decent place in the next three days. Whoever had a broken-down garage or root cellar would rent it to you at a ridiculously high price, provided you could come up with the money in advance for a month's rent and a month's security. I am not exaggerating. I was actually offered a root cellar, complete with a dirt floor. I cannot remember how much the owners were asking for such a domicile, but at today's prices in 2002, it would be equivalent to $3,000 or $4,000 a month.

It looked like I was stuck with that home away from home, but could I bring Vivienne to such a place? I wrestled with that. I wanted her. I missed her. *Should I tell her to go back to New York?* I wondered. Maybe the Hotel Beal had a better room, one where the plaster wasn't falling off the wall in chunks and there weren't brown stains all over the ceiling. They didn't. They were even a little peeved at my indicating that there might be something negative about their establishment. I figured I'd better not do any more complaining lest they deny me access altogether. *Who knows? It might be a restricted hotel,* I thought. So far, they didn't know I was Jewish.

I put in a phone call to Vivienne. The lady who owned the shack lived in the house next door and was obliging about calling us to the phone. We had been separated for only a few days, but I missed her terribly. I was, however, determined to be stoic and tell her to go home. As soon as I heard her voice, my stoicism went out the window. I waffled.

"Listen, honey, I haven't been able to find any place yet, and I thought maybe you might think about going home."

"What about the hotel you're in? We could stay there until we find a place."

"Yeah, ah, we could, but, ah—"

"What's the matter? Don't you want me to come?"

"Yeah, yeah, sure. It's just … The hotel is not so great."

"So? It's clean, isn't it?"

"Oh yeah, I guess. It's just a little seedy."

"I'm sure we can survive it for a few days. I love you."

"I love you. Come. I miss you like crazy."

"What's the name of the hotel? What's the address?"

"There is only one. You can't miss it—the Hotel Beal. Honey?"

"Yeah?"

"Don't expect too much." Oh, I hated myself. I'd lied to her. Well, I hadn't lied, but I hadn't told her the truth, all because of my own selfish desire. I'd said it was clean. It didn't look clean to me. You know what was clean? Vivienne was clean. She was going to hate me for this.

She did not reproach me. She didn't say anything about the room, which was a bad sign. This was a room you had to comment on. *She must be holding it in,* I thought. I was filling in what she must be thinking: *Boy, is he a jerk! He doesn't know the difference between seedy and downright disgusting.* Her silence was killing me.

Finally, I burst out, "It's a shithole! Right?"

"We'll find something else." She did, too. She found us a trailer. It was clean because she cleaned it. There was one problem with it: it was made for little people. Every time she turned, she banged her head on something. I don't remember banging my head, but I wasn't as active as she was. Vivienne was quick. She did everything quickly. I was more laid back. You might say I was lazy. She did things not only quickly but also well. She could cook a good meal out of practically anything, under any condition—except eggs. She could not make decent eggs. She wouldn't take the time to watch the pan if she fried them or the pot if she boiled them. She had a motor that was always racing, and she raced into open cabinet doors, which at first we laughed at. Vivienne could always laugh at herself, but then even she had to cry uncle. We had to find something with a few more inches of headroom.

We finally lucked out. There was a development of little hexagonal-shaped one-bedroom houses that were put up for permanent party personnel; they were difficult to get into, because they were always full. Someone, apparently, had shipped out, and we got one. I don't know that the place had any more square feet than the trailer, but there was a lot more headroom. It also had a water cooler, the forerunner of the air conditioners.

I was always in awe of my wife's intelligence. Maybe it was because she was four years older than I, but she knew so much more. I'm not putting myself down. Obviously, I knew many things she didn't know, but just her teaching me how to write a check made me feel she was so much worldlier. Sometimes I feel our marriage might have been better if I hadn't believed she was so smart. In retrospect, I can see how wrong she could be about so many things I bought into. At that time—and for many years after—I believed that if you were an actor, there had to be something wrong with you. After all, she'd read Freud. I hadn't.

The ATU in Kingman had its full complement of technicians. With our arrival from Santa Ana, they really didn't need more men, so I hightailed it over to the Special Service office to see if I could do some entertaining on the base. I was already spending a few hours a day at the hospital, doing card tricks at the bedside of the sick and wounded.

When I told them I was a comedian and a magician, the sergeant told me there was another magician on the base. He asked if I knew Lee Burchell. I didn't, but I wanted to meet him. It had been so long since I'd been with other magicians, and I felt a need for their companionship. I asked where I could find him, and off I went to his barracks.

I entered the barracks and asked some of the men where I could find Lee Burchell. They looked around and pointed to his bed. He wasn't there at the moment, so I lay down on his bed and decided to wait. He looked a bit startled when he saw me there. "That's my bed," he said.

"I know. I've been waiting for you. You're Lee Burchell, the magician? I'm Ira Stadlen."

I offered him my hand and said, "I'm also a magician." We shook hands. Neither of us could possibly have realized at that moment that we two strangers would be the closest and dearest of friends for the next fifty-eight years.

To me, that's one of the great wonders of living: life is always a surprise. That man on the corner crossing the street—might he have some effect on my life? The woman sitting across from me on the bus—will we maybe meet somewhere sometime, at a dinner party perhaps? Life is a great adventure.

Lee is eight years older than I. For most of his adult life, he's been a professional magician; he has played in nightclubs and theaters all over the country under the stage name of Lee Noble. Within days of our meeting, we were both performing in a musical revue called *About Face*. I did comedy, and Lee did magic. The show went over great. Lee told me that before my coming on the scene, he was doing comedy on the base, but after seeing my performance, he decided to stick to magic. Conversely, after seeing Lee do magic, I decided to stick to comedy.

Lee was the suavest of the suave. He had polished his act to perfection. Whenever I did a magic act, I would fly by the seat of my pants, improvising and figuring I could get out of trouble with my comedy. To watch his act was to behold flawlessness. I was, however, disappointed that Lee wasn't interested in fooling around or learning or exchanging tricks. He did his act, and that was all that interested him. But I reawakened in him what he had left behind as a kid—the same enthusiasm I had. In short order, after inundating him with the new card tricks I was doing, he became interested. The competitiveness in him took over, and we were like a couple of kids, trying to fool each other on every occasion.

Since I had sold our jalopy when I left Santa Ana, I had to buy a new one—that is, a new old one. Having been a seasoned driver for a year, I felt I knew cars. I upgraded to a 1933 Ford with a rebuilt motor and four newly recapped tires.

∞ ∞ ∞ ∞ ∞ ∞   ∞ ∞ ∞ ∞ ∞ ∞

Major Bazata was the officer in charge of Special Services, and Victor Babbit was his sergeant and majordomo. I was doing so much entertaining on the base that I was considered a member of Special Services, but I was not. Officially, I was assigned to the ATU, and they continued to pay me. The major was a big hale-and-hearty good fellow with a gravelly voice. I could impersonate him to perfection. Victor could forge his signature just as perfectly, so between us, we ran the office, and Major Bazata could spend the days in the officers' club, drinking. He was happy, and we were happy. Victor was a perfect social secretary who knew just when to send a birthday card to the CO of the base or other ass-kissing memorandums in the major's name.

The only hitch was that I could never get promoted, because I was hardly deserving of it from the ATU and I wasn't a member of Special Services. This bothered Major Bazata, who wanted to promote me as far up the line as he could. He sent an official letter to the Western Flying Training Command, requesting that I be transferred to Special Services. The WFTC sent it on to Washington, and the following answer came back: "Ira Stadlen's MOS is 617. That is the highest-priority MOS in the United States Armed Services. If you cannot find work for him in this MOS, we will find it for him. Request denied." When that letter came from Washington, I suggested to the major that we let sleeping dogs lie.

I met Vivienne in the cafeteria for lunch, and she was crying. We were about to go on furlough, and we planned to travel home. Her boss, a warrant officer, had told her that if she accompanied me home on furlough, she could not come back to work. It was outrageous, and I tried to console her. "That is an indefensible decision on the part of your stupid boss. Leave it to me. I'll fight it. What's the reason you are here, for God's sake? Don't worry about it; the furlough is eight days away."

We walked down the line with our trays, selecting our food. Vivienne didn't have the best eyesight normally, and with her eyes tearing as they were, she mistook another soldier in the line for me and removed item after item from his tray, saying each time, "You will not eat that." He would take each item back, and she'd remove it again, saying, "You will not eat that."

I was watching, waiting to see how things played out. Obviously, he was selecting fattening food. Finally, he said, "Lady, please." She looked up, saw what she was doing, and broke up laughing and apologizing. Everyone else in line cracked up as well.

I went back to the Special Services office and put a call in to civilian personnel. When they answered, I said in my Major Bazata voice, "This is the Special Services office." I was careful not to say "officer."

"Yes, Major?" Everyone knew his gravelly voice.

"Do we have some rule about wives of servicemen working on the base accompanying their husband on furlough?"

"They usually do, sir."

"I'm not asking you that, goddammit. I want to know if there's a rule that those civilian workers be guaranteed their jobs back after returning with their husband from furlough."

"I really don't know, sir."

"Well, dammit, there should be!"

"Yes, sir."

"For cryin' out loud, that's the only reason they're here, isn't it?"

"Yes, sir."

"Well, do something about it."

"We will, sir."

"Now! Do it now! Get it out to every department!" And I slammed down the phone.

Yes, a rule was announced that civilian personnel who were wives of servicemen would be guaranteed their jobs back after accompanying their husbands on furlough! Vivienne couldn't believe I had actually pulled it off.

We were to be shipped to Las Vegas—another base, another unknown. Kingman, too, was to be turned into a base hospital. Major Bazata called Victor and me together and suggested we get in his staff car, go to Vegas, and get ourselves living quarters before everyone else arrived and rented every available place to live.

Remember how tight living quarters were in Kingman when we first got there? Now probably half the base would be falling in on Las Vegas, fighting over every available place to live. We would beat them by a few weeks. All three of us rented houses in Henderson, a short commute from the air base. It was sort of like a homesteading invasion back when the West was settled.

We drove onto the base and headed for the ATU. Captain Toth from Santa Ana was now the CO. We greeted each other, and Major Bazata introduced himself and said, "Captain, I have a favor to ask you. I am going to be the new Special Services officer, and you know Stadlen here. He's a great talent. I don't know what I'd do without him. I was wondering if you might lend him to me for the duration of his stay here. He's married and lives off the post anyway, so you don't have to billet him.

I'll take care of everything else if you would just see that he's paid once a month."

Aside from the fact that Major Bazata outranked him, Captain Toth was aware of my performing abilities. He already had more personnel than he needed, and when the rest came into the unit, he would be overrun. There was no problem. He agreed, everyone shook hands, and we drove back to Kingman. I was happy to inform Viv that we were going to live in a real house with a separate kitchen and bedroom, a dining room, and a front lawn. Victor and his wife, Lucile, had the house next to ours, and I would only be doing shows because I had been loaned to Special Services.

Things didn't happen exactly that way. While we were waiting for my orders to come through, Major Bazata's orders were changed. Instead of being shipped to Las Vegas, he was shipped overseas to the Pacific. The rest of us went to Vegas.

Viv immediately got a job on the post, but where was I? I was in no-man's-land. As far as Captain Toth was concerned, I was in Special Services, and all he had to do was see to it that I got paid. As far as Special Services was concerned, they had never heard of me. If Vivienne didn't have a job, we could go back to New York, and no one would be the wiser. It was a laughable situation, and we laughed a lot about it. Everything was turned around. She was no longer there because of me; I was there because of her.

Since I had nothing to do, I visited the gambling houses to see the dealers take over the marks. The job I made for myself was to see if I could tell which dealer was a mechanic—that is, a card man capable of cheating. You can't really tell if a good mechanic is cheating. You can only tell if he could, and most of them could. I watched one dealer at the blackjack table who dealt with one hand. When you said, "Hit me," the card shot out of his hand, turned over in the air, and landed under your money. Anyone who played against this man should have had his head examined. In those days, dealers dealt with one deck as opposed to today's method of dealing out of a shoe, with as many as five decks. For some reason, everyone seemed to believe that the house never cheated. It was a naive belief born out of their desire to believe, because after all, it was the only game in town. This was not my first time in Las Vegas. I had been sent there from Santa Ana on detached service for three weeks about a year before.

That was really an experience. I put on a magic and hypnotism show there on my first day. My first night in the barracks, I was amazed that none of the men went into town. When I asked them about it, someone answered, "We don't go in anymore. We just send our pay in."

I couldn't wait. On the main drag, there was outdoor gambling for small amounts. There was one of those large vertical roulette wheels where you could bet as little as a nickel. I put a nickel down, and my number came up; I won thirty-six to one. Then I started betting quarters on the red and black, and I continued to win and finally went inside and bet dollars. I worked out what I believed was a winning system. I ran that nickel up to $150.

When I told the men in the barracks, they all got excited. Their gambling blood was reawakened. Here was a magician with a system. Now it was worth going back into the fray. We all pooled our money and went into the Last Frontier Hotel. I selected a few assistants to place bets as I told them. I had a pad and pencil and was calling out the bets. "Put five dollars on red and four on the second-third, ten on evens," etc. We only played roulette. My winning system was simple. If black came up twice in a row, I'd bet red, and if black came up again, I would double the bet. I would not place a bet until something came up twice. There were about thirty of us from the barracks, and we were winning like crazy. It was hilarious, with everybody whooping it up and patting me on the back. After a while, word got around that some GIs were breaking the bank, and people left the other tables to gather around and watch us.

Some excited GI would tell the lookers-on, "This guy's a magician." This went on until about one in the morning, when the streak came to an end. After all, how long can you keep doubling up when it goes against you? It was amazing, after we had been winning for hours, how easy it was to go broke!

Now, you might think that the men would feel bad, that they might be disappointed or feel I had let them down. No such thing. They were carrying me on their shoulders. They had had a great time. They had had a run they would remember, they said, for the rest of their lives.

I suggest you do not try my system. It is anything but foolproof. One night, in one of the clubs, one of our gang, Civatelli, was playing blackjack. I was watching him and felt that the dealer was a mechanic, and I tried to pull him away from the table. It was no use. So I sat in an empty chair and watched. Civatelli was the only one playing, and here was his conversation with the dealer.

"You know something?" he said. "You almost caused me a divorce on my honeymoon."

"Yeah, how?" the dealer asked.

"I'm from LA. We checked in, and I told my wife I was going down for a pack of cigarettes. I sat down here and lost a hundred and fifty dollars, and we had to leave."

"Uh-huh." The dealer was unmoved. After a while, he said to Civatelli, "Your problem is you don't know how to play. You keep betting a dollar at a time till you grind yourself out. See, what you should do is this: If you win, let it ride. If you win again, let that ride. Let it ride again. You now have eight dollars, draw seven, and start over."

Civatelli did just that. It worked exactly as the dealer had suggested. When Civatelli had $150 in front of him, the dealer said, "Okay, kid, take off—we're even."

I met an amateur magician that day. Lenny Greenfader had been a New York policeman. He was one of the most skilled sleight-of-hand artists I've ever known. We stayed up one night until daybreak, exchanging tricks. If he fooled me with a trick, he would teach me how to do it and vice versa. Lenny was also a great pickpocket. He had put on shows for the police department in which he'd bring the captain up on the stage and steal his gun. Then, before he let him leave, he would hand him the bullets he'd stolen out of the gun. Lenny was a real marvel.

One of the things Lenny taught me was how to beat the one-arm bandits. It was not really an honest thing to do. It can't be done today with the electric machines, but it was possible with the old mechanical ones. First, you would put in a coin, pull the lever down halfway, and hold it. Then you would put in another coin, jiggle the arm until you lined up the three winning items, and slowly let up the arm. Nothing happened, but it showed that the machine should have paid off a jackpot. You then called over an employee and showed him that you hit a jackpot and it didn't pay off. He put a key in the bandit, and out poured the money.

It so happened that he taught me that scam about an hour before my bus was leaving to take me back to Santa Ana. I only had time to knock off one bandit. I had visions of going around to all the hotels and pulling the same scam. *Oh well, maybe next time,* I thought, *if I ever get back here.* I did return, of course, when we were shipped there from Kingman, but by then, I was wise enough to realize that it would be a stupid thing to do. It was not that I suddenly became honest. It was just that if the bandits who ran Las Vegas got wise to my knocking off their one-arm kind, they might remove my arms or even plant me in the desert.

I didn't gamble at all on that last trip to Vegas. I was just a researcher, going about the business of learning all the gimmicks and techniques of crooked gambling. I made friends with some of the dealers by showing them card tricks in which I avoided sleight of hand but fooled them with mental magic. I wheedled out of them some of the tricks of the trade.

I've had any number of discussions with people about gambling. It comes up all the time when I'm showing card tricks. Invariably, they will argue with me about the honesty of Las Vegas or Atlantic City. "They don't have to cheat," they say. "The odds are all with the house." Of course they are, but who runs these gambling houses? People who are interested in a normal markup? Get real!

∞ ∞ ∞ ∞ ∞ ∞   ∞ ∞ ∞ ∞ ∞ ∞

We were in Las Vegas when the bomb was dropped on Japan and the war ended. I know that in retrospect, there has been a great deal of hand-wringing and mea culpa about dropping that bomb. Was it a moral thing to do? Is war moral? I only know how my fellow soldiers felt, who were waiting for their orders to go over to attack Japan. What joyous shouting! It meant that all of us there were going to be able to live, to lead normal lives.

Our stay in Las Vegas was a great deal shorter than we had expected. Since the war was over, we were just marking time until the machinery of demobilization reached us. It did in Fresno, California. Viv and I packed up our belongings in the back of our 1933 Ford sedan and headed east. This car had served us well.

On one occasion in Kingman, when I treated the sedan like a racing car, something happened. I was sitting around with Lee and a few other fellows, telling them a mouthwatering story. Viv and I had visited Boulder Dam the previous Sunday, and we'd stopped at a little place called the Christmas Tree Inn. They had the greatest tuna-fish sandwich and the most delicious ice-cold milk I'd ever had. Now, this was Kingman, which was about 120 degrees in the shade. It was almost lunchtime, and the guys all begged me to take them there. We'd have to get there and back pretty quickly, and it was a long way off. As I told them about it, my tongue was dancing in my mouth, and I agreed.

I didn't drive. I flew there. We downed the sandwiches and milk, which everyone agreed were wonderful, and flew back to Kingman. We were about a mile from the base, when all four retreads on my tires melted on the road. That was about the worst thing that had happened to the car until then. They all chipped in to have the tires retreaded, and in spite of the cost, we all felt the sandwiches and milk were worth it.

When I wrote to my father about the heat in Arizona, he wrote back, "It is true that a hundred and twenty in the shade is hot, but you don't mind it too much, because it is a dry heat." I want you to understand something: my father was not joking. He's a serious man.

∞ ∞ ∞ ∞ ∞ ∞   ∞ ∞ ∞ ∞ ∞ ∞

And now, folks, back to Route 66 and an automobile trip that will remain in infamy. Vivienne and I were rolling along, happy as we could be. Radio, I'm sure, was an unheard-of thing in a 1933 car, but we made our own music. We sang every song we knew. The car behaved well. There was only one problem. Vivienne decided she wanted to drive. I wouldn't hear of it. In the first place, the only time she'd driven was the time she'd taken the car out by herself and been unable to figure out how to stop. In the second, third, and fourth place, she didn't have a license. She kept saying she wanted to drive, and I kept saying no!

"This is a perfect time for me to get some experience," she insisted.

"Not on a highway, it's not!"

"It's a straight road."

"No."

"There's no traffic."

"At the moment, no!" This went on for state after state, mile after mile.

"You drove without a license."

"That was two years ago, and I didn't know any better."

She finally wore me down. It was true there was hardly anyone else on the road. I rationalized that I was there next to her. I'd let her drive for a little while, as long as the road was straight, and maybe she'd be satisfied. We were somewhere in Oklahoma, when I stopped, and we switched seats. She drove for about five minutes. There had been no traffic. Then a car came from the opposite direction. There was no problem, but as he passed us, she jerked the car to the right, off onto a soft shoulder, and back onto the road. The car went into a shimmy and was going all over the road, when a huge truck came from the other direction. The driver blew his horn; our car was uncontrollable, with an uncontrollable driver. I realized if we went into the truck, we were dead. The car was already on the left side of the road, facing it. In a split second, I did four things: I turned off the ignition, pulled off her glasses, pushed her back against the seat, and swung the car all the way to the left, through a guardrail and down an embankment.

After turning or rolling or whatever, we came to a stop with the car on its nose in a gully. We climbed out of the car, apparently uninjured, and sat there in the dirt, laughing—I guess from the joy of being alive. I said to Vivienne that I felt like Topper. "Are we sure we're not ghosts?" By then, the truck had stopped, and the two men who were in it came to the edge, looked down, and asked if there was anyone alive down there. We assured them we were and asked if they could give us a lift to the nearest town.

I checked Viv over, and neither of us seemed hurt or bleeding. By then, a few cars had stopped to look at the wreck. One of the drivers offered to take us where we could make some phone calls; he told us we were in Bristol, Oklahoma. He was helpful, and when we reached a towing company, he was able to tell them exactly where the car was. It was totaled, of course, but we were able to get our possessions out of it. We got to Railway Express, packed up our stuff, and shipped it home. We then got a hotel room, and I jumped into a hot bath. Did I mention that when Viv was scrounging around in the dirt for her glasses, I still held them in my hand?

While I was luxuriating in the bath, Viv called home to tell her folks. While she was talking to them, I called her for help. I couldn't get out of the tub. I was in a great deal of pain. Apparently, the adrenaline that had come to my aid, allowing me to do all that was necessary, had deserted me once everything was taken care of. I was injured, and now I felt it.

Viv called a doctor. In those days, a doctor would make house calls or hotel calls. I had to go to his office for X-rays. It turned out I had broken the cartilage between my ribs. He taped me up and said it would be about six weeks before I healed. Since we had to go to Chicago to get the train to New York, we decided to visit her brother and sister-in-law, Natalie. Seymour was working in Chicago for *Time* magazine as the picture editor. Since I couldn't work in my present condition, we thought we'd hole up there for a while.

I liked both of them. Seymour and I got along great. Natalie was a lovely woman who ate like a bird. Unfortunately, that is the way she put food on the table—for birds. I was so hungry while I was there that I couldn't wait to leave. They lived across the way from the lake. I would sit on a bench there on a sunny day. It was nice, but there were no places to eat in the neighborhood. I looked in vain for a diner or a hot-dog stand. I looked in her fridge and in the cupboards. It was like Mother Hubbard's. I finally urged Viv not to overstay our welcome. She agreed. She said she was starving, too.

Chapter 5

How Do You Break into Show Business?!!

As soon as we returned to my in-laws' home, my father-in-law pounced on me to sell me on coming into his business.

"What do you want to cock around in that acting for? Come in with Dave Chassler. This is a business. It's a big business, and we're going to get bigger. You want to act? So you think I don't act in my business? Believe me, there's plenty of room for acting. I'm not asking you to work for me. You'll be a partner. With your personality, you'll be a knockout. Not only that, but you'll have money. You'll be able to drive a nice car. You love the theater; you'll be able to go to the best shows, sit in the best seats. It's one thing if it was a crappy little store or something. This is Dave Chassler's. This is the most respected name in the trade. You walk into any linoleum store in the city, any of Chassler's customers. Our trucks with *Dave Chassler* on them are all over. You'll be something. You'll be a mensch."

I did not immediately agree to his offer. First of all, I was still in pain and still taped up. He was, however, relentless, and I finally caved in.

How could I have done that? I'm an actor. That is all I ever wanted to be. How could I agree to go into the wholesale linoleum business? Whenever I've told this story, I have always blamed my decision on the fact that he caught me in a weak moment. I was taped up and in pain. I think I must stop deceiving myself—I caved in because I was a child of the Depression, and the fairy dust sprinkled over me by this man was too enticing.

For a while, the job was novel and fun. Dave Chassler was a funny man, and those first few weeks, he kept me in hysterics. He was also shrewd. Vivienne certainly inherited her sense of humor from him. He was taking me around and introducing me to his customers. He said that I would be calling on them to sell. At that time, however, selling was unnecessary. There was a big shortage of goods, and he was doling them out as a favor to his good customers.

His background was interesting. A tough kid who pulled himself up from poverty, he'd been in many businesses. He had even operated a nickelodeon in the earliest days of the movie business. I have no doubt that if he had stayed in that business, he would have been another Louis B. Mayer.

Before he became a jobber, he had a high-class floor-covering store that catered to upper-middle-class people. It was at a time during the Depression, when linoleum retailers would sell the big-name products, such as Armstrong and Congoleum, at three yards for a dollar, laid. The storekeeper would carry the goods up to the apartment and install the linoleum himself for pennies.

Dave carried unknown brands that people had never heard of, charging two or three dollars a yard and extra for installation. How did he get away with it? When a woman came into his store and heard the price, she'd say, "Why should I pay you so much? I could go across the street and get Armstrong or Congoleum for three yards for a dollar."

He would reply nicely, "Yes, I know. I do not carry those brands." Since his store was large and up to date, with everything beautifully displayed and Persian rugs everywhere—and since he implied that his wares were superior—she paid the price, provided she had the money. Of course, hers was the trade he wanted.

Many of the little linoleum storekeepers would hang out in his store and watch in amazement at the way he did business. One day, a lady came in to complain that the pattern was coming off her linoleum. She said, "I want you to come up and see for yourself."

"That won't be necessary. How much did you pay?"

"Two hundred and twelve dollars. I have the receipt right here. Look!"

He raised his hand to turn her receipt away without looking at it. "I believe you, Mrs. Walsh—please." He reached into his pocket, pulled out a roll of bills, and counted off $212, and as he handed it to her, he said, "I'm terribly sorry. I'll send a man up to re-lay your floor. There will be no charge."

The poor storekeepers in the neighborhood who were there because they had no business in their stores gasped and, after the woman left, called him a crazy man.

"I'm a crazy man, huh? That's advertising, schmuck. As long as that woman lives, she'll remember this. She will tell this story to everyone, and she will never buy from any of my competitors. You can't do that, because you don't have the clientele who can pay you that kind of money. You buy for twenty-one cents a yard, sell it three yards for a dollar, and break your balls schlepping the goods up three flights of stairs. Then you pay a kid a quarter to give out leaflets, which he throws down the sewer. You call Dave Chassler crazy! Dave Chassler is crazy like a fox. And I'll tell you something—she'll walk in here one of these days for a Persian rug, and I'll stick it to her, and she'll pay it because of what I did today."

He paid less money for an unknown brand, which he eventually turned into a known brand, and then sold his store and became the largest distributor for that brand.

He told me these stories as we visited his customers. We went into one store, where he said to the storekeeper as he hugged him, "Look at you, you momser!" He turned to me. "You know how long I know this bastard?" Then to the storekeeper he said, "Harry, meet my son-in-law. Handsome guy, huh?"

Then he turned to me again. "You know how far back we go? I was at his wedding, at his son's bar mitzvah. I remember this son of a bitch—how long already, Harry? I knew this bum when he was living in the back of the store on herring and potatoes. Am I right, Harry, or am I right? Now look at this place. A palace—right, Harry? Look at the goods." He walked around the store, tapping the rolls of linoleum, spreading his arms out in wonder at his friend's coming up in the world. "Look, tootsie—no business today. I wanted my son-in-law to meet you. You need some goods, call the office. Dave Chassler

116

takes care of his friends." He hugged him again. "I love this bastard!"

It all took place in about five minutes. We were out on the street walking, about two blocks away, in front of a drugstore, when he said to me, "Go in there and call the office. Ask them how much Harry's Floors owes us."

I came out and told him, "Thirty-two hundred."

"That fuckin' shithead. He's laying an egg."

"What?"

"He's going bankrupt."

"Who? Your friend?"

"*What* friend? He should drop dead! Only not before we get what he owes us. Come—we're going back."

I was lost. *Is he talking about the same guy—his longtime friend? Was that not true? Was it only an act? Was that what he meant when he said, "You think I don't act?"*

"Wait, I don't understand. You said he was in such good shape."

"Too good. Let me tell you something, son-in-law. You saw me tapping the rolls of goods? They are full rolls."

"So?"

"Nobody carries full rolls. They're pieces made to look like rolls. A woman comes in, says she wants that pattern. Then he calls up and orders. Besides, they are the wrong patterns."

I was finding it difficult to follow him. "What do you mean wrong patterns?"

"They are Italian patterns. He's in a Jewish neighborhood. He is sticking us, and he is sticking everyone, and he is going to unload the goods."

I started laughing. "Are you telling me the patterns care if you are Jewish or Italian?"

"No, the people care. Listen, Dave Chassler knows this business from the ground up. Look, a Jewish woman wants light patterns. Her apartment must have sunshine and double exposure. The Italians have big families, lots of children. They want dark patterns with lots of flowers; it shouldn't show the dirt. Come on—we're going back to talk to that bum."

We went back in, and Dave was solemn. He sat down and motioned to Harry to do the same. "I want to ask you something, Harry. Are we friends?"

"Sure, Dave, for years."

"So if you're in trouble, how come you don't come to Dave Chassler?"

"Who's in trouble?"

"Please, Harry, stop. Dave Chassler was not made with a finger. You're laying an egg. You know it, and I know it. You are going about it in a foolish way. You are still a young man; you are going to want to go back in business. Who will give you credit? No one. But you come to a friend like Dave Chassler; he can show you how to lay an egg and get back in business. Give me a piece of paper." He wrote a bunch of numbers and handed it to Harry.

"I want you to call my competitor and order these patterns. My truck will be here tomorrow night. We'll pick up the goods. This will wipe out your debt to us, and as soon as you want to go back in business, Dave Chassler will give you credit—and if Dave Chassler gives you credit, everyone will give you credit."

Wow! It finally was beginning to sink in. Here I was—the actor, the streetwise kid, the cynic—and I'd bought the whole caboodle. *So this is the business world?* On the one hand, I was impressed with him, and on the other, I wrestled with the morality of the situation.

Who was I to question that morality? Were my days as a candy butcher at the Bay Ridge Oval moral? I never gave it a thought then. I needed the money, and that was that. Cheating to get it was a game. Was all this a game to my father-in-law? Probably—he certainly seemed to enjoy it.

After the business at Harry's store, we went to lunch at a delicatessen. The place was crowded, so we shared the table with a stranger. In this case, he was a huge, stout man with a walrus mustache. Dave could not stand fat people. In any gathering, if there was a fat person, he or she would be the butt of his humor. If there were no fat people, he would pick on the most vulnerable. In every case, everyone would be brought to hysterics except the victim. In this case, the man sitting opposite him was also German, another of his hatreds. "Look at that fat pig," he said.

He didn't say it quietly, and I tried to shush him. That was another thing about him: he seemed to get away with saying the most outrageous things right to people's faces. Perhaps they couldn't believe they had heard him correctly or thought he was addressing someone else.

Dave was eating fat frankfurters called Specials, and the stranger, pointing to his plate, asked, "Iss goot?"

Dave answered, "Ya, iss goot. You fat turd."

The man nodded his head, smiling. Dave turned to the waiter and ordered for him. When the waiter brought the man his food, the man cut off a piece, but before he could get it to his mouth, Dave grabbed his arm and said, "Let me see if it's good enough," and ate it off the man's fork. I burst out laughing. I couldn't believe anyone would do such a thing to a stranger, and I couldn't believe the man's reaction. He sat there patiently watching Dave chew, waiting for his comment.

"Iss goot?"

"I'm not sure." Then, with the man's knife and fork, he cut off another piece, ate it, and said to me, "I'm going to eat his whole lunch." I was laughing so much that I was afraid I would toss my lunch. I was literally falling off my chair, begging him to stop. He didn't, and after eating it all, he said, "Iss no goot. Order something else."

The stranger looked at the menu and did as Dave told him. I couldn't hear what he ordered, because I was in such hysterics. Dave said, "Watch—I'll eat that dish, too." I was crying by then and couldn't stay there another minute.

"No, no!" I yelled, and I bolted out the door and into the street. I do not know how it ended. For all I know, he could have given the man our checks to pay. I had never seen anything like that outside of the movies. I certainly had never been a part of it. I could visualize W. C. Fields and Ben Turpin playing such a scene.

All this happened during my first week on the job. Though I didn't much like my father-in-law the first time we met, I was certainly warming up to him. If you make me laugh or let me make you laugh, I'm a happy man.

∞ ∞ ∞ ∞ ∞ ∞   ∞ ∞ ∞ ∞ ∞ ∞

Viv and I were living with her parents. Our bedroom was on the third floor of their comfortable house. We actually had two large rooms up there, so we had our own private place when we wanted it. We took our meals with the family, which was a mixed bag because Viv and her father couldn't exchange two words without yelling at each other.

There was no such problem with her mother. Henrietta was a sweet, placid lady. I guess she had to be to have lived so long with him. I always said that Henrietta saw no evil, heard no evil, and spoke no evil. I never heard a cross word from her. I loved her.

I stayed in Dave's business for only about eight months, for a number of reasons. The most important one was that I was an actor. Whenever he introduced me to anyone as a member of the firm, in my head, I always said, *I'm an actor.* I was also tired of being a pawn for his egocentric behavior. He always needed someone to feel superior to, and it didn't take long before he would ride me about how little I knew about the business. I think he thought I should know every pattern by the number, as he did. There were hundreds of patterns, each with a number, such as 5172. I can remember that because it was the most ordered pattern from the stores in Jewish neighborhoods. He didn't learn the patterns by numbers. He knew every pattern by having laid them, cut them, and sold them over a lifetime. To me, they were numbers stamped on huge rolls wrapped in brown paper.

My biggest beef with Dave was what he did to my wife and, therefore, to our marriage. Viv had no idea of her ability. She felt she was a nothing, because he made her feel that way. She had a love-hate relationship with him; she'd defend him to me and praise him, but she'd have the screaming meemies with him. They would get into arguments over nothing. At least, they seemed like nothing to me, but she would get so worked up that she would throw things at him.

She told me that there used to be a vase on the post of the staircase. She was always throwing it at him. One day, he glued the vase to the post, so the next time she went to throw it, she couldn't move it, and realizing what he'd done, she cracked up. She told me that story when we were in Santa Ana by way of illustrating what a great sense of humor he had. What she never told me was why she was always throwing things at him.

In later years, we both went for therapy. The shrink suggested she go to college. She felt that her marks in high school were probably not high enough to get into college. The doctor, who no doubt was aware of her lack of self-esteem, said, "Well, why don't you contact your high school and have them send you your transcript?"

She did. It turned out that she had straight As. She not only went to college in her mid-thirties but also later retired as a full professor from Fordham University.

∞ ∞ ∞ ∞ ∞ ∞   ∞ ∞ ∞ ∞ ∞ ∞

I actually had no idea how to go about breaking into show business. How could I get into radio or nightclubs or the theater? After all, I was only a shipping clerk before I was in the service. All my entertaining was either for free or for little money. The only professional jobs I'd had were the summer jobs at the Swan Lake Inn and Chester's, and even they had come to me—I hadn't gone after them. I wouldn't have known how then, and I still didn't know. All I knew was that I was a married man and I had to earn a living.

My friend Paul Hanenberg, another ATU buddy, suggested that I go to WNYC, the city station, and see his brother, who was a radio engineer there; maybe he had some ideas about getting into radio. That made sense. I took the subway to City Hall, wandered through the marble halls of the Municipal Building, and entered the studios of WNYC. I asked a young man where I could find Sid Hanenberg. He pointed to a door with a lit sign that read On Air. "He's pretty tied up at the moment. Can I help you?"

"Oh, well, I really don't know Mr. Hanenberg. His brother suggested I see him. I'm a comedian, and I'm trying to get some advice on getting into radio."

"A comedian—really? Hey, I'm the dramatic director here. He probably would tell you to see me anyway. My name is Al Marshack. Hey, let's not stand out here in the hall. We'll go into this empty studio and talk about it."

He didn't look like he could be a person as important as the dramatic director, not that I had ever seen a dramatic director. He was tall and slim, had salt-and-pepper hair, and was wearing a gray sweater and slacks. He was handsome, with a wide, smiling grin. He exuded enthusiasm. In the studio, he asked about me and listened with much interest, laughing at much of what I said. "Hey, why don't you go in there where the microphone is and do some of it for me?" He flipped on the console and sat back with his long legs spread out and his hands clasped behind his head, and he listened.

I responded so enthusiastically to this man's unassuming manner and his sense of joy in discovering a possible new talent that I kept rolling, and he kept laughing. When I finished, he jumped up and asked if I was free that night. He wanted to put me on a radio program that night—and he did.

If what I had just gone through was an audition, I had better savor it. I didn't know it, but it wouldn't be that pleasant and easy again.

There was something else I couldn't possibly have known then: the man who auditioned me, Alexander Marshack, the dramatic director, would one day turn out to be one of the geniuses of the twentieth century.

It all happened quickly. I can't remember what kind of program I was on—probably a variety show—but I do remember some of the material. There were a number of movies at the time with a psychiatric theme, and I did a routine that suggested that products and commercials would soon jump on the bandwagon and take advantage of this new trend. The important thing is that I no sooner got off the air than I received a call from Spivey, the owner of a sophisticated eastside nightclub, offering me a job. There were two requirements: I had to have a tuxedo, and I had to be able to start the next night. I said it just so happened that I could start the next night and, lying, assured her that, of course, I had a tuxedo.

The first thing I did that night was call my friend Freddy Katz to ask him to come down to Spivey's Roof as my accompanist for my opening performance. There was absolutely nothing that either of us would not do for each other.

The following day, I headed to a store that sold tuxedos. I was still flying; I told the man about my good luck and why I needed the tuxedo. He fitted me with all the accoutrements, and as I stood in front of the mirror, I felt I was on my way. I paid the man and asked how soon I could pick it up. He started figuring.

"Let's see … I have this fifty stout and the forty-two long. Then there is the wedding party and the bar mitzvah. I could skip the forty-four short till after, but then again, he's crazy if I'm late. Look, I'll put a rush on it. The best I could do is a week from Wednesday."

"A week from Wednesday! I told you I need it tonight."

"You need it tonight, you'll have it tonight."

The music at Spivey's was played on dual pianos. Spivey herself played with another person, a man. She would play and sing little double-entendre ditties, such as the following:

> They all go upstairs but me.
> They all attend to the
> Sentimental end.
> I just attend to the cashbooks.

She had quite a following and was a good performer. Her style was much understated, and her audiences loved her and kept coming back. The room was a cozy one with a bar on the left, which I would pass when making my entrance and exit. There wasn't a great deal of room for dancing, but that didn't seem to bother the dancers. She had an obviously rich clientele. Everyone was dressed to the nines.

Freddy showed up. He had just written a piece of entrance music for me, and it was delightful; Spivey loved it, as did the audience, because they started laughing as soon as they heard it. Why not? My accompanist was, at twenty-one, the first cellist in the Washington Symphony Orchestra, a man who would go on to compose concertos for Piatigorsky and mentor some of the most famous pop singers in the world.

Fred had to be there only that one night to play for me so that Spivey's accompanist could learn the music cues and some of the songs I did in the act. One was a singing commercial that led into this psychiatric routine:

> If you turn and twist at night,
> If you wake and scream with fright,
> If you are neurotic, too,
> Freud-complex vitamins are just for you.

Another song I wrote for later in the act admonished my audience for buying into all those radio commercials. The music was *Holiday for Strings*. The words were mine.

> Lucky strike is two to one,
> And Rinso gets your housework done,
> And Duz does everything in sight.
> With Eversharp, you're always right.
> Take Alka-Seltzer for a cold
> And Serratan when you get old.
>
> Sucker,
> Sucker.
>
> Venita Lacquer for your hair,
> Use Pepsodent for dental care.
> Chew Dentine for a sweeter breath,
> A Fairchild coffin at your death.
> Wear Barney's clothes and look distinct;
> See I. J. Fox for better mink.

Sucker,
Sucker.

You're afraid of chest cough due to cold.
Don't let yourself be swayed;
Be sure it's pure and genuine Musterole.
Don't buy a thing unless Sinatra sings
Its praises to the sky,
Unless you're really forced to buy.

The Dionne quintuplets always use it.
Now remember, don't confuse it.
Mrs. Truman thinks they're fine;
Her daughter wears them all the time.
Wear slacks or dress;
They won't distress.
Now you can look your very best tonight.
Good night.

I was walking along Sixth Avenue, opposite Rockefeller Center, when I saw a beautiful girl coming toward me. I have said I could always spot a Music and Art girl, and I was sure this young lady was one of them. She was wearing flat-heeled shoes and a simple tweed skirt, and she had a lovely, fresh face with no makeup. I couldn't think of her name, but I was determined not to let her get away from me.

I walked directly toward her. When she stepped to the right, I stepped to the right. When she stepped to the left, I stepped to the left. Finally, I put my hands on her shoulders, moved her up against a store window, and, bon vivant in my manner, said, "I know you. We went to Music and Art together."

She smiled at me. It was the most beautiful smile I had ever seen, other than on the screen. I must have turned a deep red, because I felt the heat of embarrassment as I recognized Ingrid Bergman. I quickly withdrew my hands from her shoulders and stammered, "Oh God, I'm terribly sorry," and she said, "That's perfectly all right."

We each continued on our way; I felt like the stupidest guy in the world. She was the top box-office actress in Hollywood. She was in New York, starring in *Joan of Lorraine* on Broadway. If that weren't stupid enough, I had seen *Casablanca* three times already, and one of the parodies I was doing at Spivey's was on the film *Spellbound*, starring her and Gregory Peck.

I put a new joke into the act that night based on when I had gone through to buy my tuxedo, only before the tailor said, "Don't get excited. You want it tonight, you'll have it tonight." I built it up and switched it to a suit that had to be imported. This joke had legs and has since entered the lexicon of jokes that I still hear from people in one of its many variations.

After I had finished my act and taken my bows, I headed for my dressing room as Freddy's run-off music was playing. It was after the late show, and as I remember it, I was not paying attention as I passed the bar. A lady slid off her barstool in front of me, blocking my way. As I tried to get around her, she said, "I know you. We went to Music and Art together."

There she was—only not in low heels and a tweed skirt. What are the odds of that happening? I was flustered and astonished. I think she said she had enjoyed my performance or "We enjoyed it" or thank you.

"No," I said, "thank you." I really don't know who said what—she or the man she was with—but I blubbered something and excused myself. Today I would not escape to the dressing room. I would like to think I'd have more savoir faire.

The following night, an important agent came to see my act. His name was Mark Leddy. It was a good night, and I had high hopes he would sign me. I sat down at his table after the show and asked, "Well, are you going to handle me?"

"No, sir."

"Why not? You saw what I did to this audience."

"Yes, I did, but how many audiences do you think you'll find like this? Your problem, young man, is that you suffer from intelligence. You would die with this act in the Copa or the Latin Quarter. They wouldn't know what you were talking about. You'll have to get yourself some broader material if you want to make it in the saloon business." I never really thought of it as the saloon business but I guess that is what it is.

So again, I still didn't know how to go about getting work in show business, but I had a hint. I needed an agent. *How does one find an agent when you know absolutely nothing?* I wondered. Today it seems simple. When young people ask me those questions, I can immediately direct them to the right periodical or published lists. But there is no guarantee that they will get an agent or that the agent will get them work.

I simply tore out a page from the yellow pages, which I carried every day as I trudged around town, checking them off from *A* to *Z*. That was a pretty frustrating experience. Nobody welcomed me with the open arms of Al Marshack. Of course, WNYC was a not-for-profit radio station, and I was thankful for the opportunity that they gave me, but they didn't pay their actors. Only the staff announcers were paid. It was part of the genius of Al Marshack that, along with the actors just starting out, all the famous actors also worked for free, attracted by the quality of the shows and his exuberance.

My rounds of agents' offices went something like this: I would enter the office and talk to the receptionist. She would usually ask the same questions, and the interviews would proceed as follows.

"Yes, what can I do for you?" she would ask.

"Ira Stadlen. I'd like to see Mr. Adams."

"Do you have an appointment?" Why do they always ask that? They have their appointment book right in front of them.

"No, I don't."

"Mr. Adams sees people only by appointment."

"I see. Then I'd like to make an appointment."

"Are you a performer?"

"A comedian."

"Are you working anywhere?"

"Not at the moment."

"Mr. Adams is not seeing any new people at the moment. When you are working somewhere, give us a call, and we'll try to catch your act. You can sign the book."

That was about it, with slight variations. Sometimes I would hit on a receptionist who was sweeter than the rest and took a moment to express interest, but aside from giving me a moment of hope, it was all the same. Of course, there are many agents who do not have receptionists, and there are those who do not bother asking anything and simply say, "Nothing today!" Most, however, ask you to sign the book. It is usually an ordinary black-and-white child's copybook. My name and phone number was on every copybook in New York, but I never ever received a call from any of them.

I had worked my way up to *L*, when I'd had it. I entered this man's office with a chip on my shoulder. It was the A. L. Lyons agency. There was no receptionist, and with his door open, I could see Mr. Lyons in his inner office. I walked in without knocking.

"Yes, young man? What can I do for you?"

"You can give me a job!"

"What do you do?"

"I'm a comedian."

"Are you working anywhere?"

"If I were working, it is probably because an agent got me the job, and no matter how small that agent is, he is probably bigger than you. So why would I come to you looking for a job if I already have one?"

"Hey, young man, don't take it out on me. I didn't make this problem."

"Maybe you didn't make it, but you're too stupid to do anything about it. How are you ever going to have a chance of hitting it big? Only by finding someone who has the ability to be a star! But you don't look at anybody, so all you can do is take someone who is on his way down. You get the dregs of what the bigger agents leave behind."

"You are absolutely right. Danny Kaye walked through this office the same as you."

"There—see?"

"All right, there is this one thing, the Entertainment Managers Association."

"What's that?"

"Every month, the Entertainment Managers Association puts on a dinner at the Hotel Astor, and they put on all the acts that have been bothering them throughout the month. I can put you on that if you want."

"Yeah, sure. I'll do anything."

I do honestly believe Abe Lyons booked me on that EMA dinner to get even with me for treating him like such a shit. I didn't get on till two in the morning, following the worst acts I had ever seen in my life. The singers couldn't sing. The dancers couldn't dance, and the comedians were not funny. By the time I got on, three-quarters of the audience had gone home. Those who were left were comatose.

While I was performing to nonexistent laughs, I could actually hear a wife berating her husband: "How long are we going to stay here, for God's sake?"

As I left the hall, a little man ran after me and said, "You were great. You killed 'em!"

"No, they were dead before I got on."

"No, really, you were terrific. Here's my card. Come see me."

Come to think of it, I had noticed one hand clap when I finished. I wasted no time. I went to see him the following morning. His office was in the old Strand Building. It was a small three-story walk-up. At the top of the stairs, on the second floor, was his door, which had a frosted-glass window with the following legend, as on his card: "Stardust Theatrical Agency, Joseph T. Cortillian, and AGVA Licensed Variety Acts of Every Description."

I opened the door into a matchbox of a room with that little man seated behind the desk, talking into a coin-operated wall phone. He had Cyclops glasses and a dead cigar in his mouth. He held up his hand to stop me from interrupting his call. "I don't know why you're so upset. They loved your act." He squinted at me and motioned to me to sit down, which was difficult to do and still shut the door.

"They said they want you back next year. Shirley, what do you want? It was a smoker. You're an exotic dancer, so they felt you up a little. You're a big success—be happy." He turned to me. "You're a hoofer?"

"A comic."

"So they ripped off your bra—how much does a bra cost?" Again, he turned from the phone to me. "When you're working, lemme know. I'll try to catch the act."

"You caught the act. You asked me to come see you."

"All right, so you'll make a new G-string. My God, it's a couple inches of material. They loved your act—I'm telling you. They want you back next year. Okay, keep in touch. Shirley, send me a check." He hung up. He was now all mine.

"I caught your act?"

"Last night. I'm the one who killed them."

"Right, right, the *Daily Mirror*-Nick Kenny Milk Fund."

"The Entertainment Managers Association."

"Right, right, at Webster Hall."

"The Hotel Astor."

"I told you to come see me?"

"And here I am."

"I don't have anything for you."

I was fuming and about to say some terrible things to him, when his wall phone rang. I decided to wait and give it to him, dammit. *He'd* asked *me* to come see *him*.

"Stardust. That's right. Joseph T. Cortillian speaking … Factory party … Yeah, yeah, we have all kinds of acts. Anything you can think of—a pickpocket? No. Has to be a pickpocket? I never heard of such a thing. That's not an act; that's a crime."

I kept tapping my chest and mouthing the word *me*. I was trying to get his attention, indicating that I could do a pickpocketing act. He paid no attention to me. He was conducting business.

"Look, gimme your number. Endicott two … Yeah, yeah. Oh, four. Right, I'll see what I can do. What are you paying? Look, I got a hot little exotic dancer … Has to be a pickpocket. Okay."

As soon as he was off the phone, I said, "Mr. Cortillian, I'm a pickpocket."

"I thought you was a comedian."

"I am. I'm also a magician. I can do a pickpocket, an act that will kill them."

Ira Stadlen, Magician

"Sonny, look, do me a favor. I got no time for games. I caught your act. You're a comic."

"Look, I'll prove it to you. Stand up." I didn't wait for him. I grabbed his wrist and pulled him up.

"What are you doing?"

"You think you still have your wallet?" He felt his back pocket to be certain.

"Yeah!"

"That's nice, but how much would you pay to get your watch back?" About the only thing I could do well to pass as a pickpocket was steal watches off people's wrists. At that, I was a crackerjack. I thought, *If I get the job, I'll improvise the rest.* Cortillian was in total shock.

"How did you do that?"

"I told you—I do a pickpocket act. I'm great. You won't be sorry. I mix comedy with pickpocketing. They'll love it."

He immediately put a nickel in the phone and called the people back with a cock-and-bull story about a pickpocket who'd just returned from playing the London Palladium. "Yeah, so gimme the particulars," he said. "When? Four p.m.? Yeah. His name? He is billed as the World's Greatest Goniff. No, you'll send me a check for twenty-five dollars. You'll pay the act twenty-five in cash at the party. Fine. Nice doing business with you."

"Wait a minute—what's this twenty-five to you, twenty-five to me?"

"Listen, you're an untried act. That's my insurance. Okay, we'll forget my commission."

Well, for sure, as a pickpocket, I was an untried act, but my attitude was "If you can't do it, fake it." Boy, did I fake it. I arrived at the party early and, after observing the people, selected a few who seemed to be extroverts and approached them to help me out in the act. They were delighted, as I felt they would be. They supplied me with wallets and keys. One woman even gave me her wedding ring. I instructed them to play along and act amazed. Almost everybody has a little ham in him or her and loves to be in the spotlight.

I went into the men's room with one fellow and rigged up his shirt so that as a finish, I would remove it in front of the audience while he was apparently wearing a suit and tie. I brought a number of people up onto the platform that served as a stage, stealing their watches on the way up. That was the only legit thing I did. With my shills, I could do anything. After supposedly stealing their wallets and returning them, I could steal them over and over again because they acted as if they felt nothing and were astonished each time.

After shaking hands with a lady, I held up her ring, asked if it was important to her, and suggested she keep it in her pocketbook, not on her finger. I would place it in her hand, actually palming it. She would stick her hand in her purse as if she were leaving it there, and later in the show, I supposedly stole the ring out of her purse. I kept going around to each person. I would steal watches again from the people who were not my shills and save my shills for all the things I couldn't do, which was everything else. I did all of this clowning around and throwing gags in all the while.

I must tell you that one extroverted shill stole the show. He was terrific. I pulled his shirt off at the end to great laughs and applause. It was all great fun, and now I'll cut to the chase. On my way home on the subway, my pocket was picked. I did the show for nothing. How is that for irony? Looking at the bright side, which I couldn't do then, I could now be unemployed in another profession.

I could do this act anywhere. In fact, now that you know my secret, you can do the act. You only have to get the jobs, and you ought to learn to steal watches. Actually, if you're good at picking shills, you don't even have to steal watches.

∞ ∞ ∞ ∞ ∞ ∞   ∞ ∞ ∞ ∞ ∞ ∞ ∞

At 10:22 a.m. on March 7, 1947, Vivienne gave birth to our son, Lewis. Unfortunately, we couldn't see him for seven days because a virus was circulating in the hospital and all the new babies were kept in quarantine. I know that parents think their newborn babies are beautiful no matter how their faces are scrunched up. Our baby was really beautiful because he was already a week old when we first looked at him. There was none of that newborn look. He looked out at us with intelligent bright blue eyes. His hair was dark like his mother's. He didn't look anything like me, with the exception of his ears. I had spent many hours doing self-portraits, and I knew every curve and dent of my ears. As he was growing up, every time someone said he didn't look anything like me, I was sure to say, "The ears. He has my ears."

Now I was not only a married man but also a father, and I was still earning next to nothing. If it weren't for the US government's 52/20 Clubs for veterans and my father-in-law's largesse, I do not know where I'd have been.

I was in the process of putting together a half-hour radio show of my own on WNYC that would air Monday nights. Hey, if a one-shot on radio got me a booking at Spivey's, maybe the exposure of a weekly show would bring me to the attention of the networks. It meant I had to put together a cast, including singers and musicians, who would work for nothing. It is a sad commentary on the acting profession that getting actors to work for nothing is never a problem. Fred Katz brought in the musicians, and I got all the best sketch actors in the business. Most of them came from *The Fred Allen Show* or *The Henry Morgan Show*, where they earned their livings. They moonlighted on *The Ira Stadlen Show* for laughs

Freddy had a friend he'd met overseas while in the army. The three of us hung out together at either Fred's house or the proverbial cafeteria. Joe Barry was a singer, and he was having as many problems with his career as I was. When I was auditioning singers for the show, Fred said, "How about Joe?"

"I was thinking about Joe, but I don't know. He has a tendency to sing off-key."

"Yeah, I know. I'm working with him, though."

I finally went with a French singer by the name of René Paul. Joe Barry became Tony Bennett.

I would write the show all week, and we'd rehearse on Monday afternoon and then do it live at nine o'clock that night. There was no tape at the time. The shows were recorded on sixteen-inch disks that were cut during the performance and were not meant to be played more than once or twice.

Our show started off with a stentorian announcer: "From coast to coast, from Rockaway to the Harlem River, *The Ira Stadlen Show*." Considering we aired at the same time as the *Lux Radio Show*, one of the highest-rated network shows, we received an amazing amount of coverage in the papers.

NBC actually called me to discuss the possibility of hiring me as a summer replacement for Jack Benny. There was a great deal of talk in *Variety* and the other trade papers that they were looking for new talent. These types of articles appear almost every year, and every year, the new talent they come up with has old names.

"Mr. Stadlen, what are your credits?"

"What does that mean?"

"Your credits. What you have done? For instance, if you wrote for Bob Hope for the past ten years, we know you could sustain a weekly show."

"I see. Well, I used to write *The Will Rogers Show*."

"Oh, well, that—"

"No, that's a joke. I'm only twenty-three years old. I couldn't have written for Will Rogers or for Bob Hope for ten years. I have written thirteen half hours. You, or someone, must have heard them—you called me in."

The new talent they hired for Jack Benny's replacement was Baron Munchausen, a German dialect comedian whose humor was based on exaggeration. He was funny, but he'd had his own show in the past, and he'd been around at least fifteen years.

Instead of becoming Jack Benny's summer replacement, I took a job with a touring puppet show, *The Suzari Marionettes*, traveling from school to school in northern New York State, doing *The Wizard of Oz.* I enjoyed doing all the voices, but I don't think Viv was happy about my being away all summer during our son's first year. I was making seventy-five dollars a week, and my sleeping accommodation was paid for. That meant I earned $750 for ten weeks' work. I was in no position to turn the opportunity down—or to turn *anything* down.

I had to face the fact that it was not really just for the money—I wanted to act. I did feel guilty—not because of Lewis but because of Vivienne. She didn't bug me about it, but I knew that was not the way for a grown man to act, at least in her lexicon. I wonder how Ida felt about Eddie Cantor being away so much that when he came home, one of his children cried, "Ma, that man is here again."

One of the nice things about the tour was that we played Ithaca. Melva, my half sister from my father's first marriage, and her husband, George, had a farm nearby in Alpine, New York. I was crazy about Melva. I had no address other than Alpine, but I thumbed my way there. Melva was a real pioneer. Their farm had no electricity or running water. There was an old hand pump outside. The kitchen had a wood-burning stove. When I walked in, she was surrounded by buckets of fruit that she was canning, and the smell of the syrup was sweet and pungent. She greeted me exuberantly, hugging and kissing me. It was a wonderful, emotional reunion.

Chapter 6

"This is the training ground, Kid."

My friend Eddie Kramer booked me on the Arthur Godfrey *Talent Scouts* show. The gimmick was that someone, supposedly a stranger, came on the show because he'd discovered a talented person, and he presented him to Arthur Godfrey. Godfrey interviewed the talent scout for as much comedy as he could get out of it and then said, "All right, let's see your talented find. Here he is! Mr. Ira Stadlen." The performer did his act; theoretically, agents or producers could then call up with offers, and the talent would be on his way up the ladder of success.

Eddie is a smart guy, and he knew that, as the scout, he had to feed Godfrey what he needed to get laughs. When asked what he did for a living, Eddie told him he was a pickle inspector. The audience laughed, and Godfrey milked it. This was the format of the show. The underlying raison d'être was that Arthur Godfrey got a show on the air for little money; I and other performers did it for the exposure.

Someone did call and offer me a job. It wasn't on Broadway or the Latin Quarter but as master of ceremonies in a hotel in New Hampshire for the summer. I took it—and the Lake Spofford Hotel turned out to be a classy place. It was still half a year until the summer, but it was nice to know that I'd have a job then at least.

Just because I was not earning any money didn't mean I wasn't busy. Thanks to the GI Bill, I enrolled in a painting class at the American Art School two mornings a week and a course in radio acting three times a week under the auspices of the American Theater Wing. In between, I was writing a full-length play with my friend Elliot Arluck and still making the rounds of agents' offices. I was as busy as any important executive, but if it weren't for my father-in-law, I'd have been on food stamps, had they been available then.

I was living in my father-in-law's house, eating his food, and depending on him financially. How did I feel about that, especially with such ambivalent feelings toward him? I didn't allow myself to dwell on it. In my bones, I knew the situation was only temporary. It also didn't seem so unusual to me. In my family, it was a fact of life that family took care of family. Wouldn't my father have done the same thing if he were capable? Didn't he do the same thing when he was? If I needed a rationalization, that was it, but I didn't need it. In my family, I was considered the one most likely to succeed. I was a good investment. If I'd sold stock in me, there would have been a line to buy it. I also had supreme confidence that I would make it.

∞ ∞ ∞ ∞ ∞ ∞   ∞ ∞ ∞ ∞ ∞ ∞ ∞

The play Elliot and I wrote was called *The Devil Wears Short Pants*. It was a farce with a serious message: our leaders should not be smug because we have a monopoly on the atom bomb. Someday even a precocious ten-year-old might be able to make one. This was 1947, before the Soviets had one, and that was exactly what the little nerd in our play did. He made an atom bomb with his friend and blew it up in Van Cortland Park in the Bronx. Of course, this was a farce, so no one was hurt. No one believed him. When his mother asked him where he was going, he told her, "We are going to Van Cortland Park to blow up our first atomic bomb."

His mother said, "That's nice. Don't stay out long—you have homework to do."

We had a great second-act curtain. He burst through the door of his parents' home, incandescent. "Don't touch me, Ma—I'm radioactive."

The play was read by some literary agents who felt it was funny but did not send it to any producers. I reread it recently and can see where it needed a great deal of rewriting. But I have seen plays go into rehearsal on Broadway that were not any more polished than ours. The writers, of course, were well known, and the producers had faith they could rewrite during rehearsals.

So now I was an unemployed playwright, pickpocket, comedian, actor, and magician, and we were all going to see the king to tell him the sky was falling.

The American Theater Wing came to the rescue, and I got my money's worth from the GI Bill of Rights. The class in radio acting for returning vets was not a class to teach acting; it was to give us an opportunity to meet some directors in the business and to let the directors see what we could do by directing us in a radio play. At each class, the director would cast the play by auditioning us, and then we would produce it. We worked under the time constraints of an actual broadcast. For each class, we'd have a different network director who was currently directing his own show. I felt it was the opportunity of a lifetime.

Everyone in my class was a dynamite actor. The same way I felt in high school—that I was in the right place at the right time—was the way I felt with this gang. My fellow actors included John Randolph, Steve Hill, Martin Balsam, Warren Stephens, Ross Martin, and Abe Vigoda. I was now part of a network of actors—people I could learn from. None of us were known. Some had more experience than others but in this radio business we were all starting out together.

I learned that I had to have a registry card—a file card with a small head shot in the upper left-hand corner. The rest of the card was divided into categories: credits, or what shows you had been in; characters, such as mugs, narrators, stooges, etc.; age range, meaning how old you sounded; dialects, such as French, Jewish, etc.; and, of course, your phone number and agent.

Despite the fact that I was always cast in the best parts and, according to my peers, was a sensational radio actor, I was not booking any shows. Why? Some of them would get an occasional part. When I confided this to my friend John Randolph, he said that was not possible. He asked to see my registry card, and after looking at it, he said, "No wonder you're not getting work with this card. They think you must be crazy. Look at it. Under characters, you have 'All characters.' Under age range, you have 'Cradle to the grave, all dialect accents.'"

"But I can do all that."

"I know it, and you know it, but no director will believe it."

"Didn't I play every kind of character in all ages for the directors in the class?"

"No. You played a character for each director. They were all different directors. None of them knew what you did for the others. We in the class knew because we were with you all the time. Look. Let me explain something. Radio directors typecast. They're busy running from one studio to the next. They do not audition anyone. As far as they're concerned, Joe Blow plays cops. If he needs an old professor, he looks in his actor file—usually one he has worked with—and calls the actor he knows is right for the part. I'm sorry, Ira, but that's the business."

I was not getting on any radio shows, but I was sure getting information. What Johnny told me was invaluable. I had a problem, and I had to solve it. I did. I made up a slew of cards with all the categories left blank. I would then research what shows each director did, and I would type in the category to fit that show. If it was *Gang Busters*, under characters, I would type in "Big, tough mugs." For voice range, I'd list "30 to 40." If they typecast, I would typecast myself differently for each show. Another thing I would do was fill in the credits category with a batch of radio shows, being careful not to list the shows of the director I was going to see. Yes, I lied.

Private Eye

Gangster

One director in class was Arthur Hannah. He directed two shows: *Perry Mason* and *Joyce Jordan*. He liked my work so much that he tried to hire me for a slot on *Perry Mason*. I then learned something else. All the working actors in radio had a phone service. Not just any service—two of them had direct lines to the third floor of NBC. When a director wanted to hire an actor, he would pick up one phone, and if the actor was not on that service, he would call for him on the other phone. The two services were called Lexington and Radio# Registry. Arthur Hannah picked up one phone and said into it, "Get me Ira Stadlen." When told I was not with them, he picked up the other phone, and when he was told the same thing, he said, "Okay, then get me Coney Evans." Art Hannah told me that himself. Johnny was right. These guys were busy, and they wouldn't take the time to look any further. He had another script to read and another show to cast. Naturally, I closed the barn door and joined Radio Registry. Since I had almost worked for Art Hannah, I put his two shows at the top of my credits for radio shows I claimed to have done.

I had an appointment with Morie Robinson, the director of World Security Workshop. Under the characters category, I listed "Narrator and politicians." Under dialects, I listed Russian and French. His office was on the second floor of NBC, and as he looked at my card, he said, "Well, you've done quite a bit of work."

I modestly shrugged. At that moment, Art Hannah passed by his open door, saw me, and decided to give me a boost. "Terrific actor, Morie."

"Oh, have you used him?"

"No, but I'll get around to it."

At that moment, Morie Robinson did a double take at my card that listed *Joyce Jordan* and *Perry Mason* on top. I quickly pulled the card out of his hand and said, "Wrong card." He looked at me, perplexed. Art Hannah came into the room to see what was happening. I pulled a stack of cards out of my pocket and said, "Pick a card, any card. I've got lots of them." Then I spread them out on his desk and said, "Can I help it if you guys won't hire anyone who hasn't got a million credits? So I give you credits."

They both cracked up, and after he finished laughing, Morie Robinson opened his drawer, took out a script, and asked me to read some narration for him. I did, and he said, "You've got it—Thursday, World Security Workshop. You'll be called with the time of rehearsal and the studio." We shook hands, and I had my first real network credit.

∞ ∞ ∞ ∞ ∞ ∞   ∞ ∞ ∞ ∞ ∞ ∞

My work on my weekly WNYC show led to a job on a local Sunday morning radio program on WHN, *The Yiddish Swing Festival*. The show starred Jan Bart, the Barry sisters, Sam Medoff's orchestra, and me. Twins, the Barry sisters made a big hit and a big record with "Bei Mir Bist Du Shoen." Jan Bart was a successful singer of both English and Yiddish songs, as were the sisters. Despite its name, the show was all in English. Like everything I was doing, it paid little. To my friends and fans, I seemed to be doing well, but believe me, financially, it was nowhere. I did them all because they were showcases. Ninety percent of actors' work is showcases. Where is the real money?

Jan Bart's agent was Harry Green. Jan told me to call him. He had praised me to him and felt he could do things for me. I didn't get anywhere with him, but months later, he called me to do a benefit for UJA at the Hotel Astor. He said it would be a chance for him to see my act. Of course I agreed. It turned out to be a big shindig, a $500-a-plate dinner, and every star who was in New York at the moment was on the program.

The MC was Broadway Sam, a ticket broker and a Runyon character. He had a stack of file cards in his hand, and he would look down at one, introduce the next artist, and then discard the card. This went on all night. Every so often, he would look at a card and put it behind the stack. He would then look down and introduce the next act. I figured that must be my card, because everyone he introduced was a star. Toward the end of his pack, he introduced Libby Holman. After she finished singing, he had two cards left. He looked down, exchanged the two cards, and introduced the hottest new act in show business. They were playing at the Capitol with Naked City and doubling at the Copacabana. They ran on dressed in white tuxedos: Dean Martin and Jerry Lewis.

I didn't know whether to cry or run to the bathroom. After they broke up the joint, he introduced Ira Stadlen, pronouncing my name as "Staidlen." Before you cry for me, I not only ended the show but also stopped the show. I had that audience in the palm of my hand. It was as if Dean Martin and Jerry Lewis were never there. Well, to be honest, they were also funny, but for that audience, I was the one. I left them sick from laughing. I had been standing on my feet all night. Now Harry Green besieged me. He grabbed my arm, holding me close to him so that I couldn't escape, and as a number of people approached us, he said, "Listen, kid, if anyone asks you, you're with me."

One of the men approaching said, "Terrific, is he with—"

Harry didn't give him a chance to finish. "He's signed to me." To me, he whispered, "You'll come in the office tomorrow; we'll sign papers. Sit down. You want something to drink? Something to eat?" People were coming over to him and congratulating him, and he kept saying, "How do you like my boy, huh?"

You cannot imagine the hubbub. People kept coming over to tell me how much they'd enjoyed my act, and he had his arm around my shoulder, hugging me to him as if he were protecting me from someone—I don't know who. I'm sure most of the people hovering over me were part of the audience; they were saying nice things, and I kept saying, "Thank you. Thank you." Perhaps there might have been some other agents he was keeping me from talking to. I wish I knew who they were. He was practically strangling me while telling me over the din how much he was going to do for me.

He called me the following morning. I don't know if he remembered that he'd told me to come into the office. He said nothing about that. What he said was "Listen, kid. This is what I'm going to do. We have to have the bookers see you. That's the first thing, so I'm going to get you on some Loews one-nighters. They pay shit, you know. I think fifteen dollars, but it's a place for me to bring the bookers to see you. Understand?"

The Loews one-nighters were stage shows that the theater threw in for free with the movie on Tuesday nights to hype business. This was 1948—everyone was staying home to watch Milton Berle on TV. Sure enough, Green called me back with a date at the RKO Prospect in the Bronx for the following Tuesday. I came early because I figured at the same time I could see the movie for nothing. This theater was one of those great movie palaces built in the twenties. It was now in probably the worst neighborhood of all five boroughs. When I entered, I saw two policemen stationed on either side in front of the stairs. There were many people in various stages of lovemaking in the aisles. The noise was deafening during the movie. Twice, somebody shot off a zip gun, a homemade gun that was in vogue with gangs at the time.

When the stage show started, the noise got louder. While the girl singer was on, someone yelled out over the din, "What a box!" It was a zoo of catcalls and four-letter words, and then there was a fanfare. The microphone rose up from the floor, the run-on music started, and I was on—well, almost. Someone was holding a person by his ankles over the balcony, which put his face directly in my line of view and amazingly close to me.

143

He held his hands to his face like a megaphone and shouted, "Get off the stage, you Jew bastard!"

I just stood there, thinking, *What am I doing here? These people are not interested in my entertaining them. Do I need this for my ego? I became a performer because my friends always wanted me to entertain them. Okay, Stadlen, you're a pro. Stop analyzing yourself, and do your act.*

I did it, but no one was listening. It was an exercise in futility. I got through it and walked off. A rummy stage manager with a pint sticking out of his pocket met me in the wings with my check. I looked around. Where was Harry Green with the bookers? Nowhere that I could see.

The next day, I walked into Harry Green's office, and this is how he greeted me: "Hey, kid, what happened to you last night?"

"You were there?"

"No, but I got the report. They told me you died."

"Did they tell you everything?"

"They told me you died."

"I mean, what was going on there?"

"Look, kid, they told me you died. Under the circumstances, I'm not going to handle you."

I stood there looking at him in disbelief. I was waiting for the punch line. He was obviously joking with me. The punch line didn't come. He was serious. I waited a minute and then burst out laughing.

"You won't handle me? You just saw me stop a show following Dean Martin and Jerry Lewis at a five-hundred-a-plate dinner in front of a well-healed, sophisticated audience. You were so hot for me you couldn't keep your hands off me. Then you book me into a douche bag of a theater where they are fucking in the aisles, and because a rummy stage manager tells you I died, you are not going to handle me? I have news for you. You couldn't handle me. You're too stupid."

∞ ∞ ∞ ∞ ∞ ∞   ∞ ∞ ∞ ∞ ∞ ∞

I booked another radio show with one of the directors I had in class. John Dietz directed *Casey Crime Photographer*. I was hired to play a gangster, and the rehearsal went smoothly. We broke for dinner, and when we came back, the director took me aside and said, "Ira, I have to apologize to you. I thought you had a deeper voice. What you are doing is fine, but I had in mind a gorilla of a man with a deep, gravelly voice, so I brought in another actor to replace you. I'm sorry. It's my fault, and I'll make it up to you."

"You mean something like this?" I said, and I did that kind of voice.

He seemed bewildered. "Yeah, that's it."

"Well, you're the director, Johnny. All you have to do is tell me."

That was a stupid thing to say. I embarrassed him. I should have kept my mouth shut, shaken hands, and walked out, and he would have used me on another show. As it was, I never worked for him again. Another lesson learned—never call the witch doctor a schmuck. He has the power.

∞ ∞ ∞ ∞ ∞ ∞   ∞ ∞ ∞ ∞ ∞ ∞ ∞

The summer of '48 was my payoff from the Arthur Godfrey show. I was the MC at the Lake Spofford Hotel. It was a tremendously enjoyable summer. I went over there like gangbusters. Spofford was a classy place where I met interesting people. Rudolph Serkin was one of the guests. I had the honor of holding his infant son while he practiced. If I ever meet that other great musician, Peter Serkin, I shall tell him he peed on me in his first year of life.

We had great guest artists come up to Spofford. Bob Fosse, then a young man, was part of a ballroom dance team, the finest I've ever seen. No wonder he rose to the heights he did.

I used to start rumors in order to keep the guests busy, but mostly it was for my own amusement. I started a rumor that Amelia Earhart had been found. It traveled around the hotel in minutes, and all the guests ran to their cars to tune in to their radios. They were harmless pranks, and they created a buzz.

I must tell you about one of the greatest pranks. At my table, there were only female guests. This was not unusual at these resorts. There were never enough men to go around. So week after week, there was a new set of ladies at my table who would hover over me, listening to every pearl that emanated from my lips. One morning, I was reading a letter from Vivienne, and as usual, she wrote something amusing that made me laugh.

I was asked what I was laughing at. I said, "Oh, it's nothing you'd be interested in." That was all I had to say. It became important to them to know whom the letter was from and why I was being so secretive. At that moment, a new prank occurred to me. "It's really something I can't talk about."

"Oh, come on."

"No, really. I just can't talk about it. It's just from a friend."

"A male friend or a female?"

"If you must know, it's a male friend. I can't talk about it. He is coming up here for a rest and doesn't want anyone to know."

"He's a celebrity?"

"No, he's not a celebrity. He's just a famous director. You wouldn't be interested."

"Who is he? Come on. Tell us."

"Are you people for real? If I told you, it would be all over the hotel in five minutes."

And I didn't tell them—until lunch. They were panting by then and wouldn't leave me alone. They swore up and down they wouldn't say a word. I tortured them for a little longer, and then, after making them swear on everything holy to them, I said, "He happens to be the most famous director in the business today: Elia Kazan." I had picked him because most people wouldn't know what he looked like, and I impressed upon them that he was exhausted and must rest.

I waited and watched as the new guests arrived in the dining room. Finally, I saw my man. He was a nerdy-looking fellow—skinny, with round shoulders and a caved-in chest. He looked around the dining room, unsure of what to do. I jumped up from the table and caught him before the maître d'. I gave his limp hand a hearty shake and, with the warmth of an old friend, said, "Welcome to the Spofford. How are you? I'm the MC here, and you're going to love this place. Have you been here before? No? Well, it's a great spot, and we're going to do everything to make your stay here memorable. Let me introduce you to our maître d." I put my arm around his shoulders, walked him over, introduced him, and said, a little more loudly, "Take care of my friend here, Victor." Okay, it was done. My job was finished.

This man had never had so much attention in his life. Women were sitting at his feet. They laughed at the unfunny things he said and found him absolutely fascinating. By the third day, he was coming down to meals with crazy hats. He had a ball of a vacation. I have often wondered what happened to him after that. Did the prank affect his life in any way? Could it have done some good, given him more self-confidence? I would like to think so, but who knows?

I remembered that incident many years later, when I took my friend's sister Florie to dinner at the Russian Tea Room. At one point, a beautiful woman came in on the arm of a short, fat, bald man. Florie looked at them and said to me, "Did you see that? Look at that gorgeous gal with that dumpy-looking man. My God, what can she see in him? A beauty like that could have any man she wants."

Remembering Lake Spofford, I said, "Do you know who that man is?"

"No. Who is he?"

"Probably the most famous director in the business—Elia Kazan."

"No, really?"

"You don't recognize him?"

"I never saw him. My God. He did *Death of a Salesman*." She never took her eyes off him. During the meal, Florie said the following things: "You know, he has a very sensitive face; I like his eyes. See how he listens to her? Most men don't listen. I wonder who she is. You know, now that I look at her, I see she's not so young—too much makeup."

She didn't go quite as far as asking what a great man like him was doing with a bimbo like her, but it wouldn't have surprised me. What do both those pranks tell me—or is *pranks* the wrong word? I think they tell me that power is a great aphrodisiac. The nerdy guy who was so unappealing became desirable to all those women at the hotel. Florie, who was so turned off by the short, fat, bald man, began having fantasies about him, I'm sure.

Lew Lair used to say, "Monkeys are the craziest people." I think people are the craziest people. And before Lew Lair or Ira Stadlen, Shakespeare said, "What fools these mortals be."

∞ ∞ ∞ ∞ ∞ ∞   ∞ ∞ ∞ ∞ ∞ ∞ ∞

I had applied for an audition at the Mutual Broadcasting System, and after a year, it finally came through. The audition was for a staff announcer's job. Their local affiliate was radio station WOR at 1440 Broadway. I went there determined to knock them dead and get the job. By that time, I knew that the networks held two kinds of auditions: one was when they actually needed to hire someone, and the other was a sop to all the actors who had applied for auditions. Obviously, I was on the sop list, but I felt that once they heard me, they couldn't help but hire me. The audition allowed me to read six different kinds of copy, including commercials, news reports, and introductions to various types of radio shows. One, a commercial, was designed to catch you out. I caught on, however, as soon as I looked at it.

"Gruen watches, the perfect holiday gift. This Christmas, give your wife the gift she is sure to love. Give her a Christmas Gruen." Of course, if one didn't give the right pause between Christmas and Gruen, it gave the reading a whole new meaning. The audition took six minutes.

When I finished, the man auditioning me came out of the control room, laughing. He said to me, "I have never enjoyed an audition this much since I've been in the business. When you did the newscast, you were not just a newscaster—you were a mature news analyst. When you introduced a comedy show, you out-Zeled Harry Von Zel. The trouble is, you sounded like six different announcers. We don't want our announcers to sound different."

"Why? I mean, I can sound like anyone."

"Yes, I see you can. But if you listen to Mutual, you'll see that not only do our announcers not sound different, they all sound alike. It is a network sound. Listen to CBS, and you will hear a specific CBS sound in all their announcers."

"Well, I can do that. I'll listen to your announcers. I can do it. I can sound just like them. Come on—give me the job."

"I'm sorry—that's not possible."

"Why? You said yourself it was a terrific audition."

"For one thing, you would have to have had two years of out-of-town experience."

"So what? I could have faked that."

"I want to tell you something. I wouldn't hire you under any circumstances."

"Why?"

"Because you make me feel uncomfortable. You're obviously very talented, and you're desperate, and I just don't want to be around you."

A sudden heat rose up from my body into my face. I was crushed. I thought I had been so close. He'd said he didn't want to be around me. *Everyone always wants to be around me. What happened to me?* I couldn't get out into the street quickly enough. I started walking, and the tears flowed down my face. I kept my head down. I didn't want anyone to see me. I was a mass of confusion and embarrassment. I wanted to hide somewhere.

As I was only a few blocks from the main branch of the public library on Forty-Second Street, I headed for it. I wanted to take refuge in the quiet and privacy of the third-floor reading room, one of my favorite places. It was where I had written most of my play. The green-shaded lamps on the table before each chair shone down in front of my space and made me feel I was by myself even if there were people on either side of me. The smell of books brought back memories of sitting on the floor in front of my father's bookcase. That room was my oasis in the midst of the city. I think it was my father's too. I would find him there on numerous occasions.

Desperate, uncomfortable to be around. These words kept going through my mind. I wanted that job. I was so near that I could taste it. *What did I do wrong? Maybe I was not close at all. Maybe it was a sham audition, just PR for the network. No! That lets me off the hook. I turned this guy off. He was right. I was desperate. I am desperate, and that is what I am projecting to people. That must stop! That's it. I will never ask for a job again. So how am I going to get one? There must be a way. I can't just wait for that break to come along.* I suddenly felt tired. I felt like sleeping. The man next to me had left some books on the table and had been gone a long time. I reached over and took one. I opened it up and closed my eyes. *I'll look like I'm reading,* I thought. In a moment, I nodded off.

I awoke as the man came back, and he said quietly, "Interesting, isn't it?"

I nodded and, for the first time, looked at the title of the book I was pretending to read: *Don't Sell the Steak—Sell the Sizzle.* It was not difficult to figure out what that book was about: selling. I went down the stairs to the circulating library on the first floor, found another copy of the book, and took it home.

The idea of being a great salesman intrigued me, but how could I be a great salesman for my product? The next day, I asked the librarian if she could direct me to books on promotion, especially self-promotion. There were quite a few. There was even a book by Robert Cummings, the actor, who had written about what he did in the way of promoting himself. I worked with him a few years later, and we talked about it. When he was visiting London, he'd watched a man changing the sign on the marquee of a West End theater. He'd offered to pay the man to put his name up there as the star of that play, just temporarily so that he could take a picture of it. He'd sent the picture to agents in the United States with a note that the English actor, Sir Robert Cummings, was coming to America. For the first few years of his career, he'd played only British parts and masqueraded as an Englishman. The Englishman bit was the sizzle.

None of the ideas in these books were lost on me. The question of how to sell myself occupied a large part of my thinking and would one day sprout into the modus operandi for my success.

∞ ∞ ∞ ∞ ∞ ∞   ∞ ∞ ∞ ∞ ∞ ∞ ∞

Meanwhile, I hardly saw my brother. He was a truck driver in the garment center and worked such long hours that even to his children, he was a vague memory. He managed to buy his own truck, which enabled him to work twice as hard to pay it off. Just as he did, along came two men known as Big Tom and Little Tom, who introduced themselves as his new partners. It was the mob's way of getting a legitimate business front to invest their ill-gotten gains. Little Tom, incidentally, was well over six feet.

Their place of business was a storefront on East Thirty-Third Street. I would go by there often in the hope of finding Cal in, but most of the time, he was out delivering merchandise. I did catch him one day, and we went into his office.

Let me set the scene for you. There were two rooms with dirty brown walls and phone numbers covering the walls. There was a hand truck in the front room and a desk in each room. In the front office, every time I passed by, I saw a scrawny little man in a coat and hat, smoking a cigarette. Sometimes there were other people, but people or not, he was always sitting there smoking up the room. We had to pass him to go into the back room. I asked Cal who he was. He answered, keeping his voice down, "That's Jake. He's a three-time loser, so he has to stay clean. The mob has great respect for him because he is supposed to have spit in Dewey's face in the death house. He is now the judge of their kangaroo court. He decides who lives, who dies, who stays in business, and who goes out."

"My God, what is it like with them?"

"It's not too bad as long as you don't cross them. The other day, I said they were wrong about something, and Big Tom picked me up by my throat and held me against the wall and said, 'You little shit, who you think you're telling we're wrong?'"

151

"Jeez, what did you do?"

"I said, 'Kill me.'"

"What!"

"That's what he said. And I said, 'Kill me. Go ahead and kill me, because if you ever do that to me again, I'm going to kill you.'"

"You said *that*?"

"That's the only language they understand."

∞ ∞ ∞ ∞ ∞ ∞   ∞ ∞ ∞ ∞ ∞ ∞

Doing my daily rounds of agents, I walked into the Baum Newborn office. I would hit them at least once a week. They were always open to a little schmoozing, and I would kid around with them. They were just starting off in the business, and they were a couple of go-getters. Marty Baum was a little redhead with freckles, a sort of a hotshot, fast-talking guy. He was the ideas man. Abe Newborn was more laid back and imagined himself a philosopher. They were a good team, able to play good guy and bad guy if the need arose. This time, I hit them on a good day. A comic playing a club in Merrick, Long Island, had taken sick, and they needed a replacement that night. They gave me the job.

The club was called the South Shore Terrace. They didn't do much business during the week but were packed on weekends. Marty and Abe showed up on Saturday night and caught my act when I was breaking up the place. Marty descended on me à la Harry Green. "Hey, kid, I haven't seen anyone kill an audience like this since Milton Berle. I got plans for you. I'm gonna send you out of town, one club after another. I'll have you making a thousand a week in no time."

It seemed to me I'd heard this song before.

The following week, he booked me into a club in Erie, Pennsylvania, for $150 a week. I arrived at a club, which looked more like a bar, and asked the bartender where the room was. "You're standing in it."

"What do you mean? Where do I work?"

He pointed to the top of the bar.

Oh my God, I'm a geek, standing on a bar like the Café Metropole. It's not like they never saw my act. I do a lot of physical stuff, pratfalls and everything. I suddenly lost my voice. *What am I going to do up there?*

I sat in my room and wrote Marty a long, stinging letter. But I did what always happened to me when I was hurting: I wrote in a funny way. When I'd finished the letter, I had created a bar act. My voice came back. "Hi, folks. You're probably wondering what I'm doing standing here. Let me tell you about my agent."

A few days later, Marty called me. I started screaming at him.

"What are you screaming for?" he said. "They love you. They want to hold you over."

"On the bar? I'm working on a bar. I had to write a whole new act for this place."

"That's right. This is the training ground, Kid. When I get through with you, you're going to be able to play anywhere under any conditions. You're a trouper, and that's the business." I think Marty had seen too many Hollywood movies.

In my next booking, he got my salary up to $175 dollars a week. I can't remember the name of the club, but it had a marquee, and on the marquee was the name Arky Stanton. I asked the owner why he had that name up there. "I have a contract to play here," I said.

He said, "That's the name your agent gave us."

I called Marty in New York, and he said, "Oh yeah, we changed your name. Ira Stadlen sounds like a girl."

"Thank you, Mr. Baum, but if anyone is going to change my name, I'll do it."

When I got home, I discussed the situation with my father. "Dad, I have to pick a stage name, and I don't want it to be a stupid name like Arky Stanton. I don't know that this is all I'll do with my life. It should be a name that could be a comedian's name, but I want it to have some dignity."

My father thought about it and then said, "Well, my favorite humorist is Jonathan Swift."

"And mine is Fred Allen—so how about Allen Swift?" The moment was history in the making.

153

My next booking was the Lepis Club in Pittsburgh, Pennsylvania. True to his word, Marty got me $200 a week. I was getting up there. I took a cab from the train station, giving the driver the address. It seemed to me we were going right past the city. In fact, we were out in the country when we pulled up before a beautiful home. It was completely dark, and I was sure we had the wrong address. "You better wait, driver. Let me see if this is the place."

I walked up to the door and tentatively rang the bell. I waited, and then a little panel opened in the door, and a man, visible through the panel, said, "Yes?"

"Is this the Lepis Club?"

"Who are you?"

"I'm the comedian. I'm supposed to play here." There was a buzz, and the door opened. The man, who was wearing a tuxedo, opened another door and ushered me in.

It was a club all right—a gambling club. The place was alive with formally dressed people gambling at craps tables and roulette. There was the tinkling of glasses and laughter and the hum of many people having a good time. *Wow, this is just like the movies.* It dawned on me that working here could maybe get me arrested along with everyone else if the police raided the place. I soon found out there was nothing to fear. Sophie Tucker had played there the week before. And in fact, we *were* raided one night.

The management made an announcement that we were going to be raided. "Ladies and gentlemen, the gambling will have to stop for a while. The police will be looking in on us in about fifteen minutes. There is nothing to worry about. It is just a formality." That said, the craps tables turned into pool tables. Gambling was nowhere to be seen. At the appointed time, the police captain arrived with a few of his men, gave a cursory look around, had a few words in private with the owner, and left. It was indeed like the movies.

Playing in this club was a mixed blessing. The gambling stopped when the show went on. You might think that was nice for the performer, as it would keep the audience's attention on me. True—however, if the house was winning when they

154

had to stop, the management hated me. When the people were winning and they stopped the gambling for the show, the audience hated me. It shouldn't surprise you that considering who the management was, I preferred the audience to hate me.

My next booking was at the Top Hat Club in Montreal. I would be getting $250 a week.

"See?" Marty said. "I'm getting you up there. Oh, by the way, we had to go through the May Johnson office in Montreal, so you will have to pay another ten percent to them."

Okay, I thought, *so I'll get two hundred instead of two twenty-five net.* Not so! You see, I was paid in Canadian dollars, which were worth 15 percent less than American dollars. So I ended up with $162.50 net.

It turned out that the money was not the biggest problem at the Top Hat Club. I called a friend of my brother's, who had roomed with Cal in California, to come down and visit with me. He was there on the first night. There was not a snicker in the audience—not even a smile. I was mortified. Cal had, no doubt, touted me up to the sky. But his friend knew exactly what was wrong. I was in a French-speaking club in the French part of town, and nobody could understand me. Thank you, Marty Baum. I know, I know: "It's all part of the training ground." You'll pardon me if I do not swallow that garbage. I believe my agents would have booked me into an audience of people who could not hear or see if there were a 10 percent commission in it for them.

I cannot claim to have solved the problem of not speaking French. I did not take a speed course at Berlitz. I tried as much pantomime as I knew, but at the Top Hat, I was a fiasco. For some reason, that ended my nightclub bookings from the Baum Newborn office. Who knows? Maybe I got a bad report like the one I'd gotten from the RKO Prospect in the Bronx. With all due respect to them, though, the nightclub business was dying all over. But they did keep me busy playing the mountain resorts in the summer.

I really liked those two guys. We had a nice, fun relationship, and I felt they were my friends. Abe invited Vivienne and me to his wedding, and their office was always open to me. During the summer, I would play two, three, or as many as four hotels a weekend. Some of them were in the Catskill Mountains, the borscht circuit, or the White Mountains of New Hampshire, which I called the Vichyssoise circuit. Both areas catered to a Jewish clientele, but the Jews at the New Hampshire hotels had more money and tried to distance themselves from those in the Catskills. I found this amusing and would often give them their comeuppance in a subtle way. Many times, a woman at my table would ask me something like this: "Mr. Svift, hev you ever been to the borscht circuit?"

"Oh yes, many times."

"Really, vot is it like?"

"It's the same as here, only instead of calling it filled fish à la Balsoms, they call it gefilte fish. And instead of calling it beet soup, they call it borscht."

I was playing at the Balsoms the summer of '48. The Truman versus Dewey election was coming up. The Balsoms catered mainly to German Jews. I was sitting at a table in the Balsoms nightclub, waiting to be introduced, when I overheard this conversation at my table. A well-dressed gentleman of about fifty, smoking a cigarette through a holder, said, "Za trouble vit diss country iss dare iss no leedership. Vat diss country needs iss a Hitler."

I was ready to explode, but I held myself in check.

"Excuse me. Did you say what this country needs is a Hitler?"

"Yes."

"Isn't the reason you are in this country because of Hitler?"

"Yes, but dat's because Hitler persecuted za Jews. If he did not persecute za Jews, he did vunders for za country."

"May I ask you what you do for a living?"

"I em in finance."

I was looking around for something to throw at him or some liquid to fling in his face, when I heard, "And here he is—Allen Swift." I walked out on the floor, hating everyone.

That was not the right kind of warm-up for going out there and being funny. I never do impersonations in my act, but I needed time to get over my anger and into a better frame of mind. I started with FDR's "The only thing we have to fear" speech. Throughout the audience were gasps and comments like "My God, it sounds just like him." There was no applause. There was knocking. They all had little knockers at the tables—round little wooden balls on sticks. They couldn't be bothered putting their hands together. That was a first for me. I had never seen anything like that.

∞ ∞ ∞ ∞ ∞ ∞   ∞ ∞ ∞ ∞ ∞ ∞

About that time, Viv and I rented our own apartment. It was in the Trump development in Brooklyn, owned by Donald Trump's father. It figured every week in my WNYC show as the Trumped-up apartments. It was so tiny that when Vivienne's aunt and uncle came for dinner, after some crackers and cheese in the living room, her uncle wanted to know why we were all sitting in the foyer.

Our great joy and entertainment at the time came from our son, Lewis. He was born able to carry a tune and with an innate ability to entertain. He would sit in his high chair and, before he could speak, rock back and forth humming "The Anniversary Waltz" from the record of *The Jolson Story*—and I mean perfectly. Viv and I might not have been too happy with each other, but Lewis brought sunshine into our lives.

The summer was clearly the time I would make most of our money, so I was always looking for a way to augment my earnings. I talked my way into a part-time teacher's job at the School of Radio and Television Techniques. Using my script for *The Devil Wears Short Pants*, which was professionally bound, I presented myself as a playwright and, therefore, able to teach scriptwriting. I do not know if they actually read my play before they gave me the job or were simply impressed by the look of the script and my line of malarkey. The funny thing was that Brooklyn College sent their students there for these courses, so I could say I taught at Brooklyn College. At any rate, a number of my students through the years became professional writers and told me how much they learned from me.

Through a friend, Mel London, I landed another part-time job, teaching radio announcing at the Cambridge School of Broadcasting. Here, unfortunately, I had many students who were just wasting their GI Bill money on something they could never do.

Yet I also experienced in this job the great sense of accomplishment a teacher feels when he gets through to a student and really makes a difference in his or her life. One of my students, Bruce Palladino, had a rich, deep voice but an atrocious Brooklyn accent. I mean, he sounded stupid. When he said to me, "Hey, Mister Swif', wadaya tink? Coo' I make a goo' radio 'nouncer?" the entire class would break up.

"Bruce, nothing is impossible if you really put your mind to it. I'll work with you in class on your speech, but you'll have to do a great deal of practicing at home."

He took the task seriously, and one day, he said, "I don't know. Sometimes I want to say something, like when we practice an interview, and I don't know the word to use."

"You mean you do not have the vocabulary. Okay. Let me give you a great idea, and this is for everyone. Go into the Five and Ten, and get yourself one of those little pocket dictionaries. Every day, pick out one word you do not know the meaning of, learn its meaning, and use it as much as you can all day. You have plenty of time on the subway, coming here and going home. It is only one word a day. If you do this every day, at the end of the year, you will have three hundred and sixty-five new words. Think about this. The average person uses no more than two hundred words in his or her vocabulary."

He was the only one in the class who did the assignment. He was amusing, coming up with some words that seemed alien to him. One day, he said to me in his best but self-conscious speech, "You know, Mr. Swift, my friends on the block are laughing at me. They say I'm talking like a fairy. I am just trying to do as you say. I keep speaking the way you say is correct, but boy, are they giving me the business."

"Sure they will. But let me forecast the future for you. A year or two from now, you are a radio announcer and your friends are still hanging around the corner, and you know what they are saying? 'Hey, you know dat Bruce Palladino on radio? I know 'im. He use to live here. I know 'im poisonally.' See if they call you a fairy then."

I spent most of my time, in class and out, working with Bruce. I felt like Henry Higgins. He was worth the time. Now that he was rid of the "dees, dems, and does" accent, I realized that his voice, with its deep timbre, was pleasant. I worked with him to make an audition tape and helped him create a résumé. He was tall and presentable when he dressed up, and I included his picture on his résumé. We sent it to all the out-of-town radio stations, and he got a job at a station in Phoenix. Now, that is what I call satisfaction. I do not know if he moved on to anything else after that, but looking back on that first day in class, what expectations did he have? Maybe he could drive a truck, be a laborer on a wrecking crew, or something similar.

Chapter 7

Finesse

In the spring of 1951, I answered an ad in the *New York Times* for artists to paint on canvas, with minimum earnings of twenty-five dollars a day. It sounded good. When I arrived at the designated address, a loft in the west thirties, as many as sixty or seventy men and women were standing around, many carrying paint boxes. Hundreds of canvases were stacked up against the walls. An easel stood in the center of the room, and on a table next to it was a palette with paint and brushes. A man walked to the easel and started talking.

"May I have your attention, please? I realize you're all wondering about this ad, and possibly, the sight of so many of your fellow artists may cause some dismay among you. Please do not leave until you hear what I have to say. We will hire as many artists as can handle the work. This is a very big company. You've probably all heard of the Globus stamp album. Well, this is the Globus International Stamp Company. We sell to millions all over the world. Now Mr. Globus has branched out into the art market.

"He's not interested in fine art. He's not even interested in good art. Mr. Globus is first and foremost a businessman and a realist, and he's painfully aware that the public is not interested in art. They are interested in pretty pictures that are colorful. Mr. Globus is going for the mass market. But instead of prints, Mr. Globus is adding a bit of glamour to his product: hand-painted pictures. We're not looking for good painting. We need a form of commercial painting that requires a certain technique. Some of you will be able to master it, and some will not. It has nothing to do with your ability as artists, believe me. You couldn't sell these people a Picasso for anything.

"If you look around the room, you will see the type of work we are looking for. You have to be able to do it, and you have to be able to do it fast. Mr. Julio here is going to demonstrate a technique that is fast and good." A man approached the easel. "Mr. Julio is able to knock off a sixteen-by-twenty painting in less than five minutes. Watch him. Notice he uses a house-painting brush for most of his work. He paints in the sky first with two or three strokes. Now he drags the brush with a little gray blue—a little darker than the sky—across the horizon, moving up and down to simulate mountains in the background.

"Mr. Julio will continue to paint so that you can watch him and learn the technique. We supply the canvases and paint and pay anywhere from two to five dollars apiece, depending on the size. I know that seems like little money, but if you master the technique, you'd be surprised how much you can make. I suggest you set up five or six canvases. Do all the skies at one time, then the mountains, et cetera. Don't worry about originality. Mr. Globus will be wholesaling these all over the world, so the chance of someone seeing a duplicate is negligible. Now, I'm sure you have seen similar paintings in galleries and department stores for two and three hundred dollars, but that is not the market Mr. Globus is going for."

At that point, someone asked if the artists had to sign their names to the paintings, and the man said, "Sign any name you like. In fact, the best thing is to make the name look indistinct."

I took some canvases and paint. I walked out with an old, bearded artist, and we talked on the way to the subway. "Can you do this kind of stuff?" I asked him.

"You mean buckeye? Yeah, I guess so, but I won't."

"What did you call them—buckeye?"

"Yeah, that's what that kind of painting is called. It started at fairs in Ohio. You know, the Buckeye State. Some guy would knock them off as an attraction in a couple minutes and sell 'em to the rubes for a couple o' bucks. I'll tell you the truth. You spend forty years painting and always trying to do better. Why in hell do you want to do worse? I didn't know this was to paint buckeyes, or I wouldn't have bothered coming down."

I lined up a number of canvases in the kitchen and soon learned what the old painter meant. I was terrible at it. Everything I knew about painting got in my way. You sort of have to unlearn what you know, or you keep trying to improve it until it's not good painting and not good buckeye and takes too long to do anyway. I threw in the towel.

∞ ∞ ∞ ∞ ∞ ∞ ∞   ∞ ∞ ∞ ∞ ∞ ∞ ∞

The summer of 1951 started with foreboding. My father, who I later learned had been suffering with angina for many years, had a heart attack and was taken by ambulance to the hospital. It was strange. I never remember my dad being sick or complaining about anything. My mom was the sick one, walking around with such high blood pressure that she was considered a walking time bomb.

I went to see him in the hospital, and we talked, mainly about my cousin Clare, who had given birth to a girl the night before. His face lit up when I told him. He really loved children. He asked how I was doing and then said something that sent shivers through me: "I don't mind dying. We all have to die, but I have nothing to leave you."

I choked up. I couldn't answer him. I had to turn away from the bed so that he wouldn't see my tears. It had never occurred to me that he was anywhere near death. I managed to mumble something about seeing him tomorrow and bolted out of the room, bawling all the way down the stairs. *How could I have lost it like that? Why couldn't I have answered him and told him how much he has left me? How much of him I have in me? What his love and guidance and belief in me meant? That was so much more important than money.*

I will tell him all that tomorrow when I am more composed. Only I never got the chance. He died that night.

∞ ∞ ∞ ∞ ∞ ∞ ∞   ∞ ∞ ∞ ∞ ∞ ∞ ∞

Meanwhile, having done some research into methods of advertising and promotion, I had devised a plan. I was going to advertise and promote my product: Allen Swift. With that new name, it became simple. I was Ira Stadlen, not Allen Swift. Allen Swift was no more than waterless cookware—a product.

If they didn't buy my product, my ego was not involved. They could no longer hurt me if they rejected my product. They were not rejecting Ira Stadlen. So I would promote my product to the hilt. I sat in the third-floor lounge at NBC and addressed registry cards with Allen Swift's picture on them. I wrote things like "On *Gang Busters* Saturday night. Catch me if you can" or "On *US Steel Hour* and *Kraft Theater* this week. Catch me if you can." I sent these out daily—naturally, not to the directors of those shows.

My friend would see me doing this and comment, "What are you doing? You're not on these shows. What if they listen?"

"Why should they listen? They never listen when I'm on a show, and if they listen, will they know which one is me?"

"But they won't hear your name on the credits."

I tried to explain. "They are not interested in me. They don't care about me. They will dump the cards in the wastebasket. But as they do, week after week, they will get an impression of a face and a name of a guy who does a great deal of work. That's all."

That was only part of my scheme. There was a callboard on the third floor. When calls came through for a certain actor, the guide on the floor would page him or her and, if the person did not answer, would put the name on the callboard. The busy actors—the ones running from one studio to the other—were always being paged, and their names were always on the callboard. I happened to find a company phone on a wall in the back of the second floor; no one seemed to know it was there. I would hop down there and call for Allen Swift. That way, I was being paged all the time, and my name was on that callboard with all the hotshots. Directors walking through the lounge, which they always had to do to put in their casting calls, would hear or see my name.

That was not all. I am a great joke teller. People like to hear my jokes, so I used that, too. I would manage to be passing by a studio when I knew its show ended. I would catch the director, always with a script in my hand and always in a hurry. I would tell him a joke, supposedly on the run, and while he was laughing, I'd apologize for having to run. This went with the promise I made to myself to never again ask for work. The only way was to make them come to me and want me—or, rather, Allen Swift.

As a teacher of playwriting back in the School of Radio and Television, I always stressed to the students that their characters had to be consistent. They couldn't just do and say anything that the character, based on his background and personality, would not say. The same was true for my character, Allen Swift. For instance, when I'd go to an audition for a show on television, which was quickly taking over radio, I would not wait around if I wasn't seen at the appointed time. Often, there would be many actors waiting their turn to audition, and I would be told to wait my turn.

In such a case, I'd ask the receptionist for a piece of paper and write a note to the director or producer in charge of the audition. I would write something like the following:

Dear Mr. Whomever,

My appointment was for two o'clock. I was here on time. I realize you are a busy man, and I suspect your time is important to you. It is also important to me. In the future, if you cannot see me at the appointed time, please feel free not to call on me.

Sincerely, Allen Swift.

After a while, when a casting agent called me for an audition, I would say, "Gee, I'd love to, but I'm so backed up that day that I can only make it if I can be taken at that time. Would you please let them know that?"

When I walked in and announced to the receptionist, "Allen Swift—I have a two o'clock appointment with so and so," she would say, "Yes, Mr. So-and-So is expecting you." I would be taken right away.

My poor waiting fellow actors would turn to me with hostility: "Hey, I've been here since eleven thirty—how come you're taken in ahead of me?"

I'd reply, "Don't blame me for standing up for my rights. Stand up for yours."

Years later, when I was on the National Board of the Screen Actors Guild, I was responsible for a union rule that paid actors who were held over a certain length of time at an audition. I can't say it did too much good. I never came across anyone besides me who would stand up to a producer for what was justly his. If I came to an audition and saw a great many actors waiting, I would go over to each one and ask, "How long have you been waiting?" If it was over the allotted time, I'd say, "You know you are entitled to be paid for this. I'm on the board of SAG, and if you give me your name, I'll see to it that you get paid."

"Who's asking you? I don't want to start any trouble."

"There will be no trouble. You don't have to do anything. You signed a time-in sheet, as did the others. I'll simply take the sheet and see to it that everyone who has been kept overtime is paid."

"Please stay out of this. It's not your business."

That was the way it was, and it still is. I worked like crazy on the board to get that law through so that actors would be treated with a little dignity. That's the reason there's a sign-in sheet at every audition. I sometimes wonder what the actors think that sheet is there for. (Ah, there's so little work, who can blame them for running scared? Not everyone knows about selling the sizzle instead of the steak.)

The promotion I was doing started to work for me. I was not getting rich, but I was getting more radio shows. I even landed a running part on a daily soap opera, which was titled, ironically, *The Brighter Day.* But I did not sit on my laurels. I continued to call the third floor for Allen Swift every day.

In *The Brighter Day*, I played the part of Buzz, the big, dumb oaf sidekick of the star, played by Johnny Larkin. Johnny was a handsome, square-jawed leading-man type. He was a nice person and a damn good actor.

Now, soap operas are to drama as comic books are to literature. At least that is my interpretation. I didn't think anyone took them seriously. One day, when we came into the studio, a lady was sitting there. We were told that she was Lady Astaire, the sister of Fred Astaire. Apparently, NBC was trying to get her for an interview, but she turned them down because she wanted to stay home to listen to *The Brighter Day*. They persuaded her to do the interview by promising her she could attend the radio performance, which was in the studio next to where the interview was to be held. We started the performance, all of us standing around the mike, and all through it, she wept and sobbed something awful. So apparently, some do take soap operas seriously.

She was not the only one. The writer of the show, who was obviously a multimillionaire and lived far off somewhere, kept a huge apartment in the Waldorf-Astoria for the few times he came into the city. He gave a party for the cast in his sumptuous digs. Everyone was sitting around him as he held forth about his writing. He spoke of the inner meaning of his characters and of what made this show a great work of art. Now, stupid me, I thought he was kidding. I thought he was satirizing his own work, so I joined in. No matter how he eulogized his work, I did him one better. I compared his writing to Strindberg and other greats.

Johnny Larkin found a moment to pull me away from the group and said to me, "I think you think he's not serious. So far, he hasn't caught on to what you're doing, but you're treading on dangerous territory. He means every word he's saying."

Wow, that was one on me. I shut up from then on and was thankful to Johnny. I could have lost my job quickly. As it was, the job was not long for this world. Johnny Larkin left the show for the pull of Hollywood. I couldn't blame him. He had all the earmarks of someone who would break many hearts on the silver screen. It turned out to be a big mistake. His marriage broke up. This man's wonderful career in radio did not translate to films. He died in Hollywood from a heart attack as a young man. My mother would say he died of a broken heart.

When Johnny left for Hollywood, the part of Buzz went bye-bye. I had to find another way to make part-time money. With actors, work is always part-time because we have to be free for auditions or actual jobs. I called my friend Eddie Kramer and asked him if they were still looking for canvassers. He assured me they were and made an appointment for me to meet his boss, the closer. That door-to-door business still made me squeamish. I discussed my feelings with the closer and Eddie. I told them about my experience trying to sell waterless cookware and how I hadn't been able to cut it when I'd realized my customers were so impoverished. His name was David Webb, a "dees, dem, and does" character. He put it to me this way: "Do you own your own home?"

"No."

"Nieder duz Eddie. Nieder do I. Deez people own deir own home. Dey are not da poverty-stricken people you were tryin' to sell pots and pans to. Da gimmick in dis business is negative sellin'. We are not selling dem nuttin'. We are pickin' their house as a sample house for our product. We love their house, see? You are da advertising rep of da Carbotex Corporation. Your boss is flying in from Cincinnati tonight, and if he agrees wit you, he will pay you fifty dollars for everyone who buys dis product from seeing it on your house."

"Do they get this for nothing?"

"You leave dat up to me."

"What if they ask me?"

"You tell dem, 'If my boss picks your house, he will make it possible for you to have dis done.' Now, don' forget. You are da advertising representative. You don' have da final woid. It's up to your boss. He is a busy man, an' he's flyin' in especially to meet wit da people whose house you pick. Unnerstan'? You gotta make a sit wit her husband."

"Yeah. Is there anything else?"

"You bet. Dat's only da beginning. You gotta find out everything from dat lady except when she has her period, cause dat's not important to da sale. I wanna know how long dey're livin' dere. What dey paid for da house. How much of a mortgage dey still got to pay off. What udder bills dey got. What dey bought on time an' how much dey still owe."

"How the hell am I going to find all that out?"

"You ask. You be surprised how much dey tells you if you ask."

I was surprised, but it was true. Maybe the average housewife lives such a lonely life during the day that she is happy to have not only someone to talk to but especially someone who is interested enough in her to ask so much about her life. Obviously, I was a bit subtler in my questions. If I saw a television in the house, I'd say, "Oh, you have a television. My wife and I were thinking of getting one. Does it cost a lot?" Remember that the TV was not in everyone's home yet. We'd talk about it—what it cost, the fact that you could buy it on time, and how much they still had to pay off. By then, I had a friendly relationship, and by the time I left her, I knew enough about her and her husband's financial situation to know if they could pass a credit check. If the deal went through, they would be signing a contract obligating themselves for a few thousand dollars. If it were not possible, there would be no sit for the closer. If he decided to try anyway, at least he had all the information.

I would receive a percentage of the sale he made from the leads I brought him. If I brought him what they called a qualified lead, I would receive a larger percentage of the sale. For a qualified lead, I had to return to the house to meet the husband and get him to agree to give my boss a definite yes or no answer that night. "My boss is waiting in the car," I would say, "and he'll only be here one night, and I can't waste his time. If he makes you this offer, are you willing to say yes or no tonight?"

"No. I can't say I'll say yes tonight."

"No, you don't have to. You can say no, a big no. All I'm saying is, he's going to pick one house tonight. This is my first choice. If he picks this house, we go no further, so can you promise me—after all, it's my job on the line. You will give him a definite yes or no tonight." If the man agreed to say yes or no that night, this was a qualified lead, and I would get a larger percentage.

I would like to point out that saying yes or no that night might seem like a fair and simple thing to agree to, but it's not. When a salesman has built a fire under you to want his product and there is no time to sleep on it or take a few days to think about it, the buyer is at a distinct disadvantage. The closer can usually close a qualified sit. The word *sit* is the vernacular of the business and is used instead of *appointment*. It is indeed a sit. The closer will sit into the wee hours in the morning until he closes the sale.

I worked as a canvasser for a few weeks and brought him qualified leads. That enabled me to sit in on the closing. When I realized that this man had no command of the English language and that by no stretch of the imagination would a casting director cast him as the big boss from Cincinnati, I decided to go into business for myself. If he made $15,000 to $20,000 a year, I could make a fortune.

It was no problem. I went to the contractor who did the work and handled the financial end with the banks. He was happy to give me all the paraphernalia that was used in the sale. I got myself a canvasser, which left my days open, and I worked only three nights a week, closing two out of three sits a week and making between $500 and $1,000 a week.

I actually found this business quite satisfying. It required acting and the slyness of a magician, to say nothing of the psychology of the con man. I was also able to rationalize to myself that the product was good. The houses looked great after the job was done, and the people were satisfied. The only thing was that they paid twice as much as they would have if they had called for estimates and taken their time making a decision. On the other hand, would they have taken care of their house, which was an eyesore, if I hadn't lit a fire under them to do so?

It is interesting how people, myself included, are able to justify the way they make their living. I have a friend who was a senior executive in a tobacco company. He is one of the most intelligent and progressive people I know, and he's a humanist. He is convinced cigarettes are not harmful. Figure that one out.

Most of my stories about my time as a highbinder siding salesman are funny. I always had to sell the husband and the wife, which entailed a great deal of psychology. I had to be able to read them. Who wanted it, who didn't, and why? What were the attitudes of the couple toward each other? Usually, the wife wanted it. Why not? She wanted a pretty house, and I sensed a feeling from her of "What does he ever do for me?" I would say to her, "You listen to your husband. He's a businessman. Of course you want a pretty house, but he is the one who is out in the world of business, and it's a tough world out there, isn't it, Mr. Baker?"

"You're damn right it is!" Mr. Baker could be a deliveryman, but I made him a businessman.

I already knew the wife was sold, so I had to build up his ego. I would say, "Look, I want you two to talk among yourselves. I'll go out of the room. Listen to your husband, Mrs. Baker. He's out there on the firing line. He knows best." They would call me back in, and it was usually a sale.

The problem was that I had to sell whoever was there in the house, not just the husband and wife. I once walked into a house where four brothers, cousins of the couple, had just finished dinner. I had to interview all of them. It turned out they were all in construction of one kind or another: a carpet layer, a mason, a carpenter, and an electrician. For an hour, I picked their brains about all the work I had to have done in my fictitious house.

By the time I started selling the couple on the fabulous merits of Carbotex—"which will not only beautify your house but will, at the same time, insulate and fireproof it as well"—I had the brothers believing that I was a prospect for them. I finished up by saying, "Look, don't take my word for this. You have four experts in construction here. Talk it over with them. If they say don't do it, don't do it." The deal was all signed and sealed in the next five minutes.

Something that came up a number of times was the guarantee. The job was guaranteed for twenty years. When I said that, I would occasionally get this reaction: "Yeah, I know all about these phony guarantees. Go try and find the company when something goes wrong."

I would then pull out our certificate of guarantee. "Did you hear what your husband said? He knows what he is taking about. See this beautiful gold certificate with the beautiful seal? I didn't even show it to you before. You know why? Because a guarantee is no better than the company that stands behind it, and don't let anyone tell you differently!" For some reason, that forceful statement satisfied everybody, though my company was no more than a phone-message service.

Another question that often came up was how long they would be getting the fifty-dollar commission for each further house we sold. I had a clincher for that: "You will receive fifty dollars for each house we sell by bringing them to look at your house. However, that will stop after you receive enough to cover the cost of the job. I want you to understand that. We are not putting you in business. Now, there is one other thing about this you may not like. There may be people coming here and gawking at your house. I don't know how you feel about that. If you feel this is an invasion of your privacy, then this is the wrong house."

There it was: the negative selling, making them want your product. This was exactly what I was doing in selling Allen Swift. This line of work actually reinforced the fact that what I was doing for my career was absolutely right. Put it this way: whether or not it was right or wrong from a moral point of view, it worked. I was not born with a silver spoon in my mouth. My mantra was survival and making it. I could not look down from a lofty position of wealth and say, "That is not nice." As long as I didn't hurt anyone or break the law, it was okay with me.

I did do something that I subsequently learned was against the law. I didn't know it at the time. It just seemed to make sense in closing some sales. If I learned that the homeowners were behind in payments on something they had bought on time—a hot-water boiler, for instance—that might jeopardize their ability to pass credit with the bank, I would take out a roll of bills, peel off three or four hundred-dollar bills, and give the money to them, telling them to go to the gas company or whoever and pay off the loan first thing in the morning. Needless to say, the people could not get over the fact that I would give them this money out of pure trust. But I'd say, "I know people. I'm a pretty good judge of character, and besides, I want this house." If that wouldn't clinch the sale, nothing would. I simply added the sum I gave them to the cost of the job.

I have no idea why this was considered illegal. Today, General Motors and all the automobile companies offer $3,000 back when you sign up for a new car. They do it for the same reason I did. They tack it on the other end. This gives the buyer the down payment for the car. They can't lose. They have his signature to guarantee payment. Nobody says that's illegal. It's just American capitalism at its best. I could have been the CEO of GM. I figured out this gimmick years ago. I'll tell you one thing: it was a great feeling, having all that money. I was able to take my family on a vacation to Florida. It was also what they call in show business "fuck-you money," meaning you didn't have to take the pushing around that actors are always experiencing. Of course, I didn't take the pushing around without the FU money. But with me, it was an act.

∞ ∞ ∞ ∞ ∞ ∞   ∞ ∞ ∞ ∞ ∞ ∞

Ken Joseph, a friend from my WNYC days, was an announcer at the station. He was a tall, good-looking guy with slicked black hair and a mellifluous voice. Aside from the fact that we made each other laugh, we had nothing in common. Our values and tastes were as far apart as could be. Ken dressed in a dapper Broadway style. I dressed casually—or, as my wife would put it, like a schlump.

After many years in the life of WNYC, some bureaucrat decided that since WNYC was a city station, it should come under the civil service. Immediately, they developed a civil service written test for announcers. The entire staff of announcers failed the test and was replaced by those who scored high on the test but couldn't put two words together. My friend Ken was out of a job and did something he swore he would never do: he went to work for his father in the dress-manufacturing business.

I had a date to have dinner with Ken and his wife, Barbara, at their apartment in New Jersey. I was to pick him up at work, and we would drive out to Englewood together. His father was a successful manufacturer. His family was quite rich.

I had known them for a year or two, and when I arrived at the office, his father gave me a hearty welcome and said, "How do you like this bum?"—meaning Ken.

Ken was obviously hurt and embarrassed in front of me, and he came back at his father with "I'm not a bum. I was not a bum before, and I'm not a bum now, and you can take the job and shove it. I quit."

When we got to his house and he told Barbara he had quit his job, the reality of the situation hit them. "How are you going to make a living? What are you going to do? Why did you just up and quit?" she said.

"Because he called me a bum."

I said, "Oh Ken, that's just a figure of speech. You know your father doesn't think you're a bum. I'm sure you can go back to work tomorrow, and it will all be forgotten."

He wouldn't be moved. Barbara was holding back tears. Ken was pacing around with a mixture of anger and worry. The roast in the oven, meanwhile, burned to a crisp. All in all, it was some enjoyable dinner. We each sat silently for the rest of the evening, as if we were at a wake.

Finally, Ken came out of his torpor and asked, "How can I make some money?"

"Are you asking me?" I replied. "Go back into work tomorrow. Make believe nothing happened."

"I can't do that, not after he called me a bum."

"Oh, stop that crap. He's your father. He probably used it as an endearment."

"You don't know him. He always called me a bum. Everybody in the goddamn family has to be in his goddamn business or they're bums. He was not joking."

"All right, so join me," I suggested. "Start by being my canvasser. Then you can really be a bum, a shingle bum. That's what they call us."

"I can't go door to door."

"I see—it's not dignified enough for you. Okay. So come on a few sits with me. See what I'm doing, and then start out as a closer. You'll be the big boss. You will only go in with an appointment."

"I can't do that."

"Why not? You'll be starting at the top."

"Think of some way to make money," he persisted. "You always come up with a way to make money."

"What are you, deaf? I got a way to make money. I *am* making money."

"Not that way. Think of something else."

"You don't like my way, you think of something else."

"No, you have that crazy imagination. You can always come up with something. Think!" Ken pleaded.

"I don't have to think."

"Make believe you have to. What if you didn't have this siding thing? What would you do?"

"Good night, Ken. I am going home. Barbara, thank you for the burnt offering you set before me. I'll give you a rain check on cooking me another meal when he comes to his senses. Kenny, take two smart pills, and call me in the morning. I'm out of here!"

On the drive home, I'm ashamed to say that all I could think about was another way to make money aside from selling Carbotex. The bastard had given me a challenge. Now I would probably stay up all night thinking. That's the way I am. My brain can lie dormant for a while, and then a challenge to my creativity pops up. When I was in school, the best I ever did on a test was when they would write a line of something like dialogue and ask us to write a story using that line. It was the same thing when I was faced with that noisy bar in Erie, Pennsylvania, and had to come up with a whole new act.

I lay in bed, thinking. I can't say what I was thinking about, but I was not sleeping. About three o'clock in the morning, my head was into Mr. Globus's buckeye paintings. Why? I can't say except that this big international businessman believed he could make a great deal of money selling those paintings. Maybe there was something there that could be translated into a business on a small scale. They sure cost little. If the department stores and the galleries were selling the likes of them for $200 or $300 apiece, we could buy them for practically nothing. We could actually give them away if we had something else to sell. Yeah, maybe some kind of a premium like the toy in a box of Crackerjacks.

Suddenly, things began to take shape. My mind exploded with ideas. The visions were coming quickly and furiously. *Announcing—Ken was an announcer. Maybe some kind of quiz show? No! A make-believe quiz show. Answer the question, and get a free hand-painted oil painting. Yeah, but how do we make money? Cal has a friend who makes frames out of some sort of composition that resembles wood. He couldn't get his business off the ground. That's it! If we can get everything cheap enough ...* I couldn't wait till daylight to call Ken.

"Ken, what, in the opinion of most art experts, is the world's most famous painting?"

"Ira, you know I don't know anything about painting."

"Try! It's important. For a hundred thousand dollars, what painting, in the opinion of art experts, is the world's most famous painting?"

"Ira, I don't—"

"Schmuck, hazard a guess like you're on the air."

"Uh, *Blue Boy*?"

"You are absolutely right!"

"I am? Gee, how do you like that? I just guessed."

"You see, Ken? You know more than you think. How fast can you get over to Hector's Cafeteria?"

"Why?"

"I thought up a business. We are going to make a million."

When Ken arrived at Hector's, about ten minutes after me, what he seemed excited about was the fact that he knew that *Blue Boy* was the world's most famous painting, which put me in hysterics. Finally, he asked what the new business was.

"We are going into the art business. Paintings, colorful landscapes."

"Are you serious? I don't know that much about art, but I know that trying to sell paintings is a terrible business."

"Who said anything about selling? We're going to give them away. Listen, you get a call from out of the blue, and a radio announcer says, 'Is this Mr. Kenneth Joseph of 200 Englewood Avenue?'" I was using my announcer voice. He was staring at me. "Come on—answer. Play along. 'Is this Mr. Kenneth Joseph of 200 Englewood Avenue?'"

"All right, yes."

"Congratulations, Mr. Joseph. This is Art Johnson of the *Art and Review* radio program. If you listen to our program, you know that throughout the week, we call some lucky person from the phone book and ask a question about art. If you answer correctly, you will receive a valuable oil painting, valued by department stores and art galleries at two and three hundred dollars. You will have sixty seconds to answer this question. Are you ready, Mr. Joseph? What, in the opinion of leading art critics, is considered the world's most famous painting?"

"I don't know where you're going with this. Sure, you know that I know—but how many people would know? What are you getting at?"

"It doesn't matter. Suppose you say *Betsy Ross Sewing the Flag* or *Washington Crossing the Delaware*. You are absolutely right! *The Charge of the Light Brigade*. You are absolutely right. There are no wrong answers. Everybody wins."

"But how do we—"

"Listen, will you? 'Now, Mr. Joseph, if you will stay near your phone, you will receive a call from our shipping department to make arrangements to have this valuable painting shipped out to you. And once again, congratulations.' Okay. A few minutes later, you get another call. Pick up the phone. This is how we make our money. *Ring, ring*. Pick it up. Now I'm a different person. 'Hello, Mr. Joseph. This is the *Art and Review* shipping department. This painting was donated by the artist and is unframed, but we have made arrangements to frame it for you at wholesale if you like."

"Yeah, for how much?"

"'Fifteen dollars.' See? We give the paintings away and sell the frames."

"We give them a two-hundred-dollar painting and sell them a frame for fifteen? The way I look at it, we lose a hundred and eighty-five dollars minus the cost of the frame."

"That's right. We lose on every sale, but we make it up on the volume."

Ken was looking at me as if he were staring at a crazy man. His mouth was wide open, and I was enjoying every moment. "That was a joke, Kenny. In fact, it's an old garment center joke, but this business is not a joke. What if I told you I could get the painting and the frame for as little as seven dollars?"

"A two-hundred-dollar painting and a frame for seven dollars?"

"Ken, what a painting sells for has very little relation to its value. Van Gogh made twenty-five dollars in his lifetime from his painting. One of them today sells for millions. When I said the paintings are valued in department stores and art galleries for two and three hundred dollars, that is what comparable paintings are selling for there. Where *we* are going to buy them, they are selling for two, three, four, and five dollars. I am going to take you there now. We'll buy a painting, and then we'll tour the galleries on Madison Avenue."

The first place we went was the Globus loft, where I picked out a sixteen-by-twenty-four canvas for which I paid seven bucks—but with the understanding that in a dozen lots, I could get them for four fifty. This was for a sample test. Ken couldn't believe how beautiful the painting was. I tried to explain how these paintings were done, but it was wasted on him. I figured he might as well like the product he sold—or, rather, gave away.

From there, we took the subway to Brooklyn to visit Danny, Cal's friend, for the frames. I explained to Ken that this guy had a process for making frames from some ersatz material into molds that looked like real wood. He'd worked on it for years but couldn't get it off the ground. Cal used to talk about him all the time as if he was some kind of genius.

His workshop was in the basement of his house and was loaded with hundreds of frames in all the standard sizes. I don't know what he used—it was his secret formula. But they looked terrific. They were light in weight. They had a grain, they were done in different wood tones, and they looked like hand-carved wood. It was hard for me to believe he couldn't market them. Apparently, it was the big failure in his life. He said he hadn't been down in the basement for a few years. He was currently working for a medical lab.

I put the buckeye in one of the frames, and it looked great. I told him we had an idea for an art business and asked him how much he wanted for it.

"Take it—it's yours. On the house," he said.

"Yeah, but if this works out, we will need a lot more."

"Good. I'd like to clear out this basement. Pay me what you can—two, three, four dollars each. You tell me. I don't want to look at them anymore. Here, I'll tack it in for you. They take regular nails, like wood. I'll even wrap it for you. I don't want it to come back to Cal that I didn't take care of his kid brother. You haven't given up acting, have you?"

"No, no, this is to eat. Acting is for the soul."

We went back in the subway and headed uptown to Fifty-Seventh Street and Madison Avenue. I wanted to find a buckeye or two in one of the galleries to show Ken and, for the hell of it, get their price.

We cruised leisurely up Madison, looking in gallery windows. On Seventy-Ninth, we hit pay dirt. There in the window, beautifully lit, propped up on a velvet cloth, was a 100 percent buckeye. We stood there for about five minutes as I tried to explain the similarity to the painting we were carrying.

"Look, you're the genius. I believe you," said Ken. "Let's find out how much it is."

As we walked in, a dapperly dressed man came toward us. "Yes, gentlemen, can I be of assistance?" I was not sure if he was English or just spoke in an affected accent.

Ken said, "The painting in the window. We were wondering—"

"Oh yes. Lovely, isn't it? A fine use of color. Are you collectors?"

I said, "No, no. We just admired it and wondered how much it was."

"Well, if you are not a collector, you have an excellent eye. This one is a steal. It is by a young Italian painter, Cammilo. The gallery has high hopes for him. Let me look at the price." He reached behind the frame and pulled out a little white card attached to it. "That would be two ten."

Ken, suddenly deflated, said, "Two dollars and ten cents?"

The man chuckled. "Very humorous. Two hundred and ten."

That was all I wanted to hear. "Aha, well, thank you."

I started to move Ken to the door, but the salesman was not giving up. "This is the last Cammilo we have in the house. I doubt you'll ever see one going for less."

"Yeah, well, thanks, but it is still too steep for me."

"One moment, please. Perhaps we can do a little better. Oh Mr. Davis, could you come here a moment? We really have such high hopes for this artist. Perhaps Mr. Davis might even forego our commission. We do like to make money, but sometimes if it means furthering a young artist's career … Ah, Mr. Davis, these gentlemen are interested in this painting, and I wondered if we could do a little better on the price."

"Ah, the Carmen."

Our salesman corrected him: "Cammilo."

"Hmm? Yes, yes, the Carmen Cammilo—only uses his last name on the canvas, apparently."

Ken said, "Actually, it's kind of hard to read his signature."

"True. Very true. Well, you know artists. I can't draw a straight line, but my signature is beautiful."

We both dutifully laughed and got the hell out of there. Once we were out on the street and had finished congratulating ourselves, Ken said, "You know something? We can put it on FM."

"What's FM?"

"It's a new kind of radio transmission. It cuts out the static, gives music more fidelity. Someday it will probably be a big thing. Right now, there are only a few FM stations, and hardly anyone has an FM radio. But I know a guy who has an FM station. We could buy time on his station for twenty,

twenty-five a month. You can write some crap about art which their announcer can do."

"But if nobody has a radio, what good is it?"

"It makes it all legal," Ken said. "We announce on the program that during the week, we will call people from the phone book and ask them questions about art. That way, when we say we're calling from the *Art and Review* radio show, we're telling the truth. It doesn't matter how many people listen."

"That, my friend, is great thinking. Do it first thing in the morning. What are the call letters?"

"WGNR-FM. Now I want to find out if the whole kit and caboodle is legal. My cousin Lazarus is a lawyer. I want to check this out with him."

"All right, call him. Let's set up an appointment."

"No, if we make an appointment, he'll charge us. Let's just drop in on him. You know, we happen to be in the neighborhood."

His cousin Lazarus's office was brand new, and though he was a recent law school graduate, he had already acquired the condescending tone of many lawyers. He spoke slowly in a nasally voice that suggested the smart kid in the class who couldn't play ball. He had a way of elongating the middle of words. When he said "Kenny," it sounded like "Kehnny." Ken introduced me as his friend Allen Swift.

"Verry pleased to meet you. Well, Kehnny, what brings you to this neck of the woods?"

"Oh, we were just out shopping, and I realized we were in your area, so I thought I'd take a chance you were in."

"Well, good, good, I'm delighted. What were you shopping for? Kehnny has always been the fashion plate of the family."

"No, actually, I just bought a painting."

"A paainting? I never knew you were interested in art. Can I see it?" While Ken was unwrapping it, he said to me, "One thing about Kehnny—he's always full of surprises." Ken held up the painting for Lazarus to see.

"Why, Kehnny, I didn't realize you had such good taste in art. That is beautiful."

Ken threw a knowing look at me. "How much do you think it's worth?" he asked.

"Oh, well, really, I wouldn't have any idea. I mean, I don't know anything about art. I know what I like, though, and I like it."

"Take a guess. What would you estimate?"

"Kehnny, I really wouldn't know. It might be worth a hundred dollars. It might be worth a thousand. I can tell you what the frame is worth, though. I have a certain expertise in that department. I just spent a fortune to have these Daumier prints framed."

"All right, what do you think the frame is worth?"

"You paid at least thirty dollars, right?"

"There you are, Allen," Ken said, "from the man who just bought all these frames."

I got excited. "Let me ask you something. If you were, let's say, out to buy this frame and we sold it to you for fifteen dollars, you would consider it a bargain, right?"

"I'd consider it a gift. Why? What are you guys—"

Now Ken got excited. "Now suppose you not only got the frame for fifteen dollars but we threw in the painting, too?

"What's the matter, Kenny? Is it hot?"

"No. It's not hot." He jumped in the air for joy. "Wow, do we have a business!"

"Hey, come on, fellas—what are you guys up to?"

"Allen here has come up with the idea of a lifetime. Listen to this. Suppose you are home. The telephone rings, you pick it up, and this is what you hear. Go on, Allen."

I then went into my quiz-show-announcer voice. "Hello, is this Mr. Lazarus Cohen of 1023 Montague Avenue?"

"You want me to play along?"

"Yeah, make believe it's a real phone call."

"Yes, this is he."

"Congratulations, Mr. Cohen, This is Art Johnson of the *Art and Review* radio program. If you listen to our show, then you know we make calls to various people during the week and ask them a question about art. If you answer the question correctly, you receive a valuable oil painting selling in leading art galleries for up to two hundred dollars. Are you ready, Mr. Cohen?"

"Kehnny, I told you I don't know anything about art."

"It doesn't matter, Laz. Just answer him."

"Are you ready, Mr. Cohen?"

"Okay. Yes."

"Here is your question. You have sixty seconds to answer. What, in the opinion of leading art critics, is considered the world's most famous painting? You have sixty seconds, Mr. Cohen."

"I told you—"

Ken prompted him. "What would you do if this actually happened to you?"

"I'd guess."

"So guess!"

"*Whistler's Mother.*"

"You are absolutely correct!"

"I am? Gosh. I just took a stab in the dark. How about that! I guess certain facts just seep into your subconscious, and you know things you thought you didn't know."

We filled Lazarus in on the whole scam, not giving away our sources, of course. The more Ken and I spoke, the wider his eyes grew. He was suddenly energized, and his lawyerly pomposity vanished.

"Oh my God, this is incredibly ingenious. Kenny, I don't know what to say. Your friend is an absolute genius. It's terrific, and you can actually deliver these paintings all framed for fifteen dollars?"

"You bet your ass!" Ken said.

"You fellas looking for another partner? I have a few bucks."

"Not at the moment—maybe later," I said. "The question is, is it legal?"

"Oh, perfectly. You are giving them the painting. All you're really selling is the frame. It's a sales gimmick—that's all. It's perfectly legal. You know who uses something like this, although it is no way as ingenious? The Fred Astaire Dance Studio."

I kept on at him. "You don't see any part of this that could get us in any trouble with the law?"

"Allen, you don't know me as well as Ken does. I graduated law school among the top ten in my class. It's legal. I'd stake my reputation on it."

We went down to Globus and bought five more paintings and five frames. It was no use making a big investment until we could actually see if it worked. We also bought a roll of brown wrapping paper, twine, and a packet of "Fragile" labels to dress the packages up to look important. Ken hadn't told Barbara about our plan yet, and I hadn't told Vivienne. Our base of operation was Ken's house in Englewood because he could make unlimited local calls. It was a perfect setup. Ken opened the phone book to the *A*s and said, "It's all yours."

I think we both felt the tension. I went through a little act of preparation, rubbing my hands together and blowing on them. "Well, here goes." I dialed, and a woman's voice answered. "Is this Mrs. Edward L. Aaron of 3410 Lincoln Avenue?"

"Yes."

"This is Art Johnson of the *Art and Review* radio program. Do you listen to our show?"

Ken whispered, "Why are you asking her that?" I shook him off and held my hand over the mouthpiece.

"Well, ah, yes, sometimes," she answered.

"Well, Mrs. Aaron, if you listen to our program, you know that throughout the week, we call one or more of our listeners and ask a question about art. If you answer correctly, you will receive a genuine oil painting, appraised by various art galleries as being worth up to two hundred dollars."

"Oh my."

"Mrs. Aaron, you have sixty seconds—and only sixty seconds—to answer. So think it over."

"Oh my. I wish my daughter was here. All right, go ahead."

"Here, Mrs. Aaron, is your question. What, in the opinion of leading art critics, is the world's most famous painting?"

"Oh my. Oh dear. Oh, it's on the tip of my tongue. Is it *Christ on the Cross*?"

"You are absolutely correct!"

"I am? Oh my."

"You have won the painting, Mrs. Aaron. Congratulations! Now, in a few minutes, someone from our shipping department will call you to make arrangements to get this painting to you, so please stand by your phone." I hung up. So far, it was working.

"Okay. Mr. Shipping Department, it's all yours." Ken was nervous. After all, he was an announcer, not an actor. "Just do it like we rehearsed it."

Ken dialed, and when Mrs. Aaron answered, he said, "Mrs. Aaron, this is the shipping department of the *Art and Review* radio program. We are going to ship your prize; however, your painting was donated by the artist and is unframed. You may have it that way, or we've made an arrangement with a framer to frame it at cost, if you so desire." I moved my head close to the phone to hear the reply.

"Oh. Well, how much does it cost?"

"Just fifteen dollars."

"Uh-huh. Well, could I have it with the frame?"

"You certainly can, Mrs. Aaron. We will ship your painting out by bonded messenger service, and it should arrive in about one hour. Will someone be home to receive it?"

"Oh yes. I'll be home all day."

"That's fine. Thank you very much."

"Thank you."

We were beside ourselves, as if we'd just won gold in the Caper Olympics. We wrapped the painting, placed the "Fragile" sticker on it, and discussed who should make the first delivery. Ken thought he should deliver it while I made other calls. So off he went, and before he returned, I had sold out our meager inventory, playing both the quiz master and the shipping department character.

When he returned, he was jubilant, and the words gushed out of him. "I opened the package for her so she could see it was not damaged in any way. I thought she was going to cream—she loved it so much. Would you believe it? She gave me a five-dollar tip. You know, I've been thinking we better open a checking account in case they only have checks."

"Let's not rush it. Most people have fifteen dollars on them, and that way, we have a cash business and nothing to report."

"I love it, but what if they don't have cash?"

"Let me think. Look, play dumb. You are only a messenger. Try to get them to make it out to cash. No, that doesn't look right. I know—tell them to make it out to Dan Kaylish. We'll be buying a lot of frames, and we can pay him with the checks. Hey, he's the frame maker, isn't he? Isn't that what they are buying? Tell them he's the frame maker. It's true."

We went back to Globus, bought two dozen more buckeyes, and then headed over to Dan for more frames. This became a daily ritual. As the money came in, we plowed it back into more and more merchandise. The gimmick was working like a clock. We had sold eighty frames, and we weren't even through the As. Best of all, no one offered us checks. And except for two people, everyone gave us tips. Everybody absolutely loved the paintings. I was wondering what would happen if we came across some art connoisseur, but so far, that hadn't happened.

I'm afraid Mr. Globus was right. The public is woefully ignorant when it comes to art. They don't know anything, but they know what they like—and what they like is junk.

Each day, we would start bright and early at Ken's house with our new business. Barbara was now clued into it, but I still hadn't shared any of this with Vivienne. Our relationship was anything but ideal. So many things bothered her that more and more, I lived my life with my friends and without her. On my way home, whether in the subway or the car, I would try to think of things I could talk to her about that would not upset her. There were not many. I knew subconsciously that our marriage was doomed but never let it into my conscious thoughts. I was so wrapped up in the life of my son that any change that would interfere with that happiness could not be countenanced.

I didn't know how Globus was doing internationally with the buckeyes, but I'm sure we must have been his best customer this side of the Atlantic. We had one case where the winner of our masterpiece did not buy the frame, and we had to set a policy about that. We simply told him (it was a man) that he would receive his painting in the mail within two or three weeks. We'd send the cheapest buckeye we could buy and absorb the loss.

We would wait until we had about seven or eight orders, and then we would take turns delivering them while the other one stayed on the phone. One bright, sunny day, I was the outside man. I had delivered about four of them, when I came to the next house. There was no answer to my ringing. I was about to walk away, when I noticed someone peering out from behind the curtain with a distinctly frightened look. I was going to ring again, when a car drew up behind my car and parked. A man got out, walked up to me, and flashed a badge. "Is that your car?" he asked.

"Yes, it is."

"Can I see your license, please?"

I had to put the packed-up painting down to get my wallet out and show him my license. He took it and said, "Follow me down to the police station." He pocketed my license.

"May I ask what I'm being charged with?"

"Nothing. Interrogation."

What the hell is this? I wondered. It couldn't be about the paintings. We had Lazarus's assurance that our operation was legal. That knowledge gave me a little confidence, but still, this was a new experience for me—one I didn't feel comfortable about. It was my first brush with the law since I'd changed swimming trunks in the Coney Island boys' room.

I pulled into the police station car lot behind the policeman and walked into the station. As soon as we were inside, he addressed a short, balding man wearing eyeglasses.

"Okay, Chief, we got him!"

My stomach started making noises. What was this—"We got him"? Within seconds, it seemed, another man came in with the packaged painting from my car, which I knew I had locked.

The chief asked, "Is this one of the paintings you're selling?"

I turned to the man who was holding it. "You have no right to break into my car."

"Who broke into your car? You can check it. It's just as you left it." The chief told him to open it, which he did. Then he asked me, "How much you selling these for?"

"Nothing. I'm not selling them. I'm giving them away."

"I see—you're Santa Claus."

"No, sir. I'm selling the frames."

"Yeah, and how much you selling the frames for?"

"Fifteen dollars."

"Is that so? You are giving away this beautiful painting free so you can sell the frame for fifteen dollars? You better think of a better story than that, kid. Where are you stealing them from?"

"They are not stolen. Look, sir, this is perfectly legal. It is a sales gimmick, but it has all been checked out. It is perfectly legal."

"We'll decide if it's legal or not. Who else is in this with you?"

"No one. I do this by myself."

"Where are you making the calls from?"

"New York City." There was no sense bringing Ken into this. *They live in this town. Besides, I might need him to get in touch with Lazarus.* I had no idea how to reach him.

The cop who brought in the painting asked, "Who is Art Johnson?"

"That's me. I'm using that as a stage name."

"And who is Allen Swift? Another alias, or is that another stage name?"

Oh shit, they went through all my papers in the car. I didn't think they had a right to do that. I thought that was against the Constitution. The chief turned to the other two policemen—I *think* they were all policemen. No one there wore a uniform.

"Take him in the back room. I'll be right back. Let him cool his heels for a while."

The back room was just that—a back room, all in gray. It had desks and desk chairs, including one swivel armchair, which I sat in. The two detectives were talking to each other quietly so that I couldn't hear and laughing at some photographs they had taken out of a file cabinet. One of them walked over to where I was sitting and dropped the bunch of photographs in my lap. "You want to see some things of beauty?"

They were all pictures of faces of men who had obviously been beaten brutally. They were really ghastly: busted noses, blood streaming from eyes. What were these officers trying to do? Frighten me? For what? I said to the one who had given me the pictures, "Why are you doing this? I'm not a criminal. I actually have a radio show, *The Art and Review Program* on WGNR, New Rochelle. You can check with the station. I don't know the phone number, but you can get it from information."

"Yeah, I might just do that. What station is that?

"WGNR, New Rochelle."

He called information, and then he was dialing. I figured now they couldn't hold me. They'd get the proof. Ken was smart to do this. He spoke into the phone.

"Is this radio station WGNR? We've arrested a con man who—"

I broke in. "You can't say that. Ask them—"

I never had a chance to finish. He grabbed my arm and twisted it behind my back, knocking me off my chair. "You cocksucker—who the hell are you, telling me what to do?"

"I want a lawyer," I croaked out from my position on the floor. My arm felt as if it were separated from my shoulder, but it wasn't. I just have a low threshold of pain. Needless to say, after such a statement from the police, I couldn't expect any help from radio station WGNR. I kept asking to call my lawyer, but they kept telling me that I'd have to wait for the captain to come back. When he finally did, toward nightfall, I said to him, "Look, Captain. I am not a criminal. If what I am doing is illegal, I will stop it, but even if it was, the first thing they teach us in high school civics is that a person is innocent until proven guilty and that he has a right to counsel. I have no idea why you are doing this or what crime you think I committed, but I am entitled to call my lawyer."

The captain applauded me. "Very good. You learned your civics lesson well. The law does say you are entitled to a lawyer—after a reasonable amount of time. And we will decide what a reasonable amount of time is, and if necessary, we will move you around from station house to station house and let a reasonable amount of time pass till doomsday."

"But why?" I never did get an answer to that question. The captain left the building. I looked at my watch and realized I had already missed an audition for an animated cartoon at Paramount. The audition was for five thirty, and it was already a quarter to six. It was the first audition I had ever had for an animated character, something I'd always felt I was a natural for.

Finally, at seven thirty, the captain came back and announced, "All right, we are booking him. Let him call his lawyer."

Once again, I was taken into the back room to make the call. One of the cops was right there, and I was going to call Ken and didn't want him to hear me or see me dial a local number. I wasted time calling information for a fictitious lawyer until the cop walked out of the room and then quickly dialed Ken's number. As soon as he answered, I said, "I'm being held at the Englewood police station, and I need a lawyer. Can you get in touch with Lazarus?"

"We know where you are; we saw your car there. A lawyer will be there shortly."

A policeman then asked me to empty my pockets and remove my belt and shoelaces. One of them counted the money in my wallet and put it all in a plastic bag. I asked what the charge was, and he answered, "Who wants to know?"

I said, "My lawyer said to ask. He said you have to tell me." It was a lie, of course, but I attended the movies a lot. It's amazing how much you learn from the likes of George Raft and Humphrey Bogart.

"Misrepresentation in advertising."

I was then escorted to a jail cell and locked in. It looked exactly like jail cells I'd seen in the movies. There was a shelf to sit or lie down on. It was attached to the wall by two chains. There was a toilet with no seat on it. The room was about eight by eight, with three walls and the bars.

I suddenly became giddy. The situation struck me as funny. I began acting out scenes from all the prison films I'd seen. I was alone. There was no one to hear me. I grabbed the bars and, in my Cagney voice, said, "All right, coppers, there are no cans can keep me." Then I looked around and said to myself, "They think I can't escape. I'll flush myself down the toilet." I was laughing at my predicament. It seemed ludicrous. How the hell had I gotten into this? I had been doing fine with the siding.

I had only been in the cell for about five minutes, when one of the detectives came with another man and said, "Okay. Here is your lawyer," and opened the cell door.

It was not Lazarus. This man appeared to be about sixty, with graying hair and eyeglasses. He introduced himself, but I cannot remember his name, probably because I didn't listen to it. I was surprised at seeing a stranger. He said, "All right. They set your bail at two hundred dollars. I'll pay it. Your friend and his wife are at my house. We'll go there as soon as you are released."

"You don't have to pay my bail. They have more money of mine than that."

"Fine, let's get your things."

When we arrived at the lawyer's home, a nervous Ken greeted me with "Did you give them my name?"

"No, what for?"

"Oh God, I'd have given them yours."

"What happened to Lazarus?"

"He can't practice in New Jersey. He called Adolph."

Adolph? He was already on a first-name basis with this man. It turned out that Barbara and Ken had been there a good part of the afternoon. This was a sumptuous home. It reeked of money. Ken took me aside and told me what a big lawyer the man was and said not to worry. "He'll have the case dismissed, and by the way, he loves the paintings and asked if he could have one."

I looked around the posh living room and couldn't help smiling despite the trouble I was in. It struck me that this whole episode was a black comedy.

The lawyer went to his bookcase, took down a big, fat law book, and started looking through it, finally coming to rest on one page. He read it and let out a triumphant laugh. "They haven't got a leg to stand on. There is no way what you have been doing can be construed as advertising. A one-on-one phone call is not advertising in any shape or form. I will go over and see the judge right now and get this thrown out. Please make yourselves comfortable in the meantime."

Meanwhile, Ken was walking around chewing his fingernails and repeating that he couldn't understand how I had not implicated him.

"If you want to know the truth, Ken, I thought of it. Since your uncle is the controller of the City of New York, I figured, in the worst scenario, if you were involved, he could spring us in five minutes."

"Oh my God, I'd kill myself."

"That's what I thought. So first of all, I couldn't believe that this was as serious as that, at least not till that bastard almost broke my arm. By then, I had already said I was in this alone, and anyway, who wanted your blood on my hands? You and Barbara live in this town. What would I gain by implicating you?"

"I don't know. My God, if this got back to my family."

Barbara said, "Ken, stop it already. Worry a little about somebody else. Ira's in trouble, not you."

Fortunately—or unfortunately, depending on how you look at it—we didn't have to wait too long for the return of the lawyer. He came in and dropped a newspaper in Ken's lap. "I walked into the judge's chamber with the book under my arm. He took one look at me and said, 'Adolph, don't show me any books. This kid is going up. It's a personal thing with the captain.' I really worked on him. I pointed out that you never had any problem with the law, that you came from a good family, went to a fine school, and just had some bad advice from a freshman lawyer. He agreed to a twenty-five-dollar fine if you plead nonvole. He'll suspend the sentence, and there will be no record."

"What the hell is nonvole?" I asked.

"It means you throw yourself on the mercy of the court. It's really a damn good deal."

"Well, if I throw myself on the mercy of the court, can't he just decide on something different?"

"No, no, it doesn't work that way. This is the deal that was offered. If you accept, it works just as I laid it out. You have until next Monday to think about it. Your case will come up at nine o'clock. My advice is to grab it."

Ken walked over and showed me the first page of the local Englewood paper. Plastered all over the front page in big letters was "Phony Quizmaster Jailed." As I read the article, I broke into a cold sweat. It told the entire story, mentioning my names, including my legal name, Ira Stadlen, and my alias—not *stage name*, but *alias*! I turned to Ken and said, "This clinches it. I have to fight this. It will destroy my reputation. I'll never get work. I'm going to plead not guilty."

The lawyer admonished me not to do it. "This is only a local paper. It comes out once a week. The possibility of other people seeing it is nil."

"Yeah, but it could be picked up by the other papers. It's too good a story. Ken, you're an announcer. You see this coming off the ticker; you need a time filler. This is a perfect human-interest story, right?"

He lamely nodded in agreement.

"Don't make any rash decisions. You have until next Monday. Sleep on it. You're upset at the moment. Believe me—you are making more of this than it really is."

I was not convinced. I was sure it would turn up—if not in the *New York Times*, then in one of the tabloids or on the evening news. I was devastated. My wife didn't even know about this, and I hoped she'd never find out. Whom could I turn to? My brother, Cal, but who else? I called Cal at home and brought him up to date on everything that had transpired and where I stood with the law. His answer was "Come in tomorrow and talk to Jake."

The next day, there I was, before a different judge, but one who apparently had as much power as the one I would meet next Monday—and possibly more. However, I was there not to be judged but to be advised. There was no one there but Jake, Cal, and me. Cal said, "Jake, this is my brother, Ira, and he has gotten himself in trouble with the law. I'd like you to hear what it is all about. Go ahead, Ira. Tell Jake everything from the beginning."

I did, from the beginning. I went through everything, including what we paid for the paintings and the frames. I acted out the announcer part and the shipping and delivering and explained how I had been arrested and how I had been treated. I left nothing out. I told him what the lawyer had worked out with the judge and why I felt I had to plead not guilty and not nonvole.

He just sat there in his coat and hat, smoking his nonfiltered cigarettes down to the ends. His expression never changed. He never interrupted or even looked at me. When I was through, he said to Cal, "Tell your brudder to cop the plea."

"What does that mean?" Cal said.

"It means do what your lawyer said. Throw yourself on the mercy of the court."

"I can't do that," I protested. "Don't you understand? I have to clear my name. I have to fight this."

"Tell your brudda to cop da plea, or they'll send him up for ten years."

"That's ridiculous. Ten years for misrepresentation in advertising?"

"Tell your brudda to cop da plea, or they'll change the charge to grand larceny. They'll get a phony witness to testify she paid him five thousand dollars and he never delivered the painting."

"But I don't understand it. Why would they do that?"

"Tell your brudda his problem is he didn't use finesse. I like your brudda. He has a little larceny in him, but he didn't go about it the right way. Jersey is the biggest racket state in the whole country, but you have to use finesse. He can do dis, if he wants, wid us. We got Jersey on our payroll already. He can run dis from here. We'll put him in a real radio station. We got our own trucks. He don't have to make his own delivery."

"Thank you, thank you, but I don't want any part of this. I want out. If you want, I'll tell you where to get the paintings. You can run it yourself."

"No, your brudda got a good brain. We would need dat."

"No, you really don't, but thank you very much." I walked out with Cal and asked him, "How come he talked only to you?"

"It's simple. He never talked to you, right? It's force of habit. That way, if he was on the witness stand and they questioned him, he never in his life spoke to you."

Monday came around before I knew it, and I was standing with Adolph, my lawyer, before the bench. Behind the bench, presiding over this court of law, was Andy Hardy's father, a kindly white-haired man. He read the charge, misrepresentation in advertising, and asked how I pleaded. Adolph stepped forward and said, "My client pleads nonvole, Your Honor."

At that point, Judge Hardy eloquently spoke about young people of good homes making mistakes and how unfortunate it was when we punished these mistakes without recognizing them for what they were: youthful mistakes. "This young man is an artist, a student of a fine school who has much to contribute to society. I am going to suspend sentence and fine you twenty-five dollars, young man."

I breathed a sigh of relief, and as we walked out into the hall, Adolph said to me, "By the way, the judge says there is no reason you cannot continue your business—you just have to use finesse. I can arrange it, and oh yes, he'd like to know if he could have a painting."

Help! I'm in an asylum. I'm in a crazy house, a hall of distorting mirrors. Up is down, and down is up. Art is crap, and crap is art. Right is wrong, and wrong is right, and I'm so dumb that I just figured out what finesse *means.*

Finesse

You may rob the public blindly,
Have the judge look on you kindly,
And never ever feel you're in distress.
You can loot the US Treasury
And do it not too cleverly;
Just remember, you must do it with finesse.

If you start a business eagerly
And run it all quite legally,
You still might find you're in an awful mess.
There is no call to fret about it.
Remember, don't forget it;
Run it well, but do it with finesse.

Everything is a learning experience. What did this art caper mean to me? I felt as though I'd created a great illusion, such as sawing a woman in half or designing Houdini's water-torture test. It had fooled everyone. Nobody had figured it out. That was all that was important to me. So we didn't make a million dollars. So what? As it turned out, the story died with that one issue of the local weekly newspaper. I never came across anyone who read it, and it did nothing to destroy my career, because so far, there had been no career to destroy. As a matter of fact, this run-in with the law marked the beginning of the end of my career doldrums.

Chapter 8

Howdy Doody: A Kid in a Candy Shop

I caught a booking on the Robert Q. Lewis television program *The Show Goes On*. It was a variety show, and I did my comedy act. Robert Q. Lewis was angry with me when I finished. He said I'd taken longer than I had in rehearsal. It was not true. He had failed to leave enough time for the laughs, which were long and loud. In fact, I went over so well that a call came through for me from the Palace Theater almost right at the moment he was berating me. They wanted to book me for the next week.

What does playing the Palace mean to an act? It means everything. It means the big time. It means you are covered by *Variety*, the bible of show business. They rave about you, and the rest is the glitter and bright lights of stardom. So I wrote myself a new act to open at the Palace. *Variety* covered the first performance. As soon as I got off the stage, a call came for me backstage. "Mr. Swift, you will do the act you did on television."

I did—and I was a smash for the rest of the run. *Variety*, though, covered only the first performance, and they wrote, "Allen Swift is a comer. With a little better material, he could do it."

Why was I so stupid as to open at the Palace with new, untried material? I was not a comer. I had arrived, but I had scuttled my own career. Why did I do that?

Would you like a little hindsight and self-analysis on the subject? I did it because in spite of my chutzpah and so-called self-confidence, I was scared, and I needed an excuse if I failed. This way, I could say, "Hey, what other comic would have the courage or the ability to write himself a whole new act to open at the Palace?" The answer, of course, is *nobody*, unless he or she was afraid of success or of failure. Believe me, it was not courage.

Allen Swift, Comic

In spite of my stupidity, things were opening up for me on a number of fronts. I had a new agent, Lew and Leslie Grade Ltd. They were a big English management company that was also in film production. Nat Debin was their New York representative, and he was booking me into good theaters.

I also found myself on the first three Bob Hope TV shows. The first one was interesting, and remember, these were all done live. Bob was concerned about how it would go over, as it was also his transitional show to television after years on radio. So before the show went on the air, he took the entire cast and orchestra to the Brooklyn Paramount to try it out. I felt this was a mistake, as I'm sure he did after the experience.

Let's face it—before a radio or TV show begins, the studio audience is directed on how to react. The announcer warms up the audience, and they're shown signs telling them when to laugh or applaud. The home listening audience is not aware of this, but it assures that when the announcer says, "*The Bob Hope Show!*" there is a burst of laughter.

At the Brooklyn Paramount, the audience was not set up. They did not expect to sit through anything other than the movie they had come to see. You can't coach a theater audience on when to laugh or applaud, so there were few laughs and no applause at the end. The show bombed in Brooklyn. There was no way to get off the stage.

Bob then walked down front and said, "You know, folks, these kids"—meaning us in the cast—"just returned with me from touring thousands of miles of army camps in Korea." This was a big lie. "Hey, kids, come on out here."

He waved us out, and we sort of lined up on either side of him as he continued. "While I was there, I walked into a hospital tent, and there was this young GI all wrapped up in bandages. I said to him, 'Come on, soldier—smile. It's not as bad as all that.' And he said to me, 'Mr. Hope, did you give a pint of blood to the Red Cross this year?' I said yes, and he said, 'Well, shake hands with the guy who got it.'"

The orchestra went into his theme song. He joined hands with the cast members on each side of him and sang "Thanks for the Memory" to an audience that was finally applauding.

I guess this was in the early vaudeville tradition of a surefire ending, waving the American flag.

I did the next two shows with him as well (afterward, he moved the show to Los Angeles). While I was on the shows, I kept coming up with gags and blackouts for sketches that didn't have any. This caused him to berate his writers: "What's the matter with you guys? What am I paying you for? This kid is coming up with all the blackouts."

On the third show, the big sketch was to be played with Bob Cummings. During rehearsal, Bob turned to Cummings and said, "Bob, would you mind? I'd like to do this sketch with this kid." Cummings agreed, and I was flying, because it was a funny part. I called everyone I knew to watch the show and was terribly embarrassed, as the show ran too long and the sketch was never done—a casualty of live television.

A masseur would come to the studio each day to give Bob a massage. While he was on the table, I'd sit by him, and he'd tell me various stories about his career and, especially, how all the big shots wanted to be in his company. He mentioned the name of a big oilman who had contacted him out of the blue and asked if he wanted to get into the oil business. He should give him $10,000, the guy said, and he'd sink ten wells for him. Bob said that he did, and all the wells came in. I was twenty-eight at the time, and Bob was forty-two. I guess he enjoyed the impression he made on this younger person.

I called my friend Harold Franklin, with whom I collaborated from time to time on writing projects, and said, "Harold, let's write a film script for Bob Hope. I have his style down perfectly. I kept giving him gags and blackouts when I was on his show. I bet we could do it." I always had to have a collaborator because I couldn't spell or type. I am not saying this to denigrate Harold, who was a fine writer.

We came up with a hilarious script entitled *All That Glitters*, about a group of convicts working on a rock pile in prison who discover gold where they are digging. Word leaks out to the underworld, and everyone tries to get into prison. They claim to have committed crimes they never committed. There was a great deal of hijinks, with Bob in the middle of it. This time, however, having been once burned, I copyrighted the script as "An Original Screenplay for Bob Hope."

Since I now had a high-powered agent, I turned it over to Nat Debin to handle. There were negotiations with Paramount and Bob Hope Enterprises, and an offer of $35,000 was made to us, which we both said to grab. Nat Debin, after consulting his home office in London, held out for $50,000. Harold and I were on tenterhooks as the entire project fell apart. We would have been satisfied with a measly $35,000.

∞ ∞ ∞ ∞ ∞ ∞   ∞ ∞ ∞ ∞ ∞ ∞

I received a call from an old friend, Jack Farren, who had played a number of parts on *The Ira Stadlen Show* on WNYC. Jack was now assistant producer on a successful children's television show, *Howdy Doody*, and they were having a big problem. The show's host and owner, Bob Smith, was also the voice of the character he'd created, a marionette named Howdy Doody. The other members of the cast did the voices of other puppets and played various live characters. They had been on the show from the beginning, and now they had joined together and demanded a percentage of the show, threatening to walk off that day if their demands were not met. The executives at NBC and Bob Smith had let them walk. Jack didn't give me details, but he assured me it was not a union issue. They still had their writer and the young actress who played Princess Summer-Fall-Winter-Spring.

What they did scriptwise was send all the marionettes away to a Changing Island and bring them back with different voices. Now they wanted new voices to suit the marionettes, and they were holding auditions. He suggested me. When I came in to audition, it occurred to me that they would probably like to have the same voices as those who had left, and I suggested this to them. They assured me that they had tried that for months and decided it was not possible, hence, the Changing Island. In my modest manner, I exclaimed, "I can match any voice in the world. If you have a recording of the voices you can lend me over the weekend, I will prove it to you." I am certain that they didn't believe me, but since I had already auditioned for them, doing what they asked me to do and with voices that sounded like they could go with the marionettes, they went to the office to get a recording and gave it to me.

On Monday, I came back and matched the voices of everyone who had left the show. Unquestionably, they were delighted, but they wanted more. They wanted to know if I was also willing to puppeteer. I said I would if they would teach me. As you might expect, they agreed to do so. There was now something else. One of the characters who had walked off played a live character on the show: the storekeeper, K Cornelius Cob. I looked too young for that, so they would have to bring in a makeup artist to see if he could age me.

They brought in Dick Smith, unquestionably the best and soon-to-be the most famous makeup artist in the business. Dick tried different things each day, and the producer, Roger Muir, kept saying, "No, he still looks too young." Finally, after many trials and errors, he seemed satisfied, with reservations that I might get away with it. The proof would come on the show, and at last, that first day arrived.

A Kid in a Candy Shop: Learning from Puppeteer
Rufus Rose for *Howdy Doody,* NBC-TV, 1954.

We started rehearsing at ten in the morning. I was up on the bridge over the marionette stage with the puppeteers. On my first day, they put a marionette in my hands. Rufus Rose, the major puppet master, gave me the most rudimentary instruction: "Hold this with your left hand. Hold this with the right." He was a nice man, but he had to handle a number of marionettes himself and sync them to my voices and the voice of Howdy. There were two card girls, one on either side of the puppet stage, with the cue cards. The entire script was on the cards. Each character's lines were underlined in a different color. I changed voices depending on the underlined color.

As I said, I also had to handle one of the marionettes without knowing what I was doing. My God, didn't anyone care what it looked like? Yes. From time to time, Rufus or Lee, the gal puppeteer, would say, "Watch it, Allen—you're sagging." So I'd lift it up. But remember, while I was trying to be a puppeteer, I was also talking for the marionette in my hand in one voice and for the others in different voices, reading the cue cards, and remembering not to move my marionette's mouth when he was not supposed to be talking!

I was a nervous wreck. All I wanted was some time alone to practice with the damn marionette. I had no trouble with the voices. My time alone finally came. Everyone cleared out of the studio, and I had a half hour to practice. Then everyone came back, and the show started. I was doing much better. Then Rufus poked me in the back, took my marionette, and told me to get down on the floor. My entrance as K Cornelius Cob was now. I jumped down and got on my mark, and the red light on the camera trained on me was on. I looked at the monitor and saw K Cornelius Cob with no costume and no makeup!

It dawned on me at that moment that that was where everyone had gone. That was what that half hour was for—to get into costume and makeup. I quickly mussed up my hair, pushed my cheek out with my tongue, mugged like crazy, and, in my down-eastern New England aged voice, said, "Howdy, folks, K Cornelius Cob here." Believe it or not, I finished the scene. I then went to my dressing room and waited for the ax to fall.

Bob Rippen, the assistant director, came in and said, "Good show, guys. Nice work, Allen."

Bob Hultgren, the director, came in and said, "Nice show. Welcome aboard, Allen."

The producer, Roger Muir, came in and said, "Great show. And, Allen, the makeup is perfect. Keep it that way." From that day on, I never wore makeup for the role.

The next day, I had a call from Nat Debin to tell me that he had booked me into the Palladium in London. I said, "You better unbook me. I just signed a three-year contract with NBC to do *The Howdy Doody Show*."

I think he was totally shocked that I would quit my stand-up career when it was getting so hot. So were all my show business friends. I could explain it quite simply: "TV is a clean business. You should see my dressing room. I can go to work every day in the daytime. I'll be able to spend more time with my kid. The nightclub business is all but dead, and how many Palace Theaters or London Palladiums are there?"

I was also making good money and would make it every week, doing what I loved to do. It was a great deal of fun being on *The Howdy Doody Show*. They kept throwing live parts at me. I played a crazy Indian, Chief Thunder Chicken; the magician, Professor Abra-K-Dab; and another silly character almost every week. It was live television, and something unexpected was always happening that required ad-libbing.

Bob Smith, as Buffalo Bob, was a large hale-and-hearty guy with the same persona on and off the little screen. The way he greeted me every day seemed ridiculous to me. Wherever I was when he spotted me, he would shout out, "Allie, baby!" and grab me around the shoulders in a bone-crunching hug, as though he hadn't seen me for years. This wasn't just once in a while; this was every day—and sometimes twice.

Bob had created the character of Howdy for a radio show that he did in Buffalo before he came to New York City, and he translated it to TV. He was a talented musician and could make music out of almost anything. He would set up glasses on a table with various amounts of water in them and play them like a xylophone. He was fine at communicating with kids, too. He brought his friend Bob Nickelson from Buffalo to play Clarabell, the clown, after the original Clarabell, Bob Keeshon, walked off with the rest of the cast. It seemed as if everyone in that show was named Bob. Nickelson was also a talented guy—actually, I should say "multitalented." He was a musician, an arranger, and a fine voice man in his own right. This was a great stock company of performers, born to delight and entertain children.

Rounding out this company was the writer, Ed Kean. He was a real find. Ed must have had an arrested development, because he was adept at infiltrating the minds of children and knowing what made them laugh and the kinds of stories and characters they enjoyed. I don't believe Bob Smith really appreciated what he had in Ed Kean. He would always make fun of him and the material he wrote, but for the kids, it was right on the mark.

I was like a kid in a candy shop. I enjoyed every minute of every day in studio 3A.

Right outside was the third-floor lounge where I used to hang out and where many of my friends were still camped. I could schmooze with them during breaks, but things were changing. No longer were the radio actors and directors running around from studio to studio. Radio was giving way to television, and it was either get into the new medium or perish.

My joy went on unabated for about ten months, and then catastrophe struck. Bob Smith had a massive heart attack in the middle of the night. His recovery was uncertain. Fortunately, he did recover, but slowly. He was out of the show for about a year. There was pandemonium at NBC. *Howdy Doody* was a gold mine to them—and to me. I prayed as much as an atheist can pray that Bob would recover and come back quickly. For me, Bob was the goose that laid the golden egg. I was fond of this man who was responsible for my good fortune. I visited him in the hospital and brought him a bottle of Scotch. One of Bob's jokes was "Who is the perfect wife? Answer: a deaf-and-dumb nymphomaniac whose father owns a liquor store." My gift was intended to make light of his illness and provide a symbol of hope that he would be well enough soon to drink it.

There was no problem hiring a different host or hosts during his convalescence, but they were frantic at NBC about what to do for the voice of Howdy. I had never tried to do that voice or even thought about it. Once, Bob had asked me if I could do the voice of Howdy. I'd said no, and he'd said, "Nobody can do that voice." I'd realized then that this was a source of pride to him and had never again given it a thought.

Now, though, in order to keep the show going and save my meal ticket, I became highly motivated to master Howdy's voice. I took some of the old Howdy Doody records home to work on it. It was not an easy voice, because it was close to Bob's actual voice. As a matter of fact, my impersonation was of the way Bob had done it early in the show. After a while, he had tended to lapse too close to his own voice, not that it mattered much.

When I felt I had the voice perfected, I tried it out on my friend Lester's little boy, who was blind. I came into his apartment, talking in that voice, and the child ran to me, calling, "Howdy Doody!" When I went up to the Howdy Doody office and did it for them, Martin Stone, one of the owners, jumped up and clicked his heels together.

I learned later that the brass at NBC were surprised that I hadn't tried to hold them up for a fortune once I mastered Howdy's voice, but such thoughts never occurred to me. I kept my fingers crossed that Bob would come back and everything would be as it had been. The man's life was hanging in the balance, and that was all I thought about. As far as I was concerned, Bob Smith's personality was the strength of the show.

A book about *The Howdy Doody Show* that came out a few years ago—*Hey, Kids, What Time Is It?*—mentions that Allen Swift saved the show twice. What it should have said is that Allen Swift saved his ass twice, because that was how I looked at it. Hi-diddle-dee-dee, this was the life for me—and that was what I was protecting. I had no desire to go back to the life of stand-up comedy, even if it meant becoming a star.

I'd accomplished my early goal: to make a living as an actor.

∞ ∞ ∞ ∞ ∞ ∞   ∞ ∞ ∞ ∞ ∞ ∞

At the time I started on the show, I went into therapy, and so did Vivienne. We began then because we could now afford it. My friend Jack Farren and his girlfriend, also named Vivian, were engaged. Vivian's uncle and aunt held an engagement party for them at their home in White Plains. Her uncle was a well-known psychiatrist, Nathaniel Breckir. Both Vivienne and I found him to be charming and loved how he dealt with his young daughter, who, at about eight years of age, was monopolizing the evening.

The following day, I called Vivian Farren for his phone number, and a wonderful relationship developed in the next three years between Nat and me. He was a gifted man who was both warm and insightful, and without going into the nuts and bolts of my therapy, he made a powerful impact on my life.

He was the only psychiatrist I ever heard of who graduated anyone. Usually, psychiatrists will hold on to a patient until death parts them or the money runs out, but not Nat. After three years, he said, "Get out. You're through. This is graduation. Go on out, and enjoy your life. You don't need me. You can handle whatever comes up."

It's been forty-six years since then, and so far, he has been right. After our professional, doctor–patient connection ended, we remained the closest of friends until his death. There were many other respects in which he differed from his colleagues. He often involved himself in his patients' lives. Also, he'd use his patients to aid other patients if he thought it would be helpful.

Shortly after I started therapy with him, I rented a cold-water studio on Third Avenue to paint in my spare time. Nat had a patient whom he probably treated on the cuff. I say that because Mr. Calabrese could not possibly have afforded his fees. He was a poor shoemaker. Nat told me his story. He was a sculptor on the side who would go to buildings that were being demolished and pick up stones to sculpt. The problem was that he couldn't work in his apartment; it was small, and his wife couldn't accept the mess. I had admired a nice piece of work in Nat's office. Nat thought I would like to meet him. I was intrigued, and Nat set up a meeting at a brownstone being demolished where Mr. Calabrese felt there might be stones worth taking.

When I arrived, he was sculpting a piece of brownstone right at the site. He was a slight, dark man with a sweet face and a thick Sicilian accent. We talked about the piece he was working on and why he was working there on the street. "My wifea, she dona likea da mess in da kitch," he said.

So that was how it started. I invited him to come work in my studio. I was only using it part-time, and even if we were both there together, the studio was big enough to accommodate the two of us. As long as I was there, I helped him carry back to the studio some of the broken stones for future carving.

Schlepping stones would be a joint effort for many years. Salvador Calabrese shared every studio I had, and they grew larger and fancier as my income increased. We loved each other's work and each other, and I became friends with his wife and family at the same time.

As the years went by, the quality of his work steadily improved, and I decided to use my connections and my marketing ability to promote my sculptor friend. My brother and I ran an art exhibit and sale of his work in my home. I sent out invitations. Cal mounted his work impressively, and we sold enough so that Mr. Calabrese never had to cobble shoes again. Then I contacted the producer of the *Today* show, who had been a lowly cue-card boy when I was on *The Howdy Doody Show*, and piqued his interest in the story of this little Italian shoemaker-sculptor.

Next, I went to the prestigious ACA Gallery and made a deal with them they couldn't refuse: "You give my client, Salvador Calabrese, a show, and I will feature your gallery on the *Today* show." It was done. He and the gallery received a great deal of publicity. The Hartford Athenaeum Museum bought his work, and my friend was launched.

All of this happened because a psychiatrist had used unconventional techniques to treat his patients. I talked for years about Nat to many people, always raving about him, even to other therapists. There were those who called his methods meddling in other people's lives or playing God. Isn't that what all doctors, psychiatrists, and therapists do—play God? Healing is not only a science but also an art, and if Nat was an artist in his field, who else should play God?

∞ ∞ ∞ ∞ ∞ ∞   ∞ ∞ ∞ ∞ ∞ ∞

Back to Howdy Doody. Now I was doing his voice along with all the other voices. Bob, however, had made a big mistake, in my opinion. Before his heart attack, he had fired the writer, Ed Kean. This threw the writing to everyone and anyone, and for the most part, the show suffered. At one point, I was so unhappy with the scripts that I asked Roger Muir to give me a crack at writing them. He did, and that too was a great deal of fun. I'd go to dinner after the show and then to my sky-lit studio on Forty-Sixth Street. I would write until about one in the morning, call a stenographer on the phone, and dictate the material to her. She would have it mimeographed and in the studio for the next day's rehearsal.

If "sky-lit studio" sounds posh and romantic, let me assure you it was anything but. It had a skylight all right, but the room was four flights up in a rickety building, with a toilet at the end of the hall. There was something romantic about it, though. I kept rabbits there for my magic tricks, and Mr. Calabrese and I worked in there.

I ran into a little problem with Roger at that time. I wrote many songs for the show, and he insisted the songs belonged to NBC. That stuck in my craw because no one else wrote original songs; they would write parodies to existing songs. I figured out how to get around that. For every song I wrote, I would write two sets of lyrics. For instance, I wrote a song called "I'm Howdy Doody's Sister." I then wrote another one called "I'm Old Kit Carson's Sister." I sold it to a music publisher who then took all my songs. On the script, I'd write the lyrics for the show with the following note: "Parody of 'Old Kit Carson's Sister,' Brighten Music." In this way, I became an ASCAP writer and earned money through ASCAP whenever the song was played on the show. As the great Durante would say, "Da flexible mind."

This period in my life was productive. Aside from *The Howdy Doody Show*, I wrote an hour-long comedy that I sold to NBC for their Matinee Theater. *The Yankee Doodler* was about a bookkeeper in a textile firm who unconsciously doodled designs and became an acclaimed artist. As a consequence, he changed from a milquetoast persona into a man of the world.

I believed it would make a terrific book for a musical. The actual performance was done live from the West Coast, so I had nothing to do with how it was cast or directed, although I sent my recommendations along with the script. I invited several producers to join me in a screening room at NBC to view the live performance, in the hope of creating some interest in the project.

As the show unfolded, I sank lower and lower in my chair, hoping that I would vanish altogether. Everything that could be wrong with it was wrong. The casting was terrible. The direction was awful. The leading actor could not remember his lines, so he repeated the same joke three times, making me look like the worst writer in the world.

I was so furious that I ran up to the story department. Just as I entered the office, a person who was on the phone looked up at me and said, "I'm on the phone to the coast. They loved it. They said, 'Take anything this guy writes. He can just submit outlines.'"

"They loved it?" I screamed. "They're butchers. Tell them as far as comedy is concerned, they are tone deaf, and I wouldn't write two words for them."

In retrospect, I think I went a little too far. It is always wise to put a little space between the anger and the expression of it. Regrettably, I was just so embarrassed about how I had come across as a writer, and the proximity of the writing department didn't allow for time to sleep on it. One often hears about writers who want the studio to take their names off a picture; it's probably for the same reason.

After my first year on the show, I was given a vacation, and Vivienne and I went to Mexico. I was totally knocked out by its beauty. The light there was so exciting that all I wanted to do was paint. My oils were back in my studio, but I did have watercolors, pens, and India ink. I sketched everything and everyone and made notes for putting them on canvas back home. For the first time, I realized how the impressionists must have felt when they experienced the light of the French countryside. I promised myself that one day, I'd have a home in this magnificent land.

In 1953, Mexico City was so clean and the air so clear that you could see Popocatepetl, the volcano, from every part of the city. Today you can see nothing, and you can choke to death on the air. But as the song goes, "That was long ago, when the world was young."

∞ ∞ ∞ ∞ ∞ ∞　　　∞ ∞ ∞ ∞ ∞ ∞ ∞

Toward the latter part of my second year on the show, I received a call from my former agent, Nat Debin. He said, "Hi, Allen. I called for a number of reasons: first of all, to congratulate you; second, to say I think you made a bad deal; and third, I think you owe me a commission."

"Nat, what are you taking about?"

"The Hope show."

"What about the Hope show?"

"Don't tell me you don't know about it."

"Know about what? Please, Nat—I have no idea what you're talking about."

"The Hope special last night. You didn't see it?"

"No."

"They did your film script. I wondered why I didn't see your credit."

"Really? Why, that's plagiarism."

"You're damn right. I'd contact a lawyer immediately!"

"My God, yeah. You're sure it was the film?"

"Allen, I handled the negotiations, didn't I? I'm telling you—it's your script."

After I got off the phone, I sat, bewildered. *How could they do such a thing? What are they—stupid? The script is copyrighted as "A Motion Picture for Bob Hope." I'll dig out the copyright.*

I picked up the phone and called Zack Becker, Vivienne's uncle, who was an executive vice president at CBS. I told him the story. He said he would put in a call to either Bill or Marshal Bratter, the best plagiarism lawyers in the business, and set up a meeting with either of the brothers for me.

I didn't have to wait long. Zack called back in about ten minutes and said I had an appointment with Bill Bratter first thing in the morning. I brought my film script and the original copyright. It was a quick meeting. He said he would get the NBC script, go over everything, and set up another date with me.

At our next meeting, as I entered the office, he shook my hand and said, "This is as open-and-shut a case of plagiarism as I have ever come across, and now that that's said, I suggest you forget about it."

"What!" I said, not believing my ears.

"Let me explain a few things to you. We would have to sue NBC, the Colgate-Palmolive-Peet Company, the sponsor of the show, and Bob Hope Enterprises. You work for NBC. Your biggest sponsor of *The Howdy Doody Show* is Colgate. The law of plagiarism states that the plagiarist is liable for the use he has put the plagiarized material to. If he had made a motion picture of your material, we could get every penny from the box office. The TV special, however, makes him liable for the going rate for a script for a special. That would be seventeen hundred dollars. My fee will be more."

Fucked by the fickle finger of fate. What could I do? I thanked Mr. Bratter and said, "I think I'll go see Bob Hope. I can't believe a man in his position would do a thing like that. Why? What does that money mean to him? Seventeen hundred dollars for a script? This may have been lifted by one of his writers. Maybe he didn't remember it. I'll talk to him."

"Well, you could try. You have nothing to lose."

I caught Bob in one of the studios at NBC. He was sitting in the audience section with his hat and coat on. The studio was empty except for us. I don't know why he was there, but whatever the show was, it hadn't started, and he didn't seem to be in any hurry. I sat down next to him, and he said, "Hi, kid, how you doing? You eating?"

"You have a few minutes, Bob? I'd like to talk to you."

"Sure, kid, what's up?"

"Bob, after I worked with you on those first three shows, I felt I had your style down so well that I wrote a film for you, *All That Glitters*. There was a negotiation at the time that broke down. The script showed up a few weeks ago on your special. I don't know how it happened. Maybe one of your writers lifted it. You may not even have remembered my original script. You're a busy guy. I know how these things are. Here are both scripts: my original copy, written as a film for you, and the NBC script. Look them over. If you tell me they're not the same, I'll fold my tent and steal quietly away. But if you agree that it's mine, pay me what you would pay for a special and give me a credit on your next show. I'd like to be able to say I wrote for Bob Hope."

"Sure, kid."

He then sat there with a script on either knee and turned the pages together one after the other through to the end. He then handed both of them back to me and said, "What can I tell you, kid? It's just one of those fucking coincidences."

I sat there for a few minutes, absorbing what the great man had said, and thought to myself, *Where is Les Brown's orchestra? Wouldn't this be a perfect cue for "Thanks for the Memory"?*

∞ ∞ ∞ ∞ ∞ ∞   ∞ ∞ ∞ ∞ ∞ ∞

The midcentury was an embarrassment of riches in friendships. I made more marvelous friends in the few years of the early fifties than in the rest of my life. Though I have been writing this memoir mainly in chronological order, I am going to fill you in on some of the lives and accomplishments of two of these incredible friends.

Alexander Marshack was the tall, handsome young man who was the creative director at WNYC and gave me my first fling at radio. I lost track of Alex for a few years but met him accidentally on the steps of the main branch of the New York Public Library. He was no longer at WNYC. I was delighted to see him, and as we spoke, he was focusing a camera on an old woman sitting on the steps. He spoke to me with the same enthusiasm that I remembered from our first meeting, but his concentration was split between me and what he saw through his viewfinder.

"I just came from Willoughby's and bought this camera," he said.

I've related this chance meeting because six months later, his photographs were part of *The Family of Man* exhibit in the Museum of Modern Art, and he was sent around the world on an assignment by *Look* magazine. He returned with the most beautiful portfolio of photographs taken in the jungles of Sumatra, plus a case of amoebic dysentery that has played havoc with his immune system ever since.

Again, I hadn't seen him for a few years when I ran into a mutual friend and asked if he'd seen him lately. "Haven't you heard?" he said. "Alex is *the* authority on International Geophysical Year."

"What? How did he come to that?"

"It seems he wrote the definitive book on the subject."

When next I heard from Alex, it was a phone call at about ten o'clock at night. "Ira? Alex. You have a sixteen-millimeter projector, don't you?"

"Yeah. How the hell are you?"

"Look, I just returned from the Soviet Union with some fantastic footage. I've been a go-between between the State Department and the Soviets on the exchange of space information. Would you like to see this stuff?"

"Yeah, sure. When?"

"Now."

"Come on over."

That evening in my studio, I saw what no one in our country had yet seen: footage of Sputnik. It might not seem like much today. Since then, we've gone to the moon and even further, but I remember how unbelievable that was then.

Alex had written one of the first books on the space project and had been given an advance from McGraw-Hill to do another one. As a hook for his new book, he decided to find out when man first became aware of space and the heavens, and his research took him into prehistory, studying ancient bones and sculptures in museums and cave paintings. Using his knowledge of photography, and with the help of macro lenses, he found a language in the markings on the bones and paintings that scholars had previously considered simply decorative designs. He broke a code of prehistory, showing that prehistoric man knew and used a seasonal calendar for planting, and he abandoned his book on space to become an archaeologist.

His work was funded by Harvard's Peabody Museum; he has delivered lectures and presented scientific papers all over the world. Instead of the book on space, he wrote another landmark book, *The Roots of Civilization.* The Museum of Natural History in New York devoted an entire exhibit to his findings, replete with full-scale replicas of his magnificent photos of the cave paintings in Le Soeur in France, and *National Geographic* has featured his work in the magazine. The question is, what is he going to do with the rest of his life?

∞ ∞ ∞ ∞ ∞ ∞   ∞ ∞ ∞ ∞ ∞ ∞

The second man I want to mention is Gene Deitch. About the time I joined *The Howdy Doody Show*, I auditioned at the UPA animation studio for some voices for *Pump Trouble*, a film for the American Heart Association. The director of animation, Gene Deitch, who was about my age, was the writer of the script, and Bill Bernal was perhaps ten years older. I had a sense of déjà vu in their presence. I realized it harked back to my audition at WNYC; these men were similar to Alex Marshack. They were real people without pretenses, and they loved what they were doing. The older man almost gushed with enthusiasm—he was that exuberant.

Gene was a bundle of nervous energy, and he enjoyed himself immensely as he went over the storyboard with me. I had the feeling that he believed this film was going to be wonderful. Whether he actually felt it, I don't know, but he inspired me to believe it about every project I later worked on with him.

I ended up doing all the voices on *Pump Trouble*, but that is much less important than the friendship that developed among the three of us. I shared many wonderful moments with Gene and his wife, Marie, and with Bill and Barbara, including the joys of the births of Gene's third son and Bill's daughter and the downs and ups of breakups and remarriages of each of us.

With Gene, however, there was great chemistry. We had much in common. Neither of us ever outgrew childhood, I think. Life was one adventure after another, and the phrase "The one who has the most toys when he dies wins" fit us to a T. We were both top-notch in our fields. Gene was super top-notch. His animation won him an Academy Award, and today, in our old age, he is considered the grand old man of animation.

Gene and I collaborated later, in the 1980s, on what we hoped would be an animated series for TV. He directed it in Prague, where he had reluctantly accepted a short-term project years before that segued into a lifetime of joyous filmmaking, marriage, and creative collaboration with the girl of his dreams. Gene wrote a wonderful memoir called *For the Love of Prague*. It is both a love story about his romance and marriage to Zdenka and a hilarious story of his life and work as an American under and post-Communism in one of the most beautiful cities in the world.

If I tell you much more about my friend Gene Deitch, I might be accused of plagiarizing his book, so I suggest you look up http://www.fortheloveofprague.com on the web. You'll be glad you did. Gene and I usually see each other about once a year, but thanks to e-mail, we are in touch almost every day. He enriches my life. I hope I do the same for him. There is nothing like a good friend.

∞ ∞ ∞ ∞ ∞ ∞　　　∞ ∞ ∞ ∞ ∞ ∞

At the time I was having a ball on *The Howdy Doody Show*, I was also studying with a famous painter of the Ashcan school, Philip Reisman. He was an old friend of the family and, I might add, a fan of mine. The classes were at night, and we'd often go out for coffee after class. On one of these occasions, Philip told me about an artist who was a real character he said I ought to meet. He felt I would get a great deal of material just by spending a little time with him. He said he had a gallery of sorts on Fifth Avenue and Twenty-Third Street; he was a magician with paints and was not beyond faking the work of some famous painters. He also felt that he was a wonderful painter in his own right who had given up. He knew I was starting to collect works of other artists and said I could probably pick up some bargains in his gallery because he had a good eye and bought paintings at auction that he sold cheaply.

One day, when I had a few hours to kill and found myself downtown, I called Phil for the actual address of the man, Jack Levitz. His place was opposite the Flatiron Building. I found the address all right but was about to pass it by because there was a barber pole outside. But when I looked in the window, I saw a beautiful eighteenth-century landscape. I cupped my eyes to avoid the reflection of the sun so that I could peer into the interior but gave up and opened the door and walked in. I couldn't believe my eyes.

It was a long, narrow store with paintings adorning every inch of wall space and hundreds of paintings stacked up on the floor against the walls. Near the door was an old desk that he had used over the years as a pallet, covered with mounds of dried paint, and an easel stood nearby. On the wall, a few feet back from the desk, was a pay phone, and about three-quarters of the way back was a barber's chair complete with a barber giving someone a haircut. There was a partial screen that did not hide the barber or his customer. I had been looking at a fine still life on the wall opposite the pay phone. This was the thought that went through my head at the moment: *If I was sitting in a theater and the curtain went up on a William Saroyan play and this was the set, I'd believe it.*

At that moment, a short, stocky man, probably in his early sixties, with a cigarette dangling from his lip and the look of an aged prizefighter, came out of the back room and put a nickel in the pay phone. He dialed, listened, and then spoke in a high voice. "Hello, is Bill Saroyan there? Oh, will you tell him his friend Jack Levitz called?"

God, I thought, *Saroyan really finds these people.*

He hung up the phone, turned, and saw me looking at the still life. "A beauty, isn't it? The man was a master. Twenty-five dollars. You won't buy it."

The door opened, and a man walked in toward the back of the store and started examining some of the paintings on the floor. A moment later, a woman opened the door and asked, "How much is the painting in the window?"

"What do you care? You won't buy it," Levitz said.

The man looking at the paintings on the floor picked one out and asked the price.

"Come back tomorrow with your wife and I'll tell you."

"I want to know how much it is. I may buy it," the man insisted.

"My dear friend, why are you wasting my time? You know what will happen if I sell you this painting? You'll bring it back Monday with a hole in the middle where your head went. What in your house did you ever pick out yourself? Is there one stick of furniture, one ashtray, one towel or pillow? Bring your wife and I'll tell you the price."

Two ladies walked in. He turned to me and whispered, "From Forest Hills. They're looking for a couch painting. It shouldn't have any red, yellow, or blue in it."

They were looking at a flat Dutch landscape, and one asked, "What is this of?"

"That is Hitler's retreat in Berchtesgaden." Then he whispered to me, "You always have to give them a story."

"Really? But it's so flat."

"That is after the bombing. It was leveled."

"Oh, how much is it?"

"Thirty-five dollars."

"Will you take twenty-five?"

"Out!" He pointed to the door.

"What?'

"Out, out, out." He was furious.

"All right, I'll pay thirty-five."

"No! You can't have it. That man was a master. Out, out!"

The women rushed out the door, mumbling that he was a crazy man. He was holding the door open for them, ushering them out. But as they were leaving, a little girl about eight years old stood in the doorway, holding a crayon drawing. Immediately, his fury abated as he took the drawing that she offered him. "Oh, that's beautiful, darling—lovely." He reached in his pocket, took out a dollar, and gave it to her, patting her hair. "Keep up the good work, sweetheart." The child ran off with her dollar. He took the drawing, opened the drawer of his pallet desk, added it to a pile of youthful scribbling, and said to me, "I collect children."

I must tell you that I fell in love with that crazy man at that moment and made up my mind to befriend him. Philip Reisman was right: Jack Levitz was a treasure trove of material. Forget the material—he was the treasure.

The first thing I did was pick out a painting and, without a word, put a hundred-dollar bill in his hand and say, "I'm taking this."

He looked at me for the first time. Before, I was just someone to whisper his inner thoughts to instead of simply thinking them. Now I was someone who loved art. "Just like that, you're buying it?"

"Just like that. It's a knockout painting."

"Wait, I'll get your change. It's fifty dollars. Here, thank you."

"Thank you. You've got some great stuff here." I took my painting and left. I had a feeling he would remember me. That was important, because I would be coming back. I had a great deal to discover about this man. Besides, his store or gallery or barbershop—whatever it was—was a goldmine of art. Those paintings were not schlock. There were no buckeyes there. Every painting on those walls was a quality painting that would sell for hundreds or even thousands of dollars uptown in the fancy galleries.

I started haunting the place. At least a few times a week, I'd spend several hours with Jack. I'd stand in his shop and watch him throw customers out if they didn't have the right appreciation of art. We became friends and would go to lunch together, and he would regale me with stories of his past. Jack had studied with Bellows at Yale Art School as a young man. I told him that Phil Reisman had said he was a wonderful painter, and I asked to see his work. "You wouldn't like it," he said. "An artist paints what he loves or what he hates. I paint what I hate. They're not pretty pictures."

"So what? Come on, Jack—give me a little more credit than that. I love a good painting—you know that. I'm not interested in pretty pictures. Let me see them."

"Some other time maybe. They're down in the cellar. You'll get your clothes all dirty."

"So I'll send them to the cleaners."

"Some other time."

That "some other time" went on for many months. Meanwhile, I learned how he was able to sell these paintings so cheap. He would buy them at auction, and as long as the quality was there, he didn't care what shape they were in. He would restore them and frame them. If it was a large painting, partly damaged or destroyed, he either painted it in, matching the artist's technique, or cut it into several smaller paintings. He was a master, knowledgeable of the chemistry of the pigments and the grounds on the canvas.

One day, I came over to go to lunch with him and found him repairing a beautiful gold baroque frame that was missing a corner. He mixed up some concoction of Bulldog linoleum cement, plaster, and various other ingredients into a putty of sorts and, looking at the corner that was there, modeled a perfect replica of what must have been hand carved. "Okay. Let's go to lunch. When we come back, I'll guild it." He did it all in minutes.

Another day, I came and found about eight Van Gogh paintings lined up against the wall, and one on the easel, which he was in the process of painting. I watched him with my mouth open. He painted the one on the easel in front of

219

me in one hour. He painted it as I imagine Van Gogh himself might have done it—he laid that paint on with a kind of fury. He was not copying anything. These were Jack's originals as Van Gogh might have painted them. "I got an idea. This movie on Van Gogh is coming out, *Lust for Life*. I figure I could rent these to the theaters for lobby displays."

Someone got hold of one of Jack's Van Gogh's, took the canvas off the stretcher, took it to Europe, and claimed he'd discovered an unknown Van Gogh. There were stories about it in the papers and periodicals, and after experts debated over it, the painting was declared not to be an original Van Gogh. But the notoriety surrounding it enabled the man to sell it for $50,000. Hey, that's the art market!

One morning, I arrived early at Jack's place. I needed a haircut, and I'd seen the barber at work there whenever I visited. I figured I could kill two birds with one stone. Jack saw me and opened the door. "Allen, what are you doing here so early?"

"I needed a haircut, so I figured—"

He put his hand over my mouth. "Shush, he'll hear you."

"That's all right. I need a haircut and—"

"Quiet! Otto will hear. You can't get a haircut here. Otto will cut your ear off. He's blind. He's all right for the bums around here but not for a fine gentleman like you. Why do you think I let him use this place? He can't see anymore."

So that is the story of the barber in the art gallery. It was something I couldn't understand before. He needed a place to work, so Jack gave him space in his gallery. It might seem incongruous to someone else but not to Jack.

Finally, after months of pestering, Jack took me down into his cellar to see his paintings. They were covered with years of dust, but Jack spat on them and wiped each one off with a rag for me to see. The first one I looked at was *The Painter of Ryder*. Albert Pinkham Ryder was a nineteenth-century artist famous for his paintings of night seascapes. The moon and clouds were always prominent in his work. He was a poverty-stricken artist who never had decent material to work with, so his paintings, in time, developed cracks.

Jack's painting was his swipe at the gullibility of art museums. The artist in the painting was painting Ryder forgeries. On the wall behind him were already-finished forgeries. On his pallet were yellow moons laid out in a row. At his feet were two buckets—one labeled "cloud paint" and one labeled "boat paint." There was also a brochure from Park-Bernet and a fat roll of money. The painter had a halo around his head.

"This is a self-portrait. There are more of my Ryder's in museums than Ryder's. The curator of the Ryder collection paid me to paint them for him. Who would challenge such a man? And I put a halo around my head because I didn't do anything wrong. I put a boy through medical school."

Jack told me of his experience with the noted Hollywood producer Charles K. Feldman, who had taken him to Hollywood to be an artist in residence at his palatial home. Jack was bitter about him because he felt the man had humiliated him. He showed me photographs of him painting in Feldman's swimming pool, with easel and all. Feldman sold many of his paintings to his friends, including Edward G. Robinson, who was a noted collector.

Among the paintings in the cellar were those from Jack's disgust-of-Hollywood period. In one tremendous painting, *The Ogre of Hollywood*, a magnificent nude whose face was almost ugly was controlled by a monster who also held little men in tuxedos on strings. On another, titled *Zanuck's Casting Couch*, a pretty nude teenage girl was lying on a couch with a jelly apple in her hand. Every one was a little gem or a big gem. Why were these paintings hidden away in a cellar? All of his work had stories attached to them, and they were fascinating and full of the artist's emotions.

"Jack, how much would you sell these paintings for?"

"Are you kidding? Nobody would buy these."

"I would."

"You would buy these paintings?"

"If you want to sell them. Give me a price."

"Thirty-five dollars apiece. Take what you want."

"I'll take them all. Lock the cellar. I'll come by with a car one of these days and pick them up. Let's count them and figure the bill."

"I can't believe you."

"Believe me. I'm robbing you, Jack, but let's face it—they robbed Van Gogh, too."

I finally got up the nerve to ask Jack if he would teach me. He said he was not a teacher but would like to see some of my work. I wasted no time in bringing in some of the paintings I had done in Mexico. He looked at them quickly and said, "Oh well, you're a painter. All you need is a few tricks. Your color is great. You caught the light. Phil Reisman did a whole series on Mexico, but they do not have the light." We made a date for him to come over to my studio one evening and then go out to dinner.

As promised, he showed me a few tricks—well, maybe to him they were tricks. To me, they solved problems I had wrestled with all through the years—and here were the answers all in one night. "Tell me something, Jack. I studied with Raphael Soyer, and I kept looking to him to help me solve these problems. You mean to tell me such a famous artist doesn't know these things?"

"Sure he knows them, but why should he show them to you and make a competitor?"

That was Jack—down to earth, a man of no illusions. I took him to a nice restaurant, hoping to treat him, but he'd have no part of it and insisted on splitting the bill. His way of expressing himself was interesting; his words remain in my memory. I realized that his was not the happiest marriage. He never confided anything about his family other than the pride he had in being able to pay for his son's medical education.

However, in philosophizing, he'd say things like "How is it possible that a little woman, so small, as light as a feather, can take a big, strapping man and over time, like the waves against a rock, reduce him to a pebble of a person?"

I only once visited Jack and his wife in their home in Queens. What impressed me—or, I should say, depressed me—most was that there was not one Levitz painting on the walls.

One day, in his shop, another child—a boy this time—came in and brought Jack a small painting, and again Jack gave him a dollar. I pointed out to Jack that it was not so good. It was a painting by the numbers. "How do you like that? A smart guy like me gets taken in."

∞ ∞ ∞ ∞ ∞ ∞   ∞ ∞ ∞ ∞ ∞ ∞

Howdy Doody characters in NBC'S Los Angeles parking lot, 1954 l.to r.: Allen Swift as Chief Thunder-Chicken, Bobby Nicholson as Clarabelle the Clown, Bob Smith as Buffalo Bob and Bill LeCornec as Chief Thunder-Thud.

In my third year of *The Howdy Doody Show*, Bob Smith fully recuperated and came back to the show. This was a big plus. After all, it was his baby, and even as good as Ted Brown was, he wasn't Bob Smith. However, I couldn't understand why I was continuing to do the voice of Howdy. I felt sure that Bob would resume doing it. Possibly he wanted to go back to work slowly after what he'd gone through. He was still the same hale-and-hearty guy he was before, and he still greeted me each day with "Allie, baby" and the bone-crushing hug.

Two weeks before I was due to sign a new contract, Roger Muir called me into his office and told me that my option was not going to be picked up. I was dumbstruck. I'll recount how he said it to me for its historical value, but however he said it, it was an unbelievable blow to my solar plexus. I could hardly breathe as he said, looking down and never at me, "We, ah, are having, ah, to cut back. Our ratings are, ah, running into, ah, competition from the Mickey Mouse shows, and well, I'm sorry."

Why he couldn't look at me as he said it was because it was a lie, and he knew that I knew it. It didn't even make sense financially. I was being paid scale. The puppeteers were earning the same scale as me. I was now a seasoned puppeteer, so if they really had to cut back ... Well, why belabor it? There was obviously another reason, and it was one that had never occurred to me. Bob Smith's friend Bobby Nickelson told me it was what Bob wanted. "But why, Nick?" I asked. "I saved this guy's show for him. I never asked for another penny."

"Al, you have no idea of the ego of this man," Bobby answered.

∞ ∞ ∞ ∞ ∞ ∞   ∞ ∞ ∞ ∞ ∞ ∞

This was an earthquake. The ground opened up and swallowed me. Ironically, this was my last week of therapy. My shrink had told me it was graduation week—"Over the ocean, tomorrow's promotion." I walked into his office like a zombie. "Nat, they dropped my option."

He got up from his chair, came toward me with a big, wide smile on his face, and shook my hand. "Congratulations, you're free. Don't you see what this means? There is a whole world out there for you. You think nobody knows who you are? You think this is going back to square one? If I were you, I would take a full-page ad in *Variety*: 'Thank you, Bob Smith.' What did you think, this would go on forever? Move ahead. Now there is nothing to stop you."

I walked out of his office feeling eight feet tall. I went directly to my studio and, during the next two weeks, created a sixteen-page brochure with a cover that looked official: "CONFIDENTIAL FILE: Allen Swift."

I did all the artwork and interspersed comedy with facts. I paper-clipped a handwritten note with the recipient's name and "This is important!" to the cover. On the inside first page were instructions to the reader:

1. Read this file carefully.
2. Memorize the facts about Allen Swift.
3. Use him when the opportunity arises.
4. Inform your employer of your actions.

Your display of good judgment in carrying out the above instructions will be rewarded!

The following pages were full of drawings and photographs of characters I had done on *The Howdy Doody Show*, as well as those for UPA Cartoons.

There was one dramatic page with black negative film running down the entire page and white print on the black film that read,

Over $8,000,000 was spent in 1955 on advertising using the voices of Allen Swift.

HOWDY DOODY

PHINEAS T. BLUSTER

ALLEN SWIFT

PLAYED THESE

AND 50 OTHER

CHARACTERS

ON

Howdy Doody

SANDY MAC TAVISH

HYDE & ZEKE the TWIN BEARS

DILLY DALLY

FLUB-A-DUB

"CONFIDENTIAL FILE: Allen Swift" 1956

226

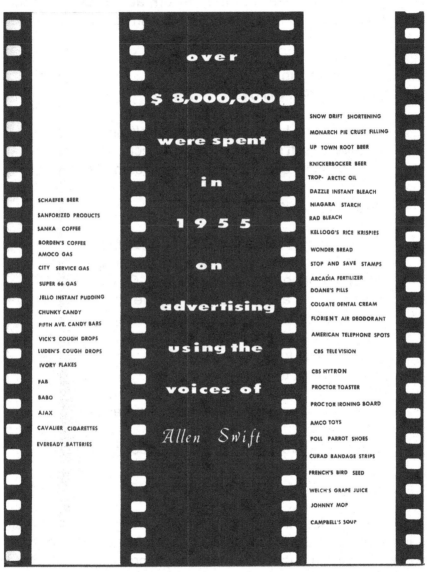

"CONFIDENTIAL FILE: Allen Swift" 1956

227

There was a great deal more puffery in the form of gags. And on the last full page was an advertisement for a free long-playing record, replete with the artwork and a replica of the kind of magazine ad for records that was in vogue at the time.

> Nothing to buy!
> No club to join!
> No salesman will call!
>
> Now you can have a ten-inch long-playing record of Allen Swift's voices, taken directly from the sound tracks of a score of revolting commercials.
>
> Absolutely free!
>
> It's yours for the asking. Spend leisure hours at home enjoying such favorite commercials as Sanka Coffee, Ivory Flakes, Bab-O, Schaefer Beer—yes, all the spots you've heard on television but never dreamed of owning.
>
> Delight your friends!
> Be the life of the party!
>
> Thirty minutes of *uninterrupted commercials*!
>
> But you must act fast! Records are being pressed now.
> Reserve your copy for future delivery!

And of course, there was a box for them to fill out their names and addresses. There was also a free mail-order card so that they didn't have to cut out anything or find a stamp. I put in the usual disclaimer: "I understand if I am not satisfied, I may return the record in ten days for a complete refund."

One-third of the people who received the brochure requested the record, and thirteen weeks from the date of the mailing, I was earning three times what I'd earned on *The

Howdy Doody Show, and *Howdy Doody* went to once a week, on Saturday mornings, and then off the air entirely.

Now, you might wonder about some of my facts. Was it a lie to say that $8 million was spent in 1955 on advertising using the voices of Allen Swift? No! I simply totaled the *Howdy Doody* budget for the year, including airtime. Wasn't that what was spent using my voices? It was creativity with numbers and even more honest than Arthur Anderson. I could not help it if *Variety* and other trade papers mistook it to read "Allen Swift did $8 million worth of commercials in 1955."

The brochure was to get me started; it was not the end. I hired a press agent to keep my name in the trade papers and place articles in the popular press. I had a front-page story in the *Los Angeles Times* and articles in the *News*, the *Mirror*, and the *New York Times*. Allen Swift became the Man of a Thousand Voices. After a while, the press agent was no longer necessary. Columnists and radio and TV shows called to interview me, and I didn't let up. I was a one-man industry in voice-overs, and I did it all without an agent. I did not have to pay anyone commission. Take that, you Harry Greens and Baums and Newborns.

I had an interesting experience soon after mailing out the brochures. One morning, I was walking my dog, Scrabble, in front of my apartment house, when a man in a convertible passed by, stopped, and called to me. "Excuse me—are you Allen Swift?" I answered in the affirmative. (Actually, I said yes, but it seems more writer-like to have answered in the affirmative.)

"I recognized you from your picture in your brochure. I'd love to talk to you. I'm the president of Young and Rubicam Advertising. Are you going into the city? Can I give you a lift?" "Yes, if you can wait till I take my dog back up to my apartment." He did, and as we rode into the city from Rego Park, he kept talking about the brochure. He seemed to have memorized all sixteen pages.

"We held a meeting with my creative staff the other day, analyzing why your brochure is a perfect promotional piece. To begin with, it looks important. Open the cover and you have to laugh at the chutzpah. Turn the page—we see who the hell you are. Turn the page again and we're hit with amazing facts—but before we get bored by the facts, we're laughing again." He went on and on, raving about it. I don't know why. I almost expected him to offer me a job as a copywriter, but he didn't. He was just pleasant. We shook hands and parted. I have done hundreds of voice-over commercials for that agency through the years, but I never saw him again.

Now, you would think that with all this publicity and reputation, ad agencies would simply hire me for their commercials. That was not the case. I auditioned for 90 percent of the jobs I did. The reason the advertising business attracts the most insecure people, I soon learned, is they have nothing tangible to sell. They are selling air. Everything is done by committees in fear of making mistakes. There are exceptions but not many. I have rarely come across one person who will say, "This is right, and it's the way I want it done, and I take full responsibility."

Everything is a trial balloon and must be tested all the way down the line. Is the copy good? Test it. Are the visuals good? Test them. Is the voice on the voice-over good? Test it. Will people buy it? Test it! In my career, I've done upward of fifty thousand commercials. A great many of them never saw the light of day—they didn't test well. I did hundreds of spots only as tests. They were never meant to be aired.

I have never taken commercials seriously. As far as I'm concerned, doing commercials was a cash cow for me. I never considered it art. Perhaps the reason was that I found it so easy to do. It was never challenging. It was not the same as acting in a play by Chekhov or another playwright, where you have to dig into a part. Twenty-, thirty-, or sixty-second commercials do not require a hell of a lot of work, and as for their importance, I was selling detergent.

You can imagine, therefore, how surprised I was when I was asked to speak at the first American TV Commercial Festival Awards Ceremony. I was sure it was a send-up. I never for one minute believed that this was not a tongue-in-cheek roast by everyone in advertising. There I was, seated on the dais with all the advertising moguls. I wrote a funny routine for this silly occasion, which I expected to bring roars of laughter. It brought cold, hard stares. As my routine went on in dead silence, I realized, *Oh my God, they are all serious about this.* I finished and sat down in a silent Waldorf Astoria banquet room.

Someone sent a note up to me, asking, "What was that all about?" The next speaker was the president of the American Association of Advertising Agencies. He was the high llama of the industry. This was the context of his speech:

"I have just spent the past seventy-two hours screening television commercials, and I want to tell you it was the most exciting seventy-two hours I have ever spent." There was tremendous applause. "You people are to be congratulated. You have created a new art form—an American art form." Again, there was tremendous applause. "You are taking the story of American business out into the hinterlands. There was a time when it was said, 'Build a better mousetrap and the world will beat a path to your door.' Be a need fulfiller. But you are more than need fulfillers. You are want fulfillers. You are making the American public want, and I say it is more important to make the American people want than it is to get a man up in space!"

You never heard such an outburst of applause and whistles. The entire audience was on its feet, yelling in a frenzy of acclaim and stamping feet. I sat there looking up at the speaker, who had been seated next to me, and thinking, *Boy, am I in the wrong pew.*

The following day, I was in a studio, doing some commercials for J. Walter Thompson. The producer walked in and said, "Allen, baby. What were you saying there yesterday?"

"Those were the funnies, Matt."

"Yeah, man, this is our bread and butter."

"It's my bread and butter too, and I have it buttered on both sides. But if I have to convince myself that what I am doing is *Death of a Salesman*, I'm going to shoot myself."

Now that I've played this back on paper and in my head, I realize how smart-assed I was and lacking in any feeling for Matt, the producer, and all the others taking this ceremony seriously. It is easy to become smug and contemptuous of others when all is going well for you. The money was rolling in, and what I was doing to make it was easy. That does not mean it was easy for everyone else. Besides, everyone has the right to feel what he or she is doing is important. I believe the president of the four As was ridiculous in going overboard, but my arrogance toward everyone else in the business was also overboard.

Chapter 9

Captain Allen Swift Sets Sail

I had not been off *Howdy Doody* and live television for more than three months when I signed a contract with Channel 11, WPIX, to host *The Popeye Show* daily as Captain Allen Swift. This, again, came about through an audition, but it was one I created myself. The powers that be had purchased the entire catalogue of Popeye cartoons and needed a host for the show who would present the cartoons and deliver the live commercials.

I went to a costume house and rented an old salt's pea coat and a captain's hat. Then I had a makeup artist fit me with a gray beard and wig. I aged my face with latex and auditioned as though I were on the bow of a ship. I waved into the camera and, in an old salt's voice, greeted the audience with "Ahoy, mateys! Welcome aboard the SS *Popeye*. Captain Allen Swift on deck here to greet you." I also did a couple of commercials for them, and that wrapped it up. That was my greeting every day for the next four years. They had a set built with a ship, and I'd come up through the hatch, head over to the rail, and start the show.

It became the most successful children's show on the air in the New York metropolitan area, and I was the hottest kids' show personality. I loved doing it. My son, Lewis, was nine years old when it started, and all of my talk was directly to him. I would bring to my audience whatever problems he was having at the time, knowing they probably had the same feelings. If it was camp time, I'd talk about the kind of anxiety kids have about their separation from home, the fear of the unknown, and concerns regarding whether they could measure up to their new peers. I signed off each night by saying, "Good night to you and Lew."

They got a lot more than they bargained for when they signed me. I did magic on the show and brought on kid guests, such as Gene Deitch's son, Kim, and his friend, who made their own animated cartoons on eight-millimeter film. They showed the kids, frame by frame, how the cartoons were made.

I had a specific purpose in presenting their demonstration. A short time before, one of the cartoons had depicted Popeye climbing up a telephone pole, pulling the wires apart, and sending a fiery charge to his enemy, Bluto. The next day, the papers reported that a young child had climbed up a pole and been electrocuted. I spoke to the president of the station and asked that he remove that segment so that it could not be aired. He refused, saying, "We paid for them. We're going to use them!" After that, I explained to the children that the things Popeye did were not real. I brought Kim and his friend on to drive that point home. Every time that cartoon was shown, I made sure to explain it to the kids both before and after.

I also got the kids interested in art. I drew various objects and scenes and introduced them to a "scribble scrabble," a way to start if they had no idea what to draw. They scribbled all over the page and then looked to find some form in the scribble that they could develop. It's a sort of Rorschach test. This led to an art contest I later ran that brought giant mailbags into the station every day with all kinds of children's art. Shades of my friend Jack Levitz! Only I didn't give out dollar bills. That was many years ago, and I still have some of the most beautiful works in my collection. I often wonder how many of those children went on to be artists. Might there even be some famous American artist who started as a child because of Captain Allen Swift?

Captain Allen Swift, host of *The Popeye Show,* with Popeye, WPIX-TV, 1956-61

I started to get requests to make personal appearances, both for charity and for business promotions. Realizing this was a new market for me, I hired a friend, Manny Demby, to manage the bookings with department stores, malls, and fund-raisers.

I did magic shows at most of my personal appearances in costume as the elderly sea captain, but at some, such as Macy's on Thirty-Fourth Street, it was impossible. There were lines around the block, weaving in and around roped-off sections of the store. As children with their parents passed by, I could only shake hands and say a few words or ask a question of each child.

The business of my playing an old man while in my early thirties had repercussions. Most of my fans think I died long ago. I hear it all the time. My grandson, Peter Stadlen, was in an off-Broadway play recently. One review said, "Peter Stadlen is the son of actor Lewis J. Stadlen and the grandson of the late Allen Swift." I know I died a number of times on stage or a nightclub floor, but at this writing, the ticker still ticks.[4]

The interludes broadcast between the Popeye films were done live, and everything I did was impromptu. I never had a script. Even the commercials were done without a script. I knew the important points the sponsor wanted stressed, and the rest was left to me.

A man came to see me one day with a toy he'd invented. He said, "I have this toy, but I haven't been able to get it off the ground. So far, I've sold about three dozen. I am buying a few spots on your show for cash. I have no advertising agency, but my kid buys everything you sell. I can't give you a script or anything. Here it is. Take it home and play with it, and just sell it the way you think best."

The day after I did the commercial, the man called to tell me he had orders for twenty thousand. He decided to go across the country and buy time on the different kids' shows. "Would it be all right if I used your words and actions for my script? I wrote them down."

---

[4]   Ed. note: Allen wrote this memoir off and on between 2003 and 2009.

I said, "Sure, go ahead."
The toy was Silly Putty.

∞ ∞ ∞ ∞ ∞ ∞   ∞ ∞ ∞ ∞ ∞ ∞

This was a hectic time and a wrenching one for me. My marriage of fourteen years was definitely at an end. There was no one to blame, no hatred. What I'd loved about Vivienne I still loved. We were just oil and water from the beginning. We agreed to wait six months while we found a therapist for our son, to help him make the adjustment to our divorce a little easier.

I doubt that it did any good. Lewis was beginning to show signs of his father's cynicism, and in spite of our concern, we had to laugh at his mimicry of the doctor. After our divorce, I learned that he lied to his friends about his parents' separation, making up stories as to why I was not around much.

There was no disagreement between Vivienne and me, even about our separation agreement. The only obstacle was the lawyers. If we'd listened to them, it could have been hell. My lawyer tried to convince me I was offering too much and that she would take me for everything I had. He forced me to confront him.

"Mr. Gates, I have not hired you for advice. Don't tell me what my wife would do. I have lived with her for fourteen years. I think I'm a better judge of her than you. I will see to it that my wife is taken care of. We will split everything we have down the middle. I shall take care of my son. I have given you all the figures. You will simply dot the i's and cross the t's."

∞ ∞ ∞ ∞ ∞ ∞   ∞ ∞ ∞ ∞ ∞ ∞

While the divorce was going on, I was doing so many commercials that I was running around to different recording studios all day. In the early evening, I did *The Popeye Show*. When that finished, I would drive like crazy to Hyde Park, New York, where I was producing a season of summer stock.

I got into the summer-stock deal because my actor friend John Marley wanted to be a director and kept bugging me to get a theater so that he could direct. That sounds crazy, but it's true. I was making all this money, and what was I doing for my friends? He found a beautiful summer-stock theater that was on the grounds of the old Vanderbilt estate stables. I was hooked. It sounded exciting. I called my friend Charlie Zitner, who was always looking for things to invest in. He loved the idea, so we each put up $10,000 and formed a corporation. Since we had met in the Altitude Training Unit, we called it ATU Productions.

Now, I already had a suite of ten offices. Did I need ten offices? No, but it was cheap: $250 a month for a reception room and nine other offices in a horseshoe arrangement like an ad agency. It was cheap because it was a walk-up -- only one long flight -- and the building was not long for this world. I had a month-to-month lease.

My office was grand, with a fireplace and a large terrace over a Chinese restaurant. The other offices were only about ten by ten. I gave one to my friend Paul Ashley, a puppeteer and puppet maker, another to my friend Sam Engler, who had a public relations company, and a third to Mr. Calabrese, the sculptor. I charged rent only to one person, Ernie Pintoff, an animator who was an acquaintance but not actually a friend.

So there I was, a producer, which meant I was the publicity department, the advertising department, and the man who went around tacking posters on telephone poles. We brought in touring shows and produced our own. The first show of the season was the musical *Pajama Game*, and of course, I had an idea for how to sell it. Telephone answering machines had just come out. They couldn't take messages yet; they could only make announcements. They were perfect for theaters and were used to announce the shows and the performance times. I leased one and then brought my friend Zel deCyr up to the theater. Zel had the sexiest voice in the business, and I wrote this announcement for her to record: "Hello, did you ever play the pajama game? It's such fun. We're playing it every night at the Hyde Park Playhouse, and I so want you to come. You can dress any way you like. I'll be in my pajamas. Bye."

I then walked around to some bars and restaurants, handed a few people dimes, and said, "You want to have some fun? Call this number."

That was it. It cost me about sixty cents. Within twenty-four hours, we tied up all the telephone lines in Hyde Park, Rhinebeck, and Poughkeepsie. I was back in my office when I received a call from the telephone company, telling me I had to turn off the recording.

I said, "No, I'm not turning it off. Put on more lines." This went on all day, with calls back and forth between the playhouse, the phone company, and me.

The following morning, an executive of the phone company called me. "Mr. Swift, we realize we cannot turn off your answering machine without your permission. We even advertise it to be used for theater announcements. You are using it for that purpose, only no one ever did it just that way. Our engineers forecast if we put on a hundred extra lines, it wouldn't make a dent. We've reached a point where hospitals are being affected. It is really an emergency."

"Okay. If you call all the newspaper wire services and give them this story, I will turn it off."

"Thank you. I will do it personally immediately."

I believe this story hit every newspaper across the country. We were a sellout. Too bad we didn't have the show for the entire season with that kind of publicity. I only went up to Hyde Park for the opening of each show. The rest of the week, I was slaving away in the office, preparing the mechanicals for the ads and arranging swaps with radio stations in the area. I would do promos in various voices for time on the air. I was working until two or three in the morning, and I was exhausted. I needed help.

During the day, John was casting other shows we were to do. We used my private office, which was anything but private, as a waiting room. It was the only one that had comfortable places to sit. I was behind my desk in shirtsleeves, answering phone calls.

I am certain—in fact, I know—that most of the people who came through my office thought I was the gofer. This particular day, John was interviewing actresses. They would wait in my office until called. There was a lull in the traffic, when a beautiful girl walked in and said she had an appointment with John Marley. Now, none of these girls, by any stretch of imagination, could have been called plain, but this one dazzled me.

I remember she was wearing a yellow dress. She was willowy, but there was meat on her bones. Her eyes were large and liquid, and her skin! I never saw Deborah Kerr close up, but I imagine she had such skin. I stopped what I was working on and engaged her in conversation. Her voice and speech were lovely, and she was intelligent and real. Before I could advance the conversation further, my alarm watch went off. I had to go to a recording session. Fortunately, the studio was directly across the street. I excused myself and ran down the steps. I ran into that studio, did the job in one take, and ran back across the street and up the stairs. She was gone. I asked John, "Who was that girl?"

"What girl?"

"The pretty one."

"They're all pretty." He wasn't any help, so there was nothing to do about it.

I needed help. I was overworked, but how could I go about getting help? I called my friend Zel. We were good friends and kind of stuck on each other, but nothing had ever happened between us. I was sort of her mentor and actually helped her become a successful voice-over artist. "Zel, hiya, honey! I need a favor. I am inundated with work here. I need a Girl Friday—you know, a secretary but more. Maybe you know someone? Maybe an actress doing some other kind of work who would like to work on a production job for the summer?"

"As a matter of fact, I do. I was talking to her the other day. She works for an engineering company and is bored to death. When can she see you? She works a full day."

"Anytime. She can come in after work. I'm here till two, three in the morning. Look, talk to her. You know where I am. Tell her she should just knock on my door."

The gal must have been really interested in the job, because she came that evening. I was on the phone, talking to Manny Demby, when she knocked. I yelled, "Come in!" She did. I looked up and held up my hand as if to say, "I'll be right with you." I told Manny I'd call him back and hung up.

It was her—the beauty in the yellow dress from the other day. How lucky could I get? I offered her a seat and proceeded to interview her in a businesslike manner, which took some acting because I was so excited. I looked at her as she answered my questions, but I'm not sure I heard everything she said. We haggled a bit about the salary because I figured that was the thing employers do, but I would have paid her anything. This time, she was not going to get away.

Now, in movie parlance, we have a fast cut, or in video, we fast-forward. I have been married to that beauty for forty-one years. She is still beautiful. She is still willowy with the right amount of meat on her bones. Her eyes are liquid, but she doesn't see as well anymore, because when she looks in the mirror, she sees lines that aren't there.

If that encounter happened today, we probably never would have married. She would have sued me for sexual harassment. Fortunately, we met prior to the politically correct years. No wonder there are so many single men and women today. Everybody walks through life with blinkers on—or at least through the office.

Lenore—that's her name—actually was a great secretary. I was lucky all around. I'm a disorganized person. I let things pile up and then panic as to what to do next. Lenore calmed me down. "Just make a pile of everything. Deal with the item on top. When you're finished with that, go to the next item. Forget what's under the pile. Take it one at a time."

I have always remembered that advice, and someday I am going to use it. It is difficult to change habits.

The third show of the season was *Show Time with George Jessel*. My Girl Friday picked me up after *The Popeye Show*, and we drove like the wind to Hyde Park for the opening. We arrived just before the curtain went up. The Hyde Park Playhouse seats four hundred people. There were maybe fifty people in the audience. To say I was disappointed would trivialize how I felt, coming after two sellout shows. What could have happened? George Jessel was funny. His opening line was "Well, they didn't like Roosevelt here either."

He went on from there to do a wonderful show before mostly empty houses. I could not figure out what had happened to our audience. After two sellout weeks, we'd expect that word of mouth about our productions would engender a certain amount of interest and ticket sales. I could understand dropping down to three-quarters of a house or even half a house, but something like this defied explanation.

I went to see the woman who owned the theater and who had run it herself for years before she'd rented it to me. "Oh yes," she said, "I forgot to tell you. There are two IBM plants in the area. That is where most of the theatergoers come from. IBM closes for two weeks and sends all their employees away to a summer camp they run for them."

"Hey, thanks for telling me! Had you told me that before, I might not have booked such expensive shows for this period!"

At least I knew what the problem was. The question was, what could we do about it? John and I sat in an all-night diner, drinking many cups of coffee and mulling over the problem. If this trend kept up for two weeks, it would be financially disastrous. It was no good expressing our anger at the owner for keeping that secret from us. *There must be a solution. We just can't give up. Our audience went bye-bye, so how can we get another audience? Not everybody works for IBM. What about the rest of the people?* With so few people at our opening night, we couldn't even count on any word of mouth.

Hold the presses—word of mouth. I must generate word of mouth immediately. My flexible magician's con-man mind went into overdrive—I had it!

The next morning, I roused all the apprentices into the rehearsal hall and set up a line of telephones and phone books. "Okay, kids, you all want to be actors? You're going to act from now on. Watch and listen to what I do, because you are going to do the same."

I opened the phone book to the A's and started calling strangers as though I were a familiar friend. Here is how it went (with both sides of the conversation):

"Hello?"

I turned the receiver so that the actors could hear the person who answered. "Hey, character," I said. "Did you guys miss a great show last night. That Georgie Jessel show was hilarious. We had such a great time we're going again tonight and taking the kids. How about you and Andy joining us?"

"I think you have the wrong number."

"Oh, you're not Alma? Oh, I'm terribly sorry."

"No, that's all right—what was that show?"

"Oh, *Show Time with George Jessel* at the Hyde Park Playhouse. Look, I'm sorry to have—"

"No, no, thank you. Maybe we'll go see it."

"Now," I said to the apprentices, "that is the way it went just now with me, but it will be different each time. You not only have to act; you have to improvise. Each call will be an improvisation. The important thing is that you come on with great enthusiasm and get the whole thing out before the other party has a chance to answer. Be very believable. Don't stay on the line too long. Answer any question, of course, but remember you are trying to reach your friend."

There were six apprentices on the phone continuously, and we continued the calls until the day of closing night. We pulled it off. We were nowhere near sellout, but we didn't lose either, and we inveigled many people into doing something new—going to the theater.

What took on the character of a black comedy was the arrival of Jessel's manager, who insisted on my paying him as an independent contractor. I think Jessel was embarrassed, but his manager heated him up about it, explaining that since he paid the cast, he was entitled to that status. In truth, he certainly was, but his manager should have negotiated it that way and not allowed Jessel to sign an equity contract. I was not able to accommodate him, because it was against union regulations.

The manager told him not to go on with the show. The last thing I wanted was a brouhaha. I took Jessel aside. "George, you say this will cost you more money out of your pocket. How much would it cost you?"

"It would cost me another three hundred dollars."

"Listen, I have to say this. You have been an inspiration to me all my life. When I was able to book you up here, it was like a dream fulfilled. When I walked into that theater and saw so few people there to see you, I felt sick, but what did I see? I saw a great performer give that almost empty house a performance like they were hanging from the rafters. George, I cannot, according to the rules, pay you as an independent contractor. But I am not going to let anything cause animosity between us. I want to give you three hundred dollars from my own pocket. Here, please take it."

There was a long pause, and then he said, "Forget it. You hear? Forget it." He turned to his manager and said, "Stop it! I don't want to hear any more about this. Forget it!"

It was shameless on my part. I admit it. But on the other hand, if it had failed, I had put my money on the line. During the rest of the season, there were no more demands to be paid as independent contractors. I acted in one play that season for my soul, *The Seven Year Itch*. Lenore got to act in *Merton of the Movies* with no less a star than Buster Keaton. We ended the season with a loss of half our investment. It could have been much worse. The week after Jessel's show really killed us. I think we used up whatever audience was left in the area. I couldn't keep using that phone gimmick on the same people.

As Richard Sherman with Salome Jens as
The Girl in George Axelrod's *The Seven Year Itch*,
The Hyde Park Playhouse, Hyde Park, NY 1957

∞ ∞ ∞ ∞ ∞ ∞ ∞   ∞ ∞ ∞ ∞ ∞ ∞ ∞

Back in the city, Manny Demby had lined up quite a few personal appearances for me. I think it's time to tell you about Manny. His company was called Demby Associates. To my knowledge, he only had one associate: Myron Broun—or, as he was called, Mike. These two men were as different as a hawk and a dove, and I could never figure out how they came together. It wouldn't be difficult to find out—I could simply ask Mike, who's remained my friend all through the years and is editing this memoir. That wouldn't be fair. This, after all, is my recollection of what I perceived at the time.

Manny was the greatest con artist I ever knew, and Mike was the straightest shooter. Manny was always sloppy, with cigar ashes all over his clothes, and hyper. Mike was always neatly dressed and appeared thoughtful and serene.

Prior to working with me, Manny had been the public relations counsel for the government of Indonesia. He was a man of great ability to con his way into many ventures that would lead him to the heights and depths of the free enterprise system.

I realized that Manny was involved in various deals, any one of which might pay off big, but I only knew of them by rumor. For example, I heard he was the brains behind Dr. Ernest Dichter, a psychologist who was coining money from advertising agencies by selling them on the idea of using psychological testing to determine what the public wanted and how to sell to them.

Manny was anathema to me. There were things about him that repulsed me and, at the same time, drew me to him. Undoubtedly, he had a superior mind and a charm that overcame his many shortcomings.

I heard from him later, when he was down on his luck. He called and asked to use the typewriter in my office over the weekend. He wrote and sent out releases about a motivational research study he'd done that would cause a revolution in the automobile industry. In the release, he wrote that copies of the study were available for $1,000 each. The release was picked up by most of the newspapers and by the trade journal *Advertising Age*. Orders poured in from all the auto companies and ad agencies. There was one problem: there was no study.

Everyone who knew Manny agreed he was the fastest typist imaginable. He sat in my office and typed a thousand-page report, complete with fabricated interviews with people all over the country, including footnotes. The study concluded that what the public wanted was compact cars. I don't remember what year this was, but the following year, the auto industry came out with compact cars.

Now, think about this. While he was typing at breakneck speed, he was creating all these interviews. Since none of these interviews ever took place, the conclusions had to be Manny's. He decided what the public wanted, probably on the basis of what he wanted. At any rate, this stunt got Manny back on his feet.

The next time I met Manny, some twenty years later, he was Dr. Emanuel Demby of Motivation Research Associates. He was now making a fortune. He had offices in New York, Paris, and The Hague and was recovering partially from a stroke. His New York offices were posh, with a large staff. I was delighted by his success but not by his health. This glib man could hardly make himself understood. He passed away shortly after that. I don't know whether Manny went back to a university to get a doctorate or came by it through other means. It doesn't matter. He was brilliant.

∞ ∞ ∞ ∞ ∞ ∞   ∞ ∞ ∞ ∞ ∞ ∞ ∞

Not long after my stint as a summer-stock producer, I received a call from an old friend from our making-the-rounds days in radio. Walter Collins had been a child actor; he had played on Broadway in *Junior Miss*. The theater was, to him, a temple. He was steeped in its history. His mother was a Broadway star in the twenties. Her name was Anna Wheaton, and the song "Tea for Two" was written for her.

Walter was a member of the Lambs Club, a stodgy old actors' club, and was always after me to join. I feel like Groucho

Marx in that I wouldn't join any club that would have me as a member. Actually, I don't like to dress up with a suit and tie. All these clubs demanded it.

All of this happened before the call from Walter from New Orleans, which I will get to after filling you in on our halcyon days when he was still an actor. I finally gave in to Walter's request to join the club. I had no idea what this entailed. I figured I'd say okay, I'd pay my dues, and that would be that. But no such thing! First, he had to propose me. Then I had to go before the admitting committee and answer some questions. Walter was afraid I would kid around. He told me over and over again that the committee took this seriously, and he begged me to play it straight.

When the solemn day arrived, I put on my blue suit and red tie, combed what little hair I still had, and appeared before the tribunal. Walter sat there with fear in his eyes. The chairman asked me the all-important question: "Mr. Swift, why do you want to be a Lamb?"

I had thought about that. What could I say? *I really don't want to be a Lamb. I think it's all very silly, but my friend Walter is begging me.*

I looked at Walter. I couldn't do that. How could I phrase my answer so that Walter would know I was not serious but, at the same time, join his beloved Lambs Club?

I replied, "Well, gentlemen, all I can say is I have been an actor all my life, but it just isn't official."

Tears welled up in the chairman's eyes as he said, "That is very well put."

Walter was no longer acting. He was the creative production head of the Fitzgerald Advertising Agency in New Orleans. When he called, he said, "Allen, I have a big problem here, and I figured, of all people, you could help. We have the Jax beer account. The sponsor has shot down every idea for a commercial that we've come up with. We're only three weeks from the air campaign and have no commercials. We need sixteen one-minute spots in three weeks. Who could possibly do that? You could. You could write them, and if you could get ahold of some puppets, you could do all the voices and probably shoot them and bring them in on time."

"That's no problem. I already have access to the puppets. Paul Ashley is using one of my offices for his puppets."

"Yeah, but there's another problem," Walter groaned. "You'd have to sell this joker, and he is one ball breaker. I've already given you a tremendous buildup, but you will have to come down here tomorrow and sell the pants off him. You'll have to dazzle him in order to keep him from bolting."

"Don't worry," I assured him. "I'll surround him with all my albums, brochures, newspaper and magazine articles, and awards. I'll lay everything around him on the floor. He won't be able to stand up without stepping on them. I'll dazzle him with my thousand commercials. I'll handle it. I'll book the airline tickets and get back to you."

I did just that. And I met with Walter and his pain-in-the-ass sponsor the following morning. He might have been a problem to Walter, but to me, he was a pussycat. He hardly said a word while I was going through my pitch. He seemed overwhelmed. As I'd promised, he couldn't move out of his seat. I had him surrounded with all my junk. At the end, he asked, "What kind of campaign do you visualize?"

"Comedy. After all, what are you selling when you sell beer? Enjoyment. And what better way to convey that enjoyment than through laughter? I want your audience to tell each other Jax commercials: 'Have you heard the latest Jax commercial? It's a scream!' I want each one to be different. For example, one of them might have a Russian who claims they invented Jax beer: 'Jaxavitch, ve called it.' Every one will end with your song, 'Hello mellow, Jax, li'l darlin', that's the beer for me.' Look, there isn't much time. I have to get right back to New York and start writing if you want these on the air in three weeks. If you agree, it will cost you twenty-seven thousand dollars."

"Yeah, but I'll have to okay the scripts."

"I wouldn't have it any other way."

On the way back to the airport, Walter was unhappy about his okaying the scripts. "You did great, but now your trouble begins. He won't like the scripts. He'll waste more time going over them. We'll never get it done."

"He'll never see a script, Walter."

"He'll have to—you don't know him."

"Come on, Walt—you know as well as I do that almost nobody can read comedy. You think I'll trust him to read my scripts? He is going to hear them. I will send tapes—the sound tracks done right."

"I don't think you'll get away with that."

"My friend, listen to me. This is how it's going to work. I am going to write sixteen one-minute commercials. I shall record them and start production right away. I will have the engineer dub each commercial a number of times. Each dub will have a different take number. One spot may have seven takes, another twelve, et cetera, but they will all be the same take. For the purpose of speed, I will ask your client to go through every spot and every take and pick out each one he thinks is the best and let me know so I can rush them into production. That is going to keep him busy. I guarantee he will find a different take in each one he thinks best, and he'll feel he has made the choice. He can take as long as he wants. We will already be shooting them."

Of course, I had no idea what I was going to write, but I had access to Paul Ashley's puppets—a slew of different characters—and I wrote sketches based on them. They turned out funny. I wrote them in one night and shot them in three days. We had plenty of time to edit in the Jax jingle and logo and make the deadline.

By doing it in this way, the sponsor was hearing the finished spots with all the different voices as he might listen to them on radio, as opposed to reading the written word. Walter told me everyone in the agency laughed his or her head off, including the sponsor. That didn't keep him from spending a number of sleepless nights picking out the best takes. Aside from the fact that the campaign was a commercial success and was on the air on time, it won the Art Directors Award that year.

I had the money paid to ATU Productions. I cut the losses on our summer-stock adventure for my friend Charlie Zitner.

He then stepped out of the company, leaving me to do with it whatever the future might bring.

∞ ∞ ∞ ∞ ∞ ∞   ∞ ∞ ∞ ∞ ∞ ∞ ∞

Milton Berle's obituary appeared recently in the newspapers. Despite my personal unhappy experience with him, I find myself saddened at his death because he was a great comic who had an influence on most of the young comedians of my day and certainly on me.

While I was in rehearsal for *The Eddie Cantor Show* on the *Colgate Comedy Hour*, I received a call from Bart Swift, an agent at the William Morris Agency. He said Milton Berle was looking for someone who could impersonate Jimmy Durante. He wanted to know if I would audition for him that evening at his rehearsal in the Malin Studio. I was thrilled at the prospect of going directly from *The Eddie Cantor Show* to *The Milton Berle Show*. I said yes, of course, and showed up about five minutes before Milton returned to the studio after his dinner.

The rehearsal had not yet started. Most of the actors were standing around in groups, drinking coffee and talking. Milton came through the door like a whirlwind, removing his camel-hair coat and hat and screaming, "Fatso!" The actor who played that part on the show turned from the conversation he was having as Milton threw his garments at him. Apparently, this actor doubled as his flunky as well as a sketch artist on the show.

Bart Swift went up to Milton and said, "Milton, this is Allen Swift, the actor who does the Durante impersonation."

Milton turned to me. He was hyper. He seemed agitated, as though he had a number of things on his mind and had just been reminded about needing a Durante impersonator. "Durante … Durante. You do Durante? That's not a Durante hat." He yanked my (new) hat off my head and punched his fist into it.

I pulled it away from him. "I don't walk around as Durante, but I can impersonate him."

"Yeah, what can you do? What can you do? Can you sing? You know a Durante song?"

"I know all of them."

"'Umbriago'! 'Umbriago.' You know 'Umbriago'? Can you sing 'Umbriago'? Sing 'Umbriago.' Harry, give him—Harry, you goddamn fuck, get at the piano."

The musician scrambled up from where he was sitting and rushed to the piano.

"Give him a four-bar intro to 'Umbriago'!"

The moment I started singing, Milton turned away from me and walked across the studio. At a distance of about thirty feet, with his back to me, he was talking to someone. The moment I finished the song, he turned around and snapped his fingers.

"Okay. Let's hear it. Let's hear it."

"You heard it!" I said as I put on my coat and headed toward the door.

Bart Swift caught up with me and asked, "Where are you going?"

"Tell him to get someone else."

"Come on—that's the way he is."

"Tough! I'm not Fatso."

I can appreciate the strain he must have been under, doing a full-hour comedy show live each week, but this behavior was more than strain. This was a need to humble people. Still, as I've said, I am sad. I'm sad because this is the end of one of the great comics who honed his craft in vaudeville. His like will never be seen again. Television is no place to develop new comedians who make you fall down laughing. Now you have to settle for a smile.

I remember seeing Milton Berle at the Paramount when I was in high school. Friday was the day the new shows started there, and as I mentioned earlier, you could always find me there on Friday. If it wasn't Berle, it was another comedian, but there was always a big band.

I happened to have been there on a historic occasion. It was the day the Paramount was raided. To my knowledge, it happened only once, but I was there. Who raided the Paramount, and why? Truant officers, aided by the police.

The truant officers had evidently noticed that Friday was a low-attendance day in New York City high schools. All of a sudden, the house lights went on, and officers appeared in all the aisles, grabbing kids and pulling them out of their seats.

I not only saw them before they got to my row but also heard them berating my fellow truants. I managed to kick my books a few seats away, and when the officer entered my row, I said quite loudly, in a deep voice, "What seems to be the problem, Officer? The children playing hooky?" He stepped right over me, grabbed the kid next to me, and pulled him out of the row.

The following day, all the truants' names were published in the newspaper. There was a big hubbub in school about it. Miss Ridgeway remarked that she couldn't believe my name was not among them. I, of course, feigned hurt at such a remark, but she maintained that it was not possible for anyone to be sick only on Fridays. I never missed any of the great comedians or the near great.

Chapter 10

Lew's Laces, Economics 101 in a Communist State, and Affordable Housing in Park Slope

After my separation from Vivienne, I rented an apartment on West Fifty-Seventh Street. I saw an ad in the *New York Times* and grabbed it. That street has always had an aura of sophistication and adventure for me, dating back to my high school romance with Zora. It was landmarked in my head as the most creative street in the world. It had everything: the Russian Tea Room, where, at that time, actors and playwrights spent hours actually drinking tea and dissecting the latest Broadway play; Carnegie Hall; art galleries; and a bustling life of people in the arts, students coming and going from the Art Students' League, and musicians carrying their instruments. This was the place for me.

I had an adjustment to make to being a part-time father. Vivienne and I agreed that Lewis would be with me every other weekend and on holidays, but we were flexible about the arrangement. Lew was eleven when we separated and soon was able to hop on the subway from Rego Park and be at my place in twenty minutes. The apartment was a duplex. My office was downstairs, and the living quarters were upstairs. There were many rooms, and I filled them with things Lewis and I could have fun with. We had a professional Ping-Pong table in one room and every type of competitive game imaginable.

When Lewis was young, I played a "Guess which hand" game with him. I'd come home with some little toy that could fit in a closed fist and ask him to guess which hand it was in. If he guessed right, he'd get it; otherwise, he got nothing. He always guessed right, because I always had something in each fist, and I'd make a big fuss about how lucky he was. I did this because I wanted him to grow up believing he was a lucky person. I'd also lose many competitive games to him so that he'd feel like a winner. As far as that was concerned, however, his agility and reflexes quickly surpassed mine, and from then on, I had to fight to win.

I did this because my brother, Cal, always felt he was unlucky. It was something that depressed me. Although he was a capable person and projected a kind of swagger, he entered every situation feeling that luck was against him. I believe there must have been something in his childhood that was responsible. I discounted the hard knocks he went through in life. He came out of the war in the Pacific without a scratch—when every ship in his convoy was blown to bits. That was pretty lucky. Anyway, that was my theory, and I didn't want it to happen to my son.

Much of the fun with Lew had to do with one-upmanship in sports. Lewis was a Yankees fan, and I rooted for the Brooklyn Dodgers. It wasn't enough to go to a game together; we needed some kind of competition. Lew was always more knowledgeable than me. He knew all the averages and standings of the teams. I couldn't compete with him on that level, so I played the magic card. I was omnipotent. I talked to the spirits and claimed to know what would happen next. One day, when we were going to Yankee Stadium, Lew asked me in a condescending way, "Hey, Dad, who's going to win today?"

"Who are they playing?"

"Kansas City."

I looked up, carried on a silent communication with the spirits, and then said, "Kansas City is going to win."

"Ha-ha. For your information, in the thirty-six games these two teams have played, Kansas City has won only two games."

"That is correct, and with the thirty-seventh game, Kansas City will have won three games."

That was how the day started off. During the game, the Yanks were ahead two to nothing, if my memory serves me right, and their lead continued until the seventh inning. Lew said, "Well, Dad, when are they going to make their move?"

I looked up and spoke to the spirits. "Not yet—next inning, the lead-off man is going to start it off."

Sure enough, the lead-off man got a single. Lew looked at me, a little shaken, but with bravado, he asked me what the next man was going to do.

I said, "How about a walk?"

Sure enough, the next man walked. I figured the pitcher might now be a bit nervous about getting it over the plate and decided to go for broke. I pointed to the back wall as Lew yelled, "Cut it out!"

Kansas won three to two. What luck! It struck us both as funny.

For that split second, he thought I really was controlling the game. It mattered not that it was something I always did and that I was mostly wrong. This was pure luck. Luck is the power of the predictor. If you predict many happenings, some are bound to come true, and those are the ones that are remembered. It is the same with a so-called clairvoyant or your favorite stock analyst's predictions. How come you never see the headline "Psychic Wins Lottery"?

Lewis had a habit, as many young boys do, of not untying his laces when putting on or taking off his shoes. It wreaked havoc on them, and I wanted him to stop. I warned him that if I ever saw him do that again, I would punish him. When he did it the next time, I was taking him back to be with his mother and wouldn't see him again for two weeks. I couldn't punish him then, but could I go back on my word? "Lew, I told you if I caught you doing that again, I'd punish you. I have to get you home to your mother, but don't think you're getting away with it. Because of this, I am going to make the Yanks lose the World Series."

Lewis was thirteen years old at the time and a sharp kid. I'll tell you just how sharp he was: he was an avid reader of *Variety* and knew exactly how much every show on Broadway was taking in. We had Jack Farren and his wife over for dinner, and during the talk at the table about show business, Jack cited a certain show as a big hit. Lew said, "That show never made a penny."

Jack looked at this pipsqueak and said, "I'm sorry, but you're wrong. That show ran three years."

"That's right, and it never made a cent. The backers never even got their investment back."

Jack looked at me as if to say, "Who is this?"

I said, "Don't bet against him, Jack. He may occasionally be wrong about baseball scores but not about the theater. You want last week's grosses? He'll give them to you!"

That was my son at thirteen. He laughed at my reluctance to punish him and my pathetic prediction of "I'm going to make the Yanks lose the World Series." However, that was to give us a great deal of competitive fun during the 1960 series between the Yanks and Pittsburgh. The series went the full seven games. The last game was a seesaw. Lew was glued to the television, and I was working all over town, going from one recording studio to the other. I was not able to see any of the games and was getting my information on the Yankees' progress by word of mouth. When I heard that Pittsburgh was ahead, I'd call home and gloat, only to be told by my son that the Yanks were now ahead. Then I heard that Pittsburgh was ahead, so I sent Lewis a telegram: "Ask your father to turn off his curse. Signed, Casey Stengel."

The seesaw continued, and my latest report was that the Yanks were ahead. My last recording session was in the Times Square area, and just in case, I stopped at one of the stands that made up dummy news headlines. I had finished for the day and was headed home. At the moment that I walked in the door, Pittsburgh won the series. I quietly entered the living room, sat down opposite Lew, and opened the paper as though I were nonchalantly reading, with the headline facing him. In typical *Variety* prose, it read: "Lew's Laces Louse Yanks."

In reality, I was no longer much of a baseball fan. I was turned off when the Brooklyn Dodgers were sold to LA. Suddenly, the game became a business. It probably had been a business all along, but it had seemed as if I were rooting for a bunch of great ballplayers who'd played together for years. They weren't being bought and sold every two weeks. They were the bums who never won a World Series. They were the underdogs. In 1955, when they won their first World Series, bonfires burned all over Brooklyn. Car horns were blaring. People were yelling. It was bigger than New Year's Eve, and it has never been equaled. I was so caught up in it that I wrote a song, which was sold and recorded that night and on the air the following morning: "Johnny Podres Has a Halo Round His Head." I can't sing it for you, but here are the lyrics.

> Johnny Podres has a halo round his head.
> Johnny knocked those great big Yankees stone-cold dead.
> Johnny Podres saved the day.
> Johnny boy went all the way.
> Johnny Podres has a halo round his head.
>
> Johnny Podres has a halo round his head.
> Every Yankee was a goner
> As his pitches caught the corner of the plate.
> He had heart, and he had soul.
> Best of all, he had control,
> And he kept those Yankees in a dizzy state.
>
> Johnny brought the crown to Ebbets Field at last.
> No more wait till next year;
> Now next year has passed.
> You could hear all Brooklyn shout.
> Casey's mighty men struck out.
>
> Johnny Podres has a halo round his head.
> Johnny Podres has a halo round his head.

There is an addendum to this story. A few years ago, the LA Dodgers put out a hundred-year video on the Dodgers, and they came to me to get the rights to the song. They offered me twenty-five dollars. I said, "Come on, guys—don't you think that's a little insulting?"

"Well, how much do you want for it?"

"I think it should be at least two hundred."

They got back to me a few weeks later to tell me they didn't have to pay me anything. My copyright had run out, and I'd never renewed it. Oh well, the lyrics will be copyrighted as part of this book perhaps, but I doubt it will have any more value in the years to come. However, if you happen to be an old Brooklyn Dodgers fan, I still have a few 45-rpm records left. I'll make you a good price on them. All you have to do is search in antique shops for an old record player.

Someone once asked me on an interview program what I enjoyed most besides acting. I answered without giving it any thought: "Fathering." I sure took to being a father. I have enjoyed every aspect of it, even the headaches and heartaches. I have two daughters with my beloved Lenore. The laughter went on with them, as with Lewis, but that is only part of the story. My wish for all of them was that they grow up to be individual, thinking people, not just cookie cutouts of their parents. I realize that where the genes take over, they cannot be altered (so far), but there are things a parent can and should do. The first rule, I would say, is the same as a doctor's: do no harm. After that, give lots of love and a great deal of listening. Show them the arts, crafts, and music and all the wonders of the world you have experienced. Accept their discoveries as new and worthwhile, whether known to you or not. Enjoy them.

When Lewis was in Little League, he showed a fine aptitude for baseball and loved it. Listening to him, I learned that there was a major Little League—something he would be old enough to try out for the following season. He spoke about it a great deal, and it was obviously important to him.

He was with me the weekend the season started. I brought him home to Vivienne early on Sunday for the tryouts. When we arrived, Vivienne told him that her brother had called and had two tickets for the Roller Derby that afternoon and could take Lewis. My son pissed and moaned about the conflict he was in and then chose to go to the Roller Derby and forgo the tryout. I was not going to let this happen. I knew Lew had no interest in the Roller Derby. He was scared he wouldn't make the majors. It was the start of the season. He hadn't played ball all year. It was fear, and this would be his excuse for not trying out.

What ensued was a knockdown drag-out fight with my son. I said, "You are going to the tryout. You have been talking about it all year. We came home early for that reason. You can see the Roller Derby any Sunday, but this is the only day you can try out for the majors."

"I want to go to the Roller Derby."

"You are not going to the Roller Derby. You are going to the tryouts."

"You can't make me!"

"Yes, I can. Get the ball and the gloves."

"No!"

"Then I'll get them myself. We are going out to practice. You have two hours before the tryouts." I got the ball and gloves myself and dragged him out of the house.

"You just want me to be a ball player—that's why."

"Sure, that's me, just like the other fathers who drive their kids crazy on the ball field. You found me out."

"I'm not going to practice."

"I'm going to throw the ball to you. If you don't catch it, that's your problem, but don't ever say you could have been in the majors."

I threw it to him, and he caught it. I think that made a big difference immediately—I could tell by the way he threw it back to me. Each succeeding throw had more confidence, and he was getting psyched and happy. There were two men watching outside the fence, and they were apparently coaches for their respective teams. I heard their conversation; Lewis was out of earshot.

"Who is that kid? He's very good."

"That's the Stadlen kid. He played for Ben's Best last year. I'm taking him."

So there he was, in before the tryouts. I was proud of myself for not letting him chicken out on something he wanted. He was bright—he knew my attitude about fathers who pushed their kids like crazy on the ball field and was using it on me. I couldn't care less. I just didn't want him to fool himself the way I had in my stint at the Palace.

∞ ∞ ∞ ∞ ∞ ∞   ∞ ∞ ∞ ∞ ∞ ∞

On November 23, 1961, Lenore and I were married. I would like to be able to describe how beautiful she looked and how cute in a little white hat that stood on the top of her head and a lovely white dress. It was not a typical bride's dress. It was not a gown, just a regular-length, form-fitted dress. I don't know that she would appreciate my recollection of that moment, but she reminded me of a young colt. It was a beautiful, sunny Thanksgiving Day. We were married in a rabbi's living room and had a small luncheon with our immediate family and friends.

When the rabbi asked me if I took this woman, I answered in my Durante voice, "Indubitably."

He almost fell back into the fireplace. He then cautioned Lenore by saying, "A simple 'I do' is all that's necessary."

That evening, we took off on an Alitalia flight to Rome. This was the first trip to Europe for both of us. Lenore told me I slept through the entire flight, leaving her to drink champagne alone while the moon was shining through the window. She was too inhibited as a new bride to wake me, something she would have no compunction about today. This was a foretaste of how we would live our lives: Lenore was a night person, and I was a day person. At ten o'clock at night, I'm out. Around one o'clock, Lenore joins me.

Our honeymoon was magical. Lenore's enthusiasm made every experience memorable. She talked to everyone; language differences didn't stop her. Somehow she managed to converse with people using only her high school French, and everyone delighted in her. Seeing Europe through her eyes made it for me. I am quite shy if I cannot express myself to my satisfaction in my own language.

We spent only two days in Rome before heading to Prague to meet my friend Gene Deitch. I was anxious to meet his new love, Zdenka. We loved Rome and swore we must come back. Getting to Prague turned out to be a problem, however.

We were supposed to fly from Rome to Prague, but the plane landed in Milan, and we were told that the Prague airport was weathered in and we would have to fly to Munich to wait out the weather.

I screamed at the airline people that I would not set foot in Germany. The war and the Holocaust were not that far away for me. I had, in fact, just turned down a commercial for Lufthansa. When they'd asked me to do it, I'd asked rhetorically, "What is the slogan—'Fly Lufthansa, the airline that shot down your brother'?"

The airline people in Milan were in a quandary as to what to do with us. They went away and came back with a new route. "How about we fly you to Vienna, and you can take a train to Prague?" I agreed to that. In retrospect, I don't know why. Vienna had as many Nazis as Germany.

The next thing we knew, we were on a bus that took us out to a Lufthansa plane that was heading to Munich, where we would have a layover before boarding an aircraft for Vienna.

I was livid. Lenore tried to calm me down, saying, "The war is over a long time."

"Don't tell me the war is over a long time!"

Anyway, there we were, buckled into our seats. I was now quietly fuming as the pilot's voice came over the loudspeaker in a warm, gracious tone with a German accent. "Gut eefninck, ladies and gentlemen. Velcome aboard Lufthansa's flight seven sixty-tree nonstop to Munich, Germany. Ve vill be flying at tirty-tree tousand feet, but ze pressurized cabin vill remain at all times at a comfortable tree tousand feet. As soon as ve are airborne, dinner vill be served …"

To Lenore, I finished his speech: "…to everyvon WHO DOES EXACTLY AS HE IS TOLD!" She and nearby passengers laughed hysterically.

I repeated the "who does exactly as he is told" story at a party in my honor at the Prague animation studio and again later on in London. By the time we arrived back in New York, Peter Ustinov told it as a joke on television, and in a few weeks, it was a sketch in an off-Broadway musical. Jokes seem to travel with the speed of light.

Gene met us at the Prague railway station and whipped us over to the animation studio. I expected to see a foreign studio with differently dressed artists, but it was as if I'd never left home. With the exception of the language, the artists were the same; their attire was the same as in New York, and so was their joking around. They asked me to do some of my voices that they had been animating. When I told the Lufthansa story, I received two sets of laughs: one when I told it and another when it was translated. They also asked me to do a Russian. That impression killed them. Russians were obviously their favorite targets to ridicule.

Gene and I wrote an animation pilot for a children's series—*Samson Scrap and Delilah*—for which I did the voices and Gene did the animation. That was one of the projects that had brought him to Prague. It was a story of two urban kids with great imaginations, and a neighborhood junk dealer, Samson Scrap, and his horse, Delilah. They were pals, and with Samson's great treasure trove of junk, they were able to create unbelievable objects that rivaled flying carpets and led to amazing adventures.

Gene's animated film was so magnificent that it took my breath away. To this day, I cannot understand why it was not bought. It encompassed both Gene's and my own passion for gadgets, especially the kind we'd made as kids.

Gene took us to a gloomy hotel in the center of town that was festooned with many red flags bearing the hammer and sickle. Then we knew we were behind the Iron Curtain.

Gene's sweetheart turned out to be a lovely blonde gal who stood well over four feet tall and expressed herself with such a rush of enthusiasm that she had difficulty catching her breath. She was a bundle of explosive energy and a joy to be with. As the manager of the studio, she had to work during the day, so we were mostly with Gene, a guide who reveled in the beauty of Prague. He knew every nook and cranny of this gorgeous city and its history.

Gene and Zdenka took us to a typical Czech beer hall one night. It was rustic, with long wooden tables where people squeezed in side by side. Czech pilsner beer is probably the best in the world. It comes in large draft mugs with a rich, creamy head that takes up half the glass. I was sitting on the end of the table, and a man at the next table was making hostile faces at me. At one point, he put his thumb on his front teeth and sort of whipped it toward me. I asked Gene, "What does this man have against me?"

"He probably thinks you're German."

"Well, tell him I'm not." Gene spoke to him in Czech, and he answered with hostility.

"He doesn't believe me. He says if you are an American, I should tell you to sing 'Beer Barrel Polka.'"

Fortunately, he had picked a song I knew. My singing brought a smile to his face, and he joined in. I guess he had as long a memory as I had. The incident was the first clue I had that English sounds like German to many Europeans.

Lenore and I were impressed by the beautiful store windows. They didn't have much merchandise in them, but the window dressings were much more artistic than anything in the United States. We finally understood the reason: either they had nothing to sell, or the people running them didn't care to sell anything. Gene explained that the average Czech was a moonlighting capitalist. You could get anything done in Prague so long as you didn't go through official channels. If you needed a plumber, carpenter, or anything similar, there were plenty of people you could hire who were working for themselves unofficially.

We saw some beautiful colored glass figurines of musicians in one of the stores. They were twenty-five dollars apiece. I thought they would make perfect Christmas gifts for all my business associates. In fact, the price was perfect, just what the IRS allowed as a deduction. I usually spent more, and these figurines would have sold for much more in the United States—if you could get them. I told the salesperson that I wanted 120 shipped to the States.

"Oh no, sir, that is not possible."

"Why? You're selling them, aren't you?"

"Yes, but we do not have the facilities."

"There must certainly be shippers here that can do it."

"I don't know."

"Well, who does?"

"Maybe you could try Glass Export."

"Fine, where are they?"

"I'm sorry—I really don't know."

I could not believe my ears. Gene had told me that they desperately needed hard currency. That was why they treated him specially—he was bringing dollars into the country by directing films there. He looked up Glass Export in the phone directory, and I went there in my pursuit of those figurines.

The gentleman in charge of the Glass Export office greeted me warmly. He didn't seem to be busy. In fact, the office was extremely quiet. I must have been there about forty minutes. The phone never rang, nor did I ever see anyone else. He offered me beer and coffee. My host was delighted to talk about the United States and drew me out about my vacation in Prague, eventually asking me what he could do for me. I told him I was in the market for 120 colored glass figurines. He immediately brought out a catalogue, which he told me to take with me.

"I don't need the catalogue. They are right here. I would like one hundred and twenty of these musicians sent to the United States. Is that a problem?"

"No, no, of course not. However, it is not quite that simple."

"Why?"

"Well, we will have to establish the usual banking drafts, letters of credit. All this takes time."

"No, that's not necessary. You figure out the cost, and I'll give you a check right now."

"That's interesting. Of course, that should save time. Unfortunately, the salesman who handles this is currently in Bavaria."

"I don't understand. We don't need a salesman. I know what I want. Just write up the order."

"I'm afraid it is not quite that simple. You see, that's his department."

"Fine! Write up the order, and give it to him with my check when he gets back. When is he due?"

"Maybe a week or two. Where are you staying? I could have him call you."

"No! I'm scheduled to leave the day after tomorrow."

"Oh, I'm sorry. I have enjoyed our chat so much. Are you sure you won't have a beer? Prague beer is supposed to be the best in the world. Please, at least take the catalogue."

I knew when I was beaten. In this Socialist country, they socialized, but please no business.

Approximately six months went by. I received a call in New York from a salesman from Glass Export in Prague. He asked if he could come see me. I said, "Indeed," and he came up. We exchanged pleasantries, and then he got down to business. His business was that he wanted to leave a catalogue with me!

"No, no. I already have a catalogue. I know exactly what I want."

"That's nice, but why don't you take a few days and look it over?"

"No. See these musicians? I want you to ship me one hundred and twenty of them. Just mix them up. You have an order sheet? Write them up!"

I was determined to keep this man a prisoner in my office until he wrote up the order. It was not easy. He wanted to make another appointment with me, claiming to have to see many others that day. It was no use. He couldn't escape, so he finally wrote up the order and gave me a carbon copy but would not figure the cost or accept a check. He said I would be billed with my shipment.

Is it any wonder the Socialist system failed? There was no incentive for anyone to do anything. But this is the capper: the shipment arrived—120 glass figurines, individually boxed. Each one was protected in excelsior, and the bill was included. Understand this: they sold in Prague stores for twenty-five dollars each. I expected to pay at least that, plus packing, shipping, and duty on top of that. The bill was for $240, or $2 apiece!

For Lenore and me, the portion of our honeymoon spent in Prague was enchanting. Old Prague, with its unbelievable beauty, unmarred by billboards or neon signs, made us fantasize about making a movie there. From Prague, we went on to Paris, then London, and, finally, home.

On our return flight, we ran into bad weather, and our flight was diverted to Canada. This was unfortunate because Lewis was waiting at the airport in New York for us, which was an important development in our three-way relationship. It signaled to me that he was accepting our marriage. He had declined to come to our wedding. In fact, it had been a traumatic moment when we'd told him about our decision to marry.

Lew was at home, watching television, when we came in. We had discussed how we would tell him. My insides were churning just thinking about it. I had it all worked out in my mind. I'd break it to him excitedly, as if it were some happy idea that had just occurred to us. We had lousy TV reception, so he was sitting with his nose a few inches from the set when I broke the happy news to him. He said nothing. He didn't move. The tears simply ran down his cheeks.

I was bereft at the sight of those tears. I didn't know what this meant. Was he crying because it was definite that I would never get back with his mother, or was it that he feared he would lose his relationship with me? I tried to reassure him that no one could ever take his place with me. I told him I loved him and loved Lenore, and just as Lenore must respect my love for him, he must respect mine for Lenore. They both already had a wonderful relationship. Lenore has a real sweetness. It is the kind that never causes anyone to feel threatened.

Anyway, learning that he had been waiting at the airport for us was reassuring about our future.

∞ ∞ ∞ ∞ ∞ ∞   ∞ ∞ ∞ ∞ ∞ ∞ ∞

During this period, I made a number of trips to Phoenix to visit my cousin Jack, who was older than I, and one of my childhood heroes. He had been on the same track team as Jessie Owens at Ohio State University. He was a great kidder and could always make me laugh. In 1954, he and his wife, Grace, contracted polio during the last epidemic before the Salk vaccine was discovered. She recovered, but he was a paraplegic from then on. Jack and Grace were both optometrists. On one trip, when I was there with Lewis, she recognized that Lew needed eyeglasses. Until then, he had gotten away with his poor vision by memorizing the eye charts.

Jack was well known in Phoenix. He was a mentor to many young college kids. While I was there, Grace and Jack were scheduled to go to a banquet that marked the final night of an optometrists' convention. Jack remembered that I did stand-up comedy and asked me to entertain at the dinner. I knew it was important to him, but I had not done stand-up in quite a few years.

I suggested instead that I be introduced as a famous Soviet optometrist during the speeches. It was arranged so that no one would know I was a fake. My cousins fixed me up with one of Jack's prewar suits, a pair of Cyclops spectacles, and a small vial of water with an eyedropper. I hid them in the empty convention hall, where I could change before my speech.

During the dinner, I watched the entertainment, which was hardly audible, as people went on talking and paid the performers no attention. When it was nearing my turn, I excused myself and slipped out to change. I noticed on one of the tables a paper that was probably given that day on the invention of the bifocal contact lens. I was now suited up with my Cyclops glasses, awaiting my introduction.

The president of the Optometrists Association announced from the dais, "Ladies and gentlemen, if I can have your attention? I know we promised to have no speeches at the dinner, but we are fortunate to have a very important guest. A famous Soviet optometrist is in our city on his way to Washington. I am sure we would all like to hear from him. It is my pleasure to introduce Dr. Nicholi Serge Kornakoff."

I entered, waving my arms, and, in a thick Russian accent, began. "Greetings from the optometrist heroes of the Soviet Union to the optometrist heroes of the great state of Arizona. While there may be a cold war between our two nations, there is no such thing as a cold war between men of science. I think it is important for the American optometrist to know of the great contributions of the Soviet optometrist and for the Soviet optometrist to know of the great contributions of the American optometrist. We in the Soviet Union are very proud of our invention of the contact lens."

There was a great stirring on the dais to my left. Senator Barry Goldwater was fuming and about to rise, when the gentleman next to him, the actual inventor of the contact lens, put his hand on the senator's shoulder, restraining him and mumbling, "It's all right, Senator—we all know who invented it."

At that moment, I pulled my glasses off and squinted in their direction as if I were wondering what was going on. I put the glasses back on and continued, "Or as long ago as the Second World War, when we invented, for our heroic Red Army, the bifocal contact lens."

Understand that the invention of the bifocal contact lens had been introduced to the convention only that afternoon. I went on. "But the reason I am in your great country is to introduce a miracle, ladies and gentlemen. We in the Soviet Union have discovered a way to do away with eyeglasses of every type. Think of it, ladies and gentlemen—what this means to medicine. We in the Soviet Union have invented liquid lenses. Anyone will be able to go to their corner chemist. We have found a way to compound any prescription into a liquid form. One drop in each eye—anyone can have twenty-twenty vision. I'll demonstrate for you."

There was a deadly silence in the room. Nobody even looked at me. I took off the glasses and proceeded to put a drop in each eye.

"It takes approximately twenty seconds," I continued, "for the lens to form, or slightly less time than to develop a picture with your American Polaroid camera. Would you believe it, ladies and gentlemen? I now have twenty-twenty vision. Anyone can test me. Who would like to try this amazing product? Anyone with my prescription, minus three diopters of myopia, can try it. Nobody? Come, come, ladies and gentlemen—there must be some people with my prescription. I can't believe it. You are men of science. I don't believe it. I am seeing with my own eyes but I don't believe it.

"They told me when I was in the Soviet Union this would happen, but I didn't believe it. They told me the American optometrist doesn't want to do away with eyeglasses, but I didn't believe it. They told me the American optometrist was nothing more than a capitalist, an eye gouger, a fee splitter. You call yourself doctors. What kind of doctors are you? You're not even doctors, dentists!"

That tirade built to a crescendo, and at the last line, they realized it was a put-on. They burst out in an explosion of laughter mixed with a great deal of relief. Senator Goldwater came over to me and solemnly said, "That's what we need— more humor."

The story of this stunt was reported in the press and on TV and led to my being asked to tell the story on *The Tonight Show*. Merv Griffin also asked me to do a similar put-on at a gathering of food editors at a dinner at the Plaza. I was to be introduced as a famous Russian nutritionist. The fun for me took place before my performance. I was seated at a table with food editors and introduced as a famous nutritionist. This being at the height of the Cold War, it was interesting to watch how my fellow Americans treated their Russian guest. I didn't give them good marks. They were not-so-slyly making fun of me. They ridiculed me in a way they thought I could not understand because of my limited English vocabulary.

I had a strange reaction to this. I was involved, as an actor, in my character, but at the same time, I felt embarrassed by my countrymen's gauche behavior. I felt a great need to get back at them. They asked me if I had anything as nice as this Plaza room in the Soviet Union.

"Da, da, vary beautiful. Ve also hev vary lovely places."

"That's nothing, Doctor. You should see Howard Johnson." They were winking at each other. This was during the Kennedy administration.

I answered, "Yes, yes, your wise president." This kind of ribbing went on throughout the meal, with stupid questions like "Have you seen food like this before?" They were treating me like a buffoon and enjoying their superiority to this foreigner.

"Tell us, Doctor," someone said, "do you have any good diets for taking off weight?"

"Yes. I understand. In America, everyone vishes to take off veight. Da rest off da vorld hev no such problem."

When I was finally introduced, I ranted about the selling of vitamins, which I said were nothing but a capitalist scheme for acquiring riches and had no nutritional value whatsoever. I wondered, after blowing my cover at the end, how the people at my table felt. I didn't like them, and I didn't stay around to find out.

∞ ∞ ∞ ∞ ∞ ∞   ∞ ∞ ∞ ∞ ∞ ∞

So I was now making a great deal of money. The question was, what was I doing with it to help the world or society or my fellow man? As usual, my friend Eddie Kramer came to the rescue. Eddie had evolved from performer to agent to shingle bum to building contractor. He was now renovating houses. Aside from his drive to make a living, Eddie had always been a man of conscience and an activist for improving social conditions. He had an idea how the two of us could accomplish this using my money and his brawn and expertise in housing redevelopment.

"Ike, listen to this." Eddie always called me Ike. Why use the two syllables for *Ira* when one would do? "There are over three thousand vacant buildings in Brooklyn that are structurally sound. They could be renovated into large apartments for poor people at affordable rents, even using the rent-control guidelines. Let's face it. What causes slums? Bad plumbing and overcrowding. I figure we could redo these buildings, making large six- and seven-room apartments that could rent for less than a hundred bucks a month and still show a six percent profit.

"There are thousands of poor black people squeezed together in two- and three-room apartments. They have lots of kids but can't afford the rents on larger ones. I've written to the city about this. I keep calling the housing commissioner. Nobody moves their ass. You could buy these buildings for peanuts. I know the banks would love to get them off their hands. This is no pipe dream. I know it will work. Let's test it. We'll start with one building."

I bought a building in Park Slope. It looked like garbage to me, but Eddie assured me it was structurally sound and that I was being turned off by its looks. "Wait and see what it's going to look like. I'll put in all-copper plumbing. Everything is going to be replastered. Those holes in the walls are nothing. Under the shit, these floors are solid. You won't recognize the place."

The truth is, I didn't. He did an amazing job. That rubble looked daunting to me, but so does the rubble on my desk. The apartments were rented before we finished. We were able to mortgage the building, so I was able to get my money back, which we immediately used to do another building. We were excited about our accomplishments. Eddie even put in a little victory garden for the tenants. He was a gadfly in bugging the City Housing Department to come look at what could be done. All in all, we did three buildings before the commissioner of housing and his entourage came to see what Eddie was annoying them about.

"Wait a minute. How much are you renting these for?"

"The most expensive apartment rents for ninety-seven a month," Eddie said. "And that's a seven-room apartment. The six rooms rent for less."

"And you're able to get a return on this?"

"A legitimate return—five, six percent."

The commissioner and the others with him seemed flabbergasted. He then told us that the city was sitting on millions of dollars from the federal government to do just this— create affordable housing. Until seeing what we had done, he didn't think it was feasible. He said this process could release all this money for similar projects. He proposed that if we bought up more of these vacant buildings, the city would give us the money to renovate them and then convert the building costs to thirty-year mortgages at a low 3 percent. Eddie was in seventh heaven. This was, in effect, what he had been bugging them to do for the past few years.

I bought three more buildings, and Eddie started working on them. As we had not yet received the building money, I had to keep putting my money into the work to keep the crews busy. To stop in the middle and wait for the checks to come through from the city would leave the buildings open to vandalism.

Eddie went to see Lou Ryder, the housing commissioner, to find out why the money was being delayed. He said he had certain problems with our making such large apartments. He wanted us to cut them down to two and three rooms. He wanted to demonstrate that he was creating more living units. Eddie pointed out to him that that was not what we wanted to do, that we were trying to stop the overcrowding that was contributing to the creation of slums.

Then Ryder asked Eddie for a kickback on each building. Eddie said, "There is no room for a kickback, Mr. Ryder. Everything is figured out down to the penny."

"So what? We'll give you a bigger mortgage."

"That will defeat the entire purpose. We'd have to charge higher rents."

"What are you—a rabbi?"

There was no sense continuing the conversation. Lou Ryder was a crooked politician. Eddie brought the news back to me. My finances were being strung out to their limits, and there now appeared a series of harassing inspectors who found ridiculous faults with everything we had done so far. They demanded that we knock down almost everything and start over. Of course, no money was forthcoming.

I said to Eddie, "Let's go to Lindsey." John Lindsey was mayor at that time.

"I thought of that, but, Ike, we don't know how far up this goes."

He was right, of course. After all, the commissioner of housing is not a little flunky job. Personally, I was a fan of Mayor Lindsey, but my opinion was based on his charisma. I didn't know the man. *So what do we do to get out of this fix? Go to the law? Ha-ha! I've had my fill of the law. Maybe I should go see Jake. He could probably have one of his cronies take care of Lou Ryder—unless Lou is one of his cronies.* I thought hard about it and then told Eddie, "I have to get out of this. We didn't start this to make money. I didn't start it to lose money either. But if I have to, I'll take my lumps. Let's find a nonprofit organization that has the muscle and the will to fight Ryder. I'll give the buildings to them."

Dr. Matthews, a black neurosurgeon from St. Albans, had been in the news lately. He was running an illegal bus route because he felt the city was ignoring the needs of the black community. He was fighting the city and getting away with it; he had the muscle. I gave the buildings to him. I was able to write off part of my losses by deducting some of it as a charitable donation.

I was out of it. The years went by. Eddie had created a nonprofit organization in Brighton Beach called Geri-pair, hiring mechanics who were seniors to make minor repairs for needy senior citizens, free of charge. It was a wonderful concept and a valuable service.

The vacant buildings we had turned into viable dwelling places had been out of my mind for at least ten years. I was spending time one day looking at the junk stores on Canal Street. I decided to call home because I was playing hooky and realized no one knew where I was. My housekeeper answered the phone and said, "Mr. Swift, there are two policemen here waiting for you."

"Policemen? Are they in uniform?"

"No, but they showed me their badges."

"Would you put one of them on the phone, Tess?"

It turned out they had a subpoena for me to appear before the new housing commissioner. I told them they didn't need a subpoena and said that I would be glad to talk to the commissioner, and I asked for his phone number. We made an appointment for the following morning. The new commissioner was a charming black man, and he told me a story that blew me away. Lou Ryder had been found guilty of fraud. He had connived with the banks and the contractors in a scheme by which he'd stolen $80 million before absconding with it to Mexico. This was how it worked: The banks sold the vacant buildings to crooked contractors. The city paid the crooked contractors to renovate the buildings. The crooked contractors kicked the money back to Ryder without doing the work. Ryder's crooked inspectors signed off on the job that the work had been completed, and the mortgage money was paid to Ryder through the crooked contractors with the collusion of the banks. How about them apples?

So why was I subpoenaed? The fact is, we looked kind of fishy. How come our buildings were the only ones that were completed? I told the commissioner that I thought, under the circumstances, Eddie and I should be incarcerated for at least twenty years for our dastardly deeds. This got a laugh, but he really wanted to know the answer. I told him the whole story from the beginning, and he said, "Well, I guess you are going to be celebrating when Lou Ryder goes to jail?"

"Commissioner, how many people who have stolen eighty million dollars go to jail?"

"You're pretty cynical, aren't you?"

"After what I've been through, Commissioner, you're either cynical or a fool."

"Yeah. I guess you have a right to be."

It is some thirty years since that interview. If Lou Ryder went to jail, I never read or heard about it. What gets me is how blatant the man was and how many people he used to pull off such a fraud. You would think someone would have blown the whistle on him. I guess maybe they all felt like we did. How far up did it go?

Chapter 11

Cal and "Syndividual Commercials" A Close Shave

My brother had to do something to free himself from the mob. Finally, he hit upon a plan. He feigned a back condition and spent a month in bed. His so-called partners came to see him, sympathy on their faces, but it soon became obvious that Cal was no longer of any use to them. He was out of the business and out of his investment but happy to be away from these men who were more and more insulted by his and Florence's refusal to socialize with them. It was a calculated risk he took in doing this, but he was desperate.

He went to work for a short time for a camera-repair service company. In contrast to my nonexistent mechanical aptitude, my brother was a genius at being able to fix anything. Since I was so successful in writing and producing the Jax Beer spots, it occurred to both of us that there was a viable business there in which both brothers could work together. It was a great idea. The only problem was to figure out his role. When we started, he was the salesman. In short order, he was everything: producer, manager, film editor, bookkeeper, and the one person in my life whom I couldn't do without.

It was wonderful for both of us. The years we worked together were the happiest of his life. It was the end of manual toil and the start of his expressing his talents and ingenuity in a new field and in a new way. For me, it was having a genie with me who could do everything I couldn't. He was completely organized. I never knew where anything was. Suddenly, all I had to do was ask, and what I was looking for was in my hand. He was my magic filing cabinet. Before he arrived each morning, my desk looked like the Staten Island landfill. Within a few minutes, it was pristine. We were a great team, and most important, we loved each other. I don't believe there ever was a bad word between us.

I gradually came to see that my hero brother, Cal, had feet of clay. He suffered from an awful inferiority complex. Certainly, there was precedent for it. He had left school at thirteen to go to work to help support the family. From then on, it was a constant parade of every type of job imaginable, none of which made use of his fine intellect. He was also funny.

When I was a child, I surreptitiously watched him holding forth at a party. He had on a funny hat, and his friends were screaming with laughter. Maybe if the timing of his life had been different, he could have had the kind of career I had—or even more success. He was a wonderful, natural dancer. He just never had the breaks I had.

Working with me in my business, he had the position and respect he hadn't had before. Did that mean he no longer suffered from that sense of inferiority? I doubt it. Those scars remain throughout life. They made him overcompensate with a bravado I doubt he felt. However, we had great fun together and many adventures. The first one was a joyous promotion to introduce Cal, the new Swift Spots salesman, to the advertising world.

We bought a portable film projector with an integral screen that could show a continuous loop of the Jax spots. This was long before videocassettes. Today he would just carry a CD. Although I couldn't understand it, he was nervous about selling. He was verbal, outgoing, and likable. At any rate, I was able to assure him that with the proper promotion, the advertising agencies would welcome him with open arms.

I devised a teaser campaign that involved sending a series of letters and a postcard to the presidents of advertising agencies throughout the country. Cal would travel by car to these agencies, and we synchronized each letter's delivery with his arrival in each town. We mailed the first letter a week and a half before his arrival. It included a purple spot—that is, a circular piece of paper the size of a half dollar. For example, the first letter would say the following:

Mr. Joseph Davenport
President
Davenport Advertising Inc.
242 Main Street
Albany, NY 65432

Dear Joe,

Look this spot over in light of our former discussion. I know it is not the right spot, but it is a taking off point, and I am working on it from my end. Everything else seems to be on target. Keep the faith.

Cal

The second letter would arrive a few days later and contained two spots of different colors. The heading was the same.

Dear Joe,

Here is another spot. I think we're getting closer. Look it over, but don't discard the other one. You know how these things can work out. I'll be in your neck of the woods soon, and we'll kick it around.

As ever,

Cal

The third letter arrived with three spots, the last one in a tint between the other earlier two.

Dear Joe,

Here it is. Now I'm getting excited. I think when I see you next Wednesday, we're going to be able to finalize it. I know it is going to happen. I feel it in my bones. Keep your day clear. We're going to do it.

Love to you know who,

Cal

Two days before his arrival, Joe got a handwritten picture postcard from Atlantic City that read,

Hey, Joe,

I'm doing a little playing. As far as Florence is concerned, I'm staying with you, so hold my mail for me. See you Wednesday.

Cal

The day before Cal was due, a business letter on Allen Swift stationery arrived with a logo on the envelope of three small magenta spots. It was addressed to the following:

Mr. Cal A. Stadlen
c/o Joseph Davenport, President
Davenport Advertising Inc.
242 Main Street
Albany, NY 65432

Dear Cal:

This is to introduce you to Mr. Joseph Davenport, president of Davenport Advertising Inc. Mr. Davenport has heard of you and is expecting you. In fact, his curiosity as to who the devil you are has reached a peak. Mr. Davenport is an astute enough advertising man to know when he has been the subject of a very ingenious tease campaign. Show Mr. Davenport Swift Spots, and show him how the same creativity that was used in this tease can be used to make Swift Spots for his company. Give Mr. Davenport my best wishes and my hope that this will be the beginning of a lasting creative relationship between our two companies.

Respectfully,

Allen Swift

In every case, the letter to Cal, care of the various advertising heads, was opened and read before his arrival. All Cal had to do was give his name to the receptionist, and he was ushered in to see the boss. Now, I don't want to break my arm patting myself on the back, but this scheme should go down in the history books. Have you any idea how far a salesman gets cold-calling a customer? If he gets in at all, he might get to show his wares to a flunky with no buying authority.

You want to know how many sales were made? Who cares? We were having fun.

That, by the way, was the motivation for every shenanigan Cal and I got up to. It had to be fun—and it was. We built castles in Spain—actually, in Mexico. We went into the recording-studio business. We opened a TV studio. If it made money, it was gravy. More often, we lost money. So what? The residuals from my commercials kept coming in, and that funded our playing in the sandbox of life.

After our initial foray into selling Swift Spots, I came up with an idea for Syndividual Commercials. Syndividual was a made-up name that sprang from the words *syndicated* and *individual*.

Instead of making generic commercials in which the local advertisers would insert the sponsor's logo, I realized that, as I was the voice-over on the commercial, I could rerecord them so that they were seamless. No one would ever know they were not custom made for the client. I wrote a series of animated

279

commercials we called *The Friendly Banker*, featuring a little animated character that resembled Alfred Hitchcock. This was done at a time when banks were all local, which was a perfect niche market.

When we launched Syndividual Commercials in 1963 it was an immediate success. We produced eight Friendly Banker commercials that would have cost over $100,000 if one bank had had to foot the bill. We rented them to banks all over the country for less than a quarter of that amount. Also, we had a wonderful gimmick. Each year, we made eight more spots, and if the banks rented them, they got to keep the first eight for free. It was a terrific hook, and the commercials looked so custom made that they won advertising awards for a number of local advertising agencies.

Advertising Age

With which is incorporated Advertising Agency Magazine, formerly Advertising & Selling

Volume 33 · Number 37

September 10, 1962

A.T.U. Offers 'Syndividual' TV Ads on Rental Basis

NEW YORK, Sept. 5—Local and regional television sponsors whose budgets don't permit the production of elaborate commercials can rent their tv ads on a yearly basis from A.T.U. Productions.

Known as "syndividual" commercials, the animated spots are produced for a product category, such as milk or beer. To give them a custom-made look for a specific client, alterations are made in both the video and audio portions to include the name and logo of the advertiser and other personal identification, Cal Stadlen, A.T.U.'s exec vp in charge of production, told ADVERTISING AGE.

■ Advertisers are able to reduce their costs through the use of "syndividual" spots because of their re-use factor, Mr. Stadlen explained. They are produced in a series. A group of eight 20-second spots, for example, would ordinarily run between $20,000 and $30,000 for complete production costs if done for one client, Mr.

SYNDIVIDUAL—*These stills are from two 60-second milk commercials which A.T.U. Productions, New York, makes available to local and regional sponsors as a part of its "syndividual" series.*

Stadlen said. A.T.U., however, would lease such a series, with the company trademark added, for a yearly charge of $1,350 and up, depending on the size of the market.

■ Clients are given an exclusive contract for their product category in a market. A.T.U. takes care of all production activities, including writing, talent relations, filming, etc. The commercials are built around puppets, handled by puppeteer Lou Bunin, who is under exclusive contract at A.T.U.

A.T.U. currently is working on new "syndividual" series in the fields of meat, savings and loan companies and two catch-all categories for retail stores. In the past, the company has produced several series for banks, milk, beer, paint and gasoline. About 14 clients have been serviced to date, Mr. Stadlen said.

The production house prefers to work through agencies, Mr. Stadlen said. The characters in the commercials can be used by a client in all of his other advertising and promotion for a coordinated effort, he explained.

■ Denver U.S. National Bank, for example, has used its tv character in its outdoor, newspaper and magazine ads, as well as in numerous mailing pieces. A.T.U. provides clients with mats of the characters at cost.

A.T.U. also produces regular commercials and recently entered the motion picture production field. #

281

the most fabulous personality in
the history of bank promotion

The Friendly Banker

is exclusively yours
at a price that fits your advertising budget

 THE FRIENDLY BANKER
OPINIONS
ON BUSINESS, BANKING AND PEOPLE

I know a Doctor who took his
patient off sleeping pills and prescribed
a Savings account at their Friendly
neighborhood bank.

Lumps in a mattress can cause
insomnia, especially if the lumps are
one's life's savings.

How effective have your TV
commercials been in stamping out
this dread disease?

THE FRIENDLY BANKER

Copyright
A. T. U. Productions, Inc.

Business conditions are such today
whereby we might look forward to certain
changes in our economy. The cost of
living index is no doubt indicative of many
things -- least of which would be the cost
of living.

As Bankers, however, it would be-
hoove us to keep uppermost in our minds
the immediate problem confronting an
overwhelming number of our depositors
-- The World Series.

Cordially,

THE FRIENDLY BANKER

Some of Swift's promotion pieces for
The Friendly Banker spots (ed. note)

One day, Cal set up a meeting with two men from a brokerage house who wanted to take our company public. Cal was excited about it. They were going to get us a lot of money to expand our business, and we were going to be on the stock exchange as ATU Productions Inc.

As far as I was concerned, this was Cal's thing, and as long as they didn't bother me, it was all right. I was happily riding around town on my folding bicycle, doing my voice-overs. My involvement in the public offering was the use of my name and my credits. All our friends were caught up in the possibility of making a killing. "How many shares should we buy?" was the big question, along with "How high do you expect it to go?"

I said, "I don't know anything about it. I'm just doing my thing. They are throwing money at us. We'll do what we can. Don't go crazy buying these shares."

I was already sorry I'd become involved in it at all. What could I tell them? I didn't understand it myself. What was I supposed to do with this money? *Maybe I should read the prospectus. I don't want to make it sound like all of a sudden I'm an innocent—far from it.* I was just so happy that my brother was basking in the limelight of the public offering that I left it all to him. Maybe 20 percent of my mind was on it. Suddenly, we had more employees: a salesman, a bookkeeper, and a receptionist. I didn't hire any of them. I didn't care. We had all this money from the public offering. The shares came out at three dollars a share and quickly moved up to four dollars before they went down to fifty cents. Polaroid it wasn't.

However, it did give us the wherewithal to try making our own TV pilot shows. We bought secondhand TV cameras and equipment and built our own TV studio. I shouldn't be using *we* here. Cal built the studio. I went to London to pick the brains of my friend Mike Broun, who introduced me to front-screen projection used by the BBC. I came back with the plans, and Cal built the entire setup. There was absolutely nothing mechanical he couldn't do or a problem he couldn't solve. This life seemed to be ideal for him.

One day, as I was heading out of the office, I passed by his desk. He was concentrating on something he was typing, so I kept running. I was almost out the door, when I realized from the momentary flash of a look at his face that something was wrong. I stopped and returned to look at him. My brother's face was twisted. That is the only way I can describe it. His mouth was crooked and off-kilter. Keeping my voice matter-of-fact, I said, "Hey, butch, let's go get something to eat."

"No, I'm not really hungry."

"Okay. So you can watch while I eat. There is something I have to talk to you about."

"Can't it wait?"

"No, it's important. Finish what you're doing later."

We went next door to the Great Northern Hotel, a seedy old hotel with many single-occupancy apartments that were home to elderly people. Its restaurant was rarely crowded, and I knew we could talk there. We were alone in the place. Cal was silent. He didn't even ask me what I wanted to talk about. He seemed distracted.

"What's the problem, butch?" I asked.

"What do you mean?"

"What's the problem? Something is wrong, isn't it?"

He tried a pathetic little smile. "What makes you think something is wrong?"

"Because I know you. You have a *facrimpta* face. What is it?"

He tried to continue his denials but then suddenly broke down weeping. I had never seen my brother cry. I didn't say anything, because I couldn't. I sat there, heartsick, waiting for the sobbing to subside. I didn't have to speak. He did.

"I was typing a suicide note."

"My God! Why?"

He shrugged helplessly and said, "I don't know."

"Then we have to find out. Sit tight—I'm going to call Nat Breckir. I'll be right back."

Nat told me to bring him right over, which of course I did. I never found out what it was that led up to Cal's writing that note, but I'm sure that in the next few years on Nat's couch, Cal found out. Maybe he already knew. That was his business. The important thing was that Nat Breckir was around. Cal thrived on the relationship with Nat, as I had a decade earlier. What amazed me about Cal's breakdown was that it came at a high point in his life. If it had happened during his time in the trucking business, it would have made more sense to me.

∞ ∞ ∞ ∞ ∞ ∞   ∞ ∞ ∞ ∞ ∞ ∞ ∞

All I need to fall in love with someone is for the person to be funny. It's not really an effective litmus test. But it has happened to me over and over again with my friends. I first met Asher Richman, known as Buddy, when my not-yet-wife ran into him in the street and brought him to the house to meet me. Obviously, she knew him before she met me. He made me laugh, and that started our friendship.

Buddy was a round, cherubic fellow with a terrible rug. A "rug" in show-business parlance is a toupee. He was a musician—a cellist in the New York Philharmonic Orchestra. I was impressed. Even though musicians are known to wear the worst rugs in show business, I felt this one didn't belong on a fine classical musician. I couldn't bring it to his attention, and it was a good thing, as it turned out that it was not a toupee after all, but his own hair. He had a thickly woven, flat head of hair that showed no sign of a hairline. To me, it resembled a flat, badly made toupee laid over a bald head.

Buddy had a slew of stories about his work with the orchestra that kept me in stitches. I remember the first one he told me, about a timpanist who came to the morning rehearsal wearing a trench coat over his pajamas and fell asleep and missed his cue. Leonard Bernstein, the conductor, shouted his name. The drummer awoke and, without a moment's hesitation, said, "You want it louder, Maestro?"

In contrast to his youthful appearance, Buddy affected the lazy, world-weary attitude of one who's been everywhere and seen everything. He let it be known that he was discontented. To me, he seemed to be someone who had reached a pinnacle in his career, playing in one of the world's great orchestras. But he described it as a dead end. I wasn't sure if this was really so or just suited his sardonic style.

Ever since my high school days at Music & Art, I've been captivated by musicians. I would have loved to be able to play an instrument. Both my siblings were given piano lessons but, according to my mother, would never practice, and that was her excuse for turning me down when I asked for them. My friend Freddy Katz was my favorite. Nobody made me laugh as he did, but he was in California for many years, and our friendship became mostly a memory.

So Buddy Richman joined the group. Although he didn't have Freddy's subtle humor, he did have many funny stories, so we hung around together. Buddy's lovely wife, Nancy, who worked as an advertising copywriter, and Lenore and I saw a great deal of each other. When I look at our wedding pictures, Buddy and Nancy are prominent in our small wedding party. He was my new best friend.

One morning, I stopped by to pick him up at his apartment. He'd just finished shaving, and he asked me if I had shaved yet. I hadn't, and he wanted me to shave right there with a small amount of a liquid the color of pearl cream. It didn't resemble any shaving cream I'd ever seen, and it was a small amount—no more than the size of a twenty-five-cent piece. I thought it was some kind of a joke, but he assured me I'd have the smoothest shave ever—without washing my face first or even using water. He told me to apply it, wait twenty seconds, and then shave. I did as he suggested. It truly was a remarkably easy and comfortable shave that left my face feeling soft and clean.

There was a method to his madness. Buddy had acquired a small bottle of the cream from a scientist he'd met when he played with the orchestra in Ecuador. He'd been a guest in the man's home, and before leaving, he had asked the whereabouts of a pharmacy, because he needed shaving cream. The man offered him a bottle of the cream, saying, "Try this. I make it myself."

Buddy was excited and suggested we take it to a lab and have it analyzed.

"Why?" I asked.

"We could market it. We could make a fortune."

"You're a musician. What about the Philharmonic?"

"I'd give that up in a minute."

"I don't believe you," I said, but he swore up and down that the orchestra was a blind alley and that I didn't understand how bored stiff he was. He claimed he was ready to work his head off for an opportunity to build a company of his own. He was painting pictures of fleets of trucks roaming the streets with his name on them. He insisted he was serious, and he wanted me to go into it with him.

"First of all, Buddy," I said, "I have a very light beard. I can even use an electric razor on it. I wouldn't go by me; I never have trouble shaving. Let me try it on Cal. He has a beard like wire. He's always complaining. If it works on him, it might be a viable product."

My brother was ecstatic over the shave he got with that pearl cream. "My God, I never felt the razor," he said, and he couldn't stop raving about it.

I was getting hooked now. It could be a new challenge. I could help my friend, have a little fun, and maybe make a fortune, too.

I suggested to Buddy that we not go to a lab. "Let's go down to Ecuador and work out a deal with the inventor. I'm sure he'd be interested. Let's call him up and make a date."

When Buddy called him, Dr. Soyka said, "This is an omen. I am coming to New York next week to visit relatives."

Dr. Soyka turned out to be delightfully warm and interesting. Heavy-set, with a slight Polish accent, he had been living in Ecuador for many years, teaching chemistry at the university. I guessed he was about sixty, and he seemed in good health, except for a bad case of asthma that made him cough a great deal. The idea of a musician and an actor teaming up to market his pearl cream amused him, and he was willing to not only give us the formula but also teach us how to make it. Our agreement was simple: I gave him a check for $500 as earnest money, plus a royalty arrangement. No one could have been easier to deal with. He was a joy. We found the ingredients we needed from several chemical companies and made our first batch in my kitchen. We bought the test tubes and other items to check the materials through the process. Buddy and I felt like Louis Pasteur. We were excited when everything came together and we had the final product.

Obviously, we could not run this chemical lab from my kitchen. We rented a loft and bought huge vats, giant heating elements, and variable speed mixers. We ordered the chemicals in fifty-gallon drums. My voice-over residuals were paying for all this. I took it as a given that Buddy had no money. He made me feel as though he were an indentured slave to the low-paying New York Philharmonic and couldn't wait to give it up to work full-time in our pilot plant.

Dr. Soyka stayed with us and oversaw everything until he was satisfied we could continue alone. He was a wonderful teacher, and when he went back to Ecuador, he regularly wrote to us about additional products that could be made from the amazing base that the pearl cream came from. I felt it could be the beginning of an entire line of cosmetics.

I chose Larousse as a name for our cosmetics company. Since the USA was in the midst of the great exploration of space, I called our shaving-cream product Count Down. A friend of mine designed a beautiful label and an impressive bottle. Everything was coming up roses except for one thing: Where was Buddy, my partner?

I found myself running to the loft between recording sessions and auditions. I was the master chemist, bottle filler, label applier, and cleanup man. My partner, apparently, was no longer interested. Perhaps he felt his work was done. I called him to find out where he was. He either was not home or had excuses about how hard the Philharmonic was working him. One day, he had an extra rehearsal; the next day, it was something else, and finally, he didn't even bother to make excuses. He just never showed up.

I would see him at an occasional poker game, and he would say something like "Hey, man, what's happening?" I didn't know if that was his way of asking for a financial report, but I doubt it. He wasn't interested in what it was costing me.

The crazy thing was that at that point, I had no idea what I was going to do with all that shaving cream other than passing out bottles of it to my friends. They agreed it was a terrific product, but how could I sell it? I figured something would come to me, and it finally did. But I couldn't go it alone.

My friend Victor Babbit was out of a job, so I hired him to manage the pilot plant. Victor was the first sergeant in Special Services when I was in the air force, and we remained friends throughout our lives. Also, he had a degree in chemistry, which I didn't know but which came in handy. Now, with Victor and my brother, I had the help I needed, and if necessary, if we were successful, they would be cut in on the profits—and my silent partner would have to agree.

Now I was ready to put my plan into action and make Count Down a household name—on a meager advertising budget. For this, I started off with my actress wife. She was to go to the various pharmacies and ask the pharmacist for Count Down. Since he had never heard of the product, she would say, "My husband asked me to get it. He bought a bottle in Pittsburgh, and he is raving about it. It's some sort of new shaving thing."

"A razor or a blade?" The pharmacist would be bewildered.

"No, it's like a cream—a liquid he shaves with. He always complained, but now he says, with this stuff, he never feels the razor, and it doesn't need water."

"What did you say the name is?"

"Count Down. I think that's the name. I wrote it down." She would fumble in her purse, come up with a slip of paper with the name, and show it to the pharmacist to impress him with the name.

"I never heard of it. It must be something new. I'll ask my jobber."

Lenore repeated this all over Manhattan. We made out a route, and after skipping a day, unemployed actors I had hired followed up by going into the stores and asking for Count Down. The first day, it was one actor; the next day, two actors asked for the product; and then three asked. On the following day, Lenore went back with an empty bottle and showed it to the storekeeper. "Will this help? My husband is desperate."

"Let me see that." The pharmacist grabbed the bottle and proceeded to write down the company name and address on a piece of paper. "How do you like that? My jobber said there is no such product. I'll get it. Try me in a day or two." One of the actors followed her in a half hour and was told he would have it the next day.

Meanwhile, I was in the loft with Victor when the first call came in. I handled it so that Vic could hear how to do it. The voice on the other end asked, "Are you the company that makes Count Down?"

I answered like an employee who was harassed. "Look, sir, we're just a pilot plant. We're not set up yet for distribution. We can accommodate you with one case if you have someone to pick it up and pay cash. The retail price is two dollars. There are twenty bottles in a case, and your price is twenty dollars. I'm sorry to be so short. We're very busy here." I hung up.

Victor looked at me. "You think it'll work?"

I shrugged. "We'll see."

It worked. Storekeepers or their employees came with their checks and left with cases of Count Down. Victor kept busy answering phone calls and making up cases, but he was skeptical. "What happens after they buy it? That has to end."

"You are absolutely right, my friend. That was plan A. We now go to plan B."

"Which is what?" he asked.

"In plan B, Vic, we start buying them back."

Vic laughed. "You have to be kidding. We sell each bottle for a dollar and buy it back for two?"

"Not all of them," I explained. "We buy back just enough, and while we do that, we teach the storekeeper how to sell it. What we are going to do is a commercial in his store, and this is the way it's going to work."

I explained that two actors would be in the store. One would be deciding what kind of gum he wanted while the other asked for a shaving cream.

"What brand do you want?" the storekeeper would ask.

"I don't care. They're all the same," the actor would say disgustedly.

Now the other actor, overhearing this, would say, "Excuse me. Did you ever use Count Down?"

"What's that?" the first actor would ask.

"It's a miracle," the second actor would say. "It's a clear, creamy liquid that you put on your face. It vanishes. You see nothing but your beard. You don't even need water. With most shaving creams, you shave the cream. With this stuff, you shave the beard, and believe me, you don't know you're shaving."

By this time, if the storekeeper didn't produce a bottle of Count Down, he was plain stupid. In our actual tests, we often found that the pharmacists had already tried the product and confirmed what the other actor said.

The actor would buy the Count Down. Not long after, another actor would walk in to buy a shaving cream to test the storekeeper. If the storekeeper tried to sell him on Count Down, he bought it, and that was the end of our buy-back at that store. The pharmacist had graduated. Handmade signs started to appear in store windows all over the city: We Have Count Down.

Of course, I was one of the actors who took part in all this. So was my brother. All the actors reported on their activities at each store. We kept charts and records on every store. We knew how much each bought, how much we bought back, and how much the store sold to the public. Many stores kept coming back to us to buy more product on the same basis as the first case.

Not all the stores called us or picked up the product. We noted which storekeepers were skeptical. Some were told by their jobbers that it was probably some kind of a promotion since they'd never heard of it. Most of us had gone back often to ask if they had it in yet, and they recognized us.

I decided on a plan for these skeptical pharmacists. I called it the "rectal treatment." I walked into one pharmacy, and no sooner had I entered than the pharmacist shook his head negatively at me. I looked around as if I thought he must mean someone behind me. His partner was standing there with him, and he said, "No! We don't have any!"

I laughed and asked, "What are you—a mind reader?"

"We don't have any Count Down," he said in a snide manner.

"Oh, no, I got that already. I need a rectal thermometer. You know, the last one you sold me didn't last very long. My wife says I shake it down too hard. Could that be the reason?"

I saw the look that passed between them. It read to me like *Maybe this is on the level.* He answered my question. I bought the thermometer, and before I walked out, he asked, "Where did you get it?"

"Get what?" I asked in all innocence.

"The Count Down."

"Oh, that? I don't know—somewhere. They had a sign in the window." I left, and immediately he called Victor and ordered a case. The other actors followed suit and gave the rectal treatment to their skeptical shopkeepers.

One of the checks we received bore the name of Gillett. They wanted to buy six cases, but we kept them to one—at least one at a time. Dr. Soyka had told us not to patent the shaving cream. He said if we did, we'd have to reveal the entire process, along with the formula. Some big company could then make a slight change in it, and that would be the end of our patent. He said that even if they broke down the ingredients, they could never duplicate it.

He explained his certainty: "This product came out of a classroom project at the university. One of my students did everything wrong, and the pearl cream was born. There is not a chemist in the world, having the formula, who would ever try to formulate it in that manner."

Not unexpectedly, we received a call from Wall Street. After all, we had baited the drugstores in that area, hoping someone with money would take the hook. It turned out to be a big fish—Allen and Company, major private investment bankers. They were interested in Count Down. The word around was that it was a terrific new product; they couldn't help seeing all the hand-printed signs in drugstore windows: "Yes, we have Count Down." When some of the bankers in their organization inquired, they were sold the product with glowing reports. They had tried it themselves and were impressed. A meeting was set up between their president, Charlie Allen, and me.

Victor, Cal, and I were excited. This was a firm noted for bankrolling some of the biggest corporations on the stock exchange. We met in their conference room. About six bankers and I were sitting around the huge mahogany table. We all sat quietly, apparently waiting for someone. I figured we were waiting for Charlie Allen, but that was not the case. It was one of his vice presidents. At any rate, no one was talking, so I decided to make a little joke. "Who has the cards?" I asked.

Each of the bankers took out his business card and handed it to me. I tried hard to keep a straight face. This was obviously a group of men whose minds were strictly on business.

They did liven up when they learned that I was, to some of the younger men, a star from *The Howdy Doody Show* of their childhood and, to the others, the Man of a Thousand Voices, whom they had read about in *Time* magazine and who, supposedly, earned oodles of money. I felt it was important to establish my credits right away. In keeping with my philosophy of negative selling learned from my days as a shingle bum, I wanted them to realize I was not coming to them hat in hand. In fact, they had come to me. I wanted them to understand that I didn't need them but was willing to listen to their proposition.

Finally, we got down to business. They asked many questions. Was it patented or patentable? I wouldn't patent it, I said, because I knew they couldn't reproduce it. They were not convinced, but I didn't go into any further explanation. Then they asked about the ingredients—did it have lanolin in it? I answered no and told them it was made from a new base that we called Nioleene, from which many cosmetic products could be made, and Count Down was simply one of them. It would rival lanolin in its many uses and could also be used in formulating industrial products.

"Mr. Swift, how much money do you think it would take to go national with this product?" one of them asked.

"I really don't know," I answered. "I simply figured we'd keep going as we had, in a small way, pouring the profits back into the business, slowly building word of mouth."

"That is all well and good," one of them said, "but by then, a well-financed company could knock off your product and steal your market."

"They'll never duplicate this product."

"Maybe no, maybe yes," he countered. "For the time being, we will take your word for it. However, with enough capital behind you, you could grab a big chunk of the market while it is hot and let the others run after you."

I went on to drive home the fact that this was not just a new shaving cream; this was a revolutionary product that did not require water. "The astronauts could shave with this in space. In fact, I intend to send them Count Down, and perhaps we'll be using that in our advertising." They loved that.

I was having a great time at this point in my negotiations with Allen and Company. I was having fun in the role I was playing. But where was Buddy? He was missing all of this. *Imagine how his fantasy of having a fleet of trucks with his name on them would take off if he were sitting here with me.* Well, I finally found out where Buddy was and why I hadn't seen him for so long. I found out when he called to invite Lenore and me to spend the day on his boat.

"Boat? What boat? What are you talking about?"

"Yeah, I bought a power boat, a cabin cruiser. I figured, what am I going to do, wait for my teeth to fall out before enjoying myself?"

I was dumbfounded. *What kind of an idiot am I? Buddy, who claimed to be an indentured slave to the New York Philharmonic, Buddy who cries poverty, bought a cabin cruiser while I run around working my butt off, shelling out my residuals money to make this dream of his a reality? Sure, I bought into that dream, too. I must be nuts.*

I was nuts. I accepted his invitation. His boat was docked at City Island. We were supposed to be there at 10:00 a.m., but my wife was time challenged, and we were late. Buddy was nasty to us, accusing us of killing his day. Buddy, whom we had hosted dozens of times in our home, treated us like garbage. He had quite a boat. It looked big to me. It had a cabin that you could eat and sleep in. We just sat on the dock, listening to his peevish complaints that it was now too late to go out. I believe his wife, Nancy, was terribly embarrassed by his actions, but she remained quiet, as Lenore and I did.

That night, I developed a sharp pain in my gut. It was horrendous and went right through from my gut to my back. I took every painkiller we had in the house to no avail. At about ten o'clock, I finally called my doctor friend, Lenny Essman. He had married my high school sweetheart, Zora Pressman. (When she'd married Lenny, she'd lost the *PR* in her name. We had remained friends all through the years.) They lived in Westchester. I called to ask his advice, but Lenny, a true healer, jumped into his car and came down to Manhattan to doctor me. I was in agony, and he gave me a shot of Demerol. I slept like a baby through the night, and in the morning, the pain was gone.

After having many meetings with Allen and Company and developing a proposal, complete with plans as to how we would merchandise Count Down, they decided that it would take $3 million. I told them that I was satisfied with how we were progressing on our own but that because of all the time I was spending with them, I was neglecting my business. I gave them six weeks to come up with the money or the deal was off. I would do it my own way, as I had until then. They found that acceptable.

I was to learn why such a demand on my part was acceptable: these types of people never put their own money into these ventures. They interest other people in putting up the money. I really can't understand why they're called bankers. They should be called brokers. In this case, they had someone all lined up—a man who had made a killing in a particular cosmetic and was looking for something new. He had tried Count Down and was told by Allen and Company of its speedy acceptance by the public. A meeting was arranged, but the night before the agreed date, he had the misfortune to drop dead of a heart attack. Allen and Company needed more time. I was not about to give it to them. It would weaken my position.

Although I didn't have Buddy to contend with at this time, Victor and my brother begged me not to cut them off. "This is Allen and Company," they said. "You'll kill it!"

"You don't understand," I countered. "They really must continue to feel that we believe we don't need them. We have to play this out according to the scenario."

"What scenario?" Victor was terribly upset. "It's your scenario. You can afford such a scenario. You don't need the money. I do. You can walk away from this."

"I'm not walking away. They will come after us."

"And what if they don't?"

"Then we're no worse off than we were before. Maybe someone else will bite."

In spite of the fact that so far my technique was working, I was unable to convince them. They were dazzled by the name and reputation of Allen and Company. In the end, I reluctantly gave in to them. I was certain I was right, but they, especially Victor, had put in a great deal of time and effort. I let the deadline pass with Allen and Company. That night, I had another gut attack. Lenny came down as usual and knocked me out with Demerol.

I wish Victor and Cal had been right and I had been wrong, but that was not the case. Allen and Company now dragged things out. They kept coming up with demands for studies and projections. Months passed—but not the spasms in my gut. They were coming pretty regularly, and Lenny was doing various tests. Lenore had a cousin who was an internist, and she suggested I see him. He said it was my gall bladder and suggested I have it removed. Lenny said, "They'll take your gall bladder out over my dead body. There is nothing wrong with your gall bladder."

My wife, who leans toward emotional diagnoses in most cases of pain, blamed the shaving-cream business, and she did this without the benefit of a medical degree.

The shit hit the fan one day when my silent partner, Buddy, came to see me on a matter of grave importance. (I would like to have used a more elegant expression, but nothing I can think of has the impact of that swirling fan to denote finality.)

"Allen, someone has offered to buy the formula from me for the pearl cream," he said. "What do you think I should do? I could use the money."

I do not remember how long I sat there looking at him before speaking, but I know it was a long time because of all the thoughts going through my mind. *Is he for real? Am I the stupidest fool living? What does he mean someone offered to buy the formula from* him? *He didn't say "us"; he said "him."*

"Okay, Buddy, sell it!"

"Really?"

"Sure, sell it. You need the money." I tried to measure his reaction. *Was he happy about it? Was he relieved by my answer, surprised by it, or was his claim even true?* I couldn't tell and was so full of anger at that moment that I didn't care.

I said, "By the way, Buddy, do me a favor—lose my address and phone number."

"Why? I, er—"

"Make believe we never met."

"I just—"

"Will you please leave?"

"But—"

"Just leave. Walk out the door. I don't want to look at you. Go!"

I made up my mind right then and there. I *was* stupid. Lenore was right. I needed this business like a hole in my gut. I was sorry about Victor. I had been paying him a salary. I didn't owe anybody anything. I decided to auction off our equipment in the loft, close up, and forget all about pearl cream, Count Down, and, most of all, Asher Richmond.

As you can see, I never did forget about it. Here I am writing of it nearly forty years later. Does anyone ever forget someone he or she fell in love with, no matter how badly it ends?

I have to recognize that in spite of my smarts, I'm a lousy businessman. I should have made a contract with Buddy right at the beginning, just as we did with Dr. Soyka, and required him to invest some money. He didn't have to invest as much as I did but something that was meaningful to him. If he refused, I should never have started. If he had invested, would he still have behaved as he did? I doubt it. But who knows?

Chapter 12

Producing and Reproducing

On March 2, 1964, my daughter Maxime was born. We talked a great deal about what to name her. Lenore suggested the name Abra, which is short for Abraham, her grandfather's name. I said the kids would call her Abrakadabra. That nixed that name. I wanted to name her after my father, Max, and suggested Maxine. Lenore loved the French language and our wonderful meal at Maxim's in Paris on our honeymoon, so we substituted *m* for the *n*, added the femine e and both parties were happy.

Lenore informed me on that March night that she was ready to deliver our first child. As I was already a father and experienced, I told her she was jumping the gun. She told me to shut up and get her to the hospital. And—voilà!—she was right.

University Hospital was spanking new at the time. We appeared to be the only people there besides the staff. While Lenore was suffering the throes of labor, I kibitzed with two Haitian nurses in the waiting room. They asked me whether I wanted a boy or a girl. I was forty years old at the time and didn't relish the idea of going through the Little League bit again during the next ten years. They assured me that they had the power to grant my wish for a girl if I danced a voodoo dance with them. There was a fifty-fifty chance of their being right, so I joined in the fun. I danced with them, and in a few minutes, my daughter was born.

The following year, we were back again at University Hospital. This time, it was March 16. All of my children, Lewis included, were born in March, which proves that at least once a year, the spirit moves me.

This time, Lewis joined me in the waiting room, and this time, the same two nurses, who took full credit for my last child being a girl, were there again. They asked me the same question: Did I want a boy or a girl? I was now a year older and still didn't wish to repeat the baseball-father routine. "I would like another girl," I said.

Were my odds the same fifty-fifty, or were they better for a boy this time? They assured me that odds had nothing to do with it—my participation in the voodoo dance was a guarantee of a girl. They chanted their incantation, I danced, and my daughter Clare was born! This time, there was no controversy over the name. We named her after a favorite cousin of mine whom Lenore loved as well.

The irony in all this is that both girls grew up to embrace the new women's-lib movement and berated me for *not* teaching them to play baseball! What could I do? I admit I am a male chauvinist at heart. I still think that boys are made of rats and snails and puppy dog tails and that girls are made of sugar and spice and everything nice. I like them with long hair, dresses, and ribbons and went through the pangs of fatherhood as their beautiful, long tresses were left on the beauty-parlor floor.

The girls were educated in their formative years at the progressive Walden School. They loved it—and why not? I would have loved going to that school myself. They might not have learned their multiplication tables, but they learned to be curious, thinking people. The school was on the Upper West Side of New York City, and I loved taking them to it every day until they were old enough to travel by themselves. On a number of occasions, I sat in on a class and marveled at the exchanges of ideas between these little people and their teachers, whom they addressed by their first names.

The paradox is that while we want our children to grow up to be themselves and not replicas of us, we might then resent their being so much their own people that it sometimes becomes difficult to understand them. Occasionally, I feel like Henry Higgins, who said, "Why can't a woman be more like a man?" I'm tempted to say, "I am so rational, so clever, so free—why can't my children think more like me?" That aside, I adore them all.

∞ ∞ ∞ ∞ ∞ ∞   ∞ ∞ ∞ ∞ ∞ ∞ ∞

At sixteen, Lewis decided to try to get an apprenticeship at a summer theater. He had already spent two summers at a theater camp, which was special for him. Indeed, from my standpoint too, it was remarkable. The productions were so creative and professional that they could have toured. Aside from that, the staff at Gray Gables imbued the children with a great love of the theater.

He showed me the résumé he was sending out to summer theaters in order to get an apprenticeship. It was basically about his camp experience and a summer class in acting. Since I couldn't possibly allow my son to walk the straight-and-narrow path that most would-be thespians walked, I revised it. I added some Broadway shows to his experience. He was shocked. How could anyone believe those credits? I explained that I selected only shows that had a bunch of kids in the cast—for example, *Gypsy.*

"But I was never in those shows. What if they saw them?" he asked.

"It's simple," I said. "You ask them when they saw the show. If they say they saw it in the beginning or even on opening night, you say you were a replacement. If they saw it after it was running quite awhile, you left the cast early. Nobody remembers who the kids are in shows. They age so quickly and are replaced in long-running shows. You claim your parents pushed you onto the stage, and you hated it. You wanted to be out playing baseball. You stopped acting and thought you'd never go back to it, but here you are, realizing that you really love acting, and you're starting over." It was a believable scenario, and since Lewis already knew these shows and was constantly singing all the songs, there could be no problem.

He sent out a batch of résumés with my made-up credits and then came to me one day, complaining. "I didn't get one answer," he said in an annoyed tone, as though it were my fault.

I answered, "How do you like that? With all those credits, you still didn't get an answer. Imagine if you sent *your* résumé out. You see, nobody is interested in you. This is a highly competitive business. This is not Gray Gables. You have got to find a way to make them interested in you."

He did eventually get a job as an apprentice that summer in New London, New Hampshire. He was the youngest one there. Since there was no doubt that my son was going to follow me into the life of an actor, I talked to him about a plan I had for him to study acting in England. I had no illusions that English acting schools were any better or worse than ours; it was simply that in this business, English actors have a certain cachet. The English accent alone has great snob appeal. In America, everything imported was better, so why not give him a little edge in this difficult business? Obviously, I would try to get him into RADA, the Royal Academy of Dramatic Arts, but if that were not possible, then some other school.

∞ ∞ ∞ ∞ ∞ ∞   ∞ ∞ ∞ ∞ ∞ ∞

The following winter was one of New York's coldest and snowiest. It was Christmas, and Lenore and I returned home from a party quite late. It was about two o'clock in the morning, and I went out in the snow to walk our dog. As I came out of our building and turned left, toward Seventh Avenue, I had a strange feeling. A taxi was parked about thirty feet to the right of the entrance, and in the light of a streetlamp, I caught a flash of the back of a head through the rear window of the cab.

As I walked in the opposite direction, I kept thinking that the shape of the head was like Lewis's. *But that is not possible,* I thought. *Lewis is at his mother's.* I couldn't shake the feeling that it might be him. I turned around, headed to the cab, and looked inside, and it *was* my son, sitting there comatose, drenched in vomit.

I opened the door as the taxi driver said, "How do you like that son of a bitch? Look what he's done to my cab! I'm gonna throw the bum out."

I handed the driver a twenty-dollar bill, dragged Lewis out of the cab, and threw him over my shoulder. I carried him up to our apartment, put him down on the bed, and cleaned him up as best I could. Lenore and I were frantic. He was out cold. I called a nice GP, Dr. Greenberg, a friend of my cousin, and he came right over. He claimed he had been up and that I hadn't woken him. Maybe he had been at a party too. He examined Lewis, gave him a shot of something, and pronounced that my son was comatose.

"He no doubt consumed a great deal of liquor and possibly some very bad liquor," Dr. Greenberg told us. "Let him sleep it off. He'll probably be all right. Call me when he wakes up, and I'll come over."

I don't think I've ever been as worried as I was that day. I kept looking in on him every half hour, but he slept and slept. Of course, he eventually joined the living, but I came to a hand-wringing realization: *My son is telling me he's not ready to go to England.* I didn't know what had precipitated this drinking binge, but I was convinced my insight was on the mark. It turned out I was right.

I am not a drinker. I never have been. There's a particular reason, and it doesn't stem from any moral conviction: I don't like the taste of liquor. Also, I've never felt the need. If I need a pick-me-up, my vice is a candy bar. I'm social in a social situation without a drink, and I certainly never need one before walking out on stage. I get high enough just acting.

But here was my son, at sixteen, dead drunk. This frightened me. If I hadn't happened upon the scene he could have been thrown out and left in the snow to freeze to death. It was two in the morning, and he could have been mistaken for some bum. He had been at a party arranged by the people who ran the theater he worked at during the summer. They'd had a great time getting this kid drunk, mixing his drinks and plying him with one after another. When he was three sheets to the wind, someone had put him in a cab and told the driver to take him to West Fifty-Seventh Street. They knew I lived there. Did they actually know the address? The cab hadn't been parked in front of my building.

Fortunately, he survived and became a wonderful and successful actor—and no doubt the envy of those foolish people who had had their fun at his expense. Nevertheless, he went back the following year to the same summer theater, perhaps a little wiser about who his friends were.

At eighteen, Lewis graduated from high school, much to his and his parents' relief. I'm afraid his schooling also followed in my footsteps. As the saying goes, "The sins of the father ..." On occasion, I was to be told by an astonished teacher that my son did not do his homework. "He turned in a perfect math homework paper," one of them told me, "but when I asked him to go up to the board and do the same problems, he was unable to do them. Someone else did his homework for him. Can you believe that?"

"I'm shocked, sir—absolutely shocked," I said. "I shall give him a good talking to!"

His mother and I constantly sent Lewis to tutors, trying to raise his grades. His tutoring sessions were usually on Sunday mornings. I would pick him up at the tutor's, and the two of us would go to the T-Bone Diner for a steak lunch. It was at one of these lunches that he told me proudly about an assignment he'd had: to read a book—any book—and write a report on it. Instead of reading a book, he'd written a report on a fictitious book by a fictitious author whom he'd claimed was a great writer, and he'd received an A for it!

I am sorry. I know, as a father, I should have reprimanded him, but I couldn't. I was pleased by his creativity. It was an excellent report. It made me want to read the book! I felt pride that my son had my genes. It showed up in his conning of his teachers and in his acting ability. Alas, though, his conning was only in his schoolwork. It went no further. In everything else, Lewis is a straight arrow. What can I do? You win some, and you lose some.

∞ ∞ ∞ ∞ ∞ ∞   ∞ ∞ ∞ ∞ ∞ ∞

Martha Schlamme, whom I had worked with when I was a nightclub entertainer—she was the singer on the bill—and in an off Broadway musical, came to dinner one evening. She invited Lenore and me to attend a cabaret night at Yale in which she and Alvin Epstein were performing the songs of Kurt Weill and Bertolt Brecht. The performances and the material, some of it in German, as it was originally performed, delighted us both. They were hoping for a production in New York. Lenore, active on the fund-raising committee for the Walden Scholarship Fund, suggested they do it as a benefit in our home. As it so happened, Alvin was an alumnus of the Walden School, loved the idea, and happily consented.

Alvin is a brilliant actor and was then the director of the drama department at Yale. Martha is a lady of enormous charm and talent and the warmth and flirtatiousness of a European diva. They were a magical combination. The evening was a resounding success, and I decided to produce them in an off-Broadway theater.

I contacted Kurt Weill's widow, Lotte Lenya, to purchase the rights, but she refused. Martha was not surprised, because Lotte Lenya was a star in her own right and would want to perform the material herself. Although it seemed like an insurmountable problem, such is my love of challenges that, for me, the more insurmountable, the better. If she wouldn't sell the rights, I had to find a way around the problem. It wasn't a book show we were doing; it was simply songs. ASCAP published these songs. If they were performed in a nightclub, since nightclubs paid royalties to ASCAP in the form of licensing fees, I would need no rights or permission from the estate, nor would it cost me anything. Ha-ha!

I leased the Bitter End in Greenwich Village as the venue. Although the performers couldn't work under an equity contract, they could under an AGVA (American Guild of Variety Artists) contract. I called our show *Whores, Wars and Tin Pan Alley*. Leroy Neiman designed a wonderful poster that became a collectors item.

I only wish that my problem-solving ability made me a better producer. It didn't. I lacked the organizational skills needed. I was a perfect example of the Peter principle. Although I had good taste, I stretched myself from being a good actor, good writer, and terrific promotion person to a screwup producer.

The Bitter End didn't have proper chairs. It had long benches with backs. I figured out how many people could sit on each bench. Why I didn't delegate this job to my brother, only God knows. He would have used a tape measure. He wouldn't have oversold the opening-night house so that all the critics had to be squeezed in like sausages. As it was, we received good reviews. But they might have been great if the critics had been in a happier frame of mind from the outset.

After playing at the Bitter End for a few months, I moved the show to the Sheridan Square Playhouse. It was an off-Broadway theater that, years before, I'd had a hand in renovating from an old restaurant. I was, therefore, on good terms with the owner-producer, Joe Berut. My first question to Joe was "What is the biggest problem you face in the off-Broadway business?"

"No-shows," he said. "People call up and make a reservation and then don't show up. Some, I'm sure, dawdle too late over dinner, or they change their mind at the last minute and decide not to go out. There can be many reasons, but it hurts business. If everyone who made reservations showed up, we'd do a hell of a lot better."

This problem seemed pretty simple to solve. At the time, there was no such thing as reserving tickets to an off-Broadway play by credit card. Why not make-believe there was such a thing? In other words, when someone called to make a reservation, we could ask for a credit-card number. When we had the card number, we could say that the ticket was guaranteed and that if it was not picked up, it would be charged to the card. Since we couldn't follow through with that, we asked them to pay when they came to pick up the tickets, explaining that they were only charged if the tickets were not picked up. It worked. Everybody gave us a number and showed up as long as the person in the box office who took the reservation asked for a card number.

Lewis, unemployed at the time, was working in the box office. He refused to do it.

"Why not?" I asked.

"Because it's not honest. You can't really charge their credit card," he answered.

This, of course, had nothing to do with honesty or the lack of it. Lewis was going through a difficult time in his life at that point. Things were in a state of flux for him. I'm sure he resented working in the box office and no doubt resented me.

Two things happened shortly after this: all theaters, both on and off Broadway, installed credit-card charging to cure the no-show problem, and Lewis became an overnight sensation on Broadway, playing the young Groucho Marx in the musical *Minnie's Boys*.

Chapter 13

Inside Tracks and Soul Food

Actors who do commercials assume that advertising agencies and sponsors keep track of repeat plays of commercials and pay accordingly. I had always figured it must be accurate because it's computerized. Also, since the agencies get their percentage based on their billing to the sponsor, they'd have no reason to cheat.

Well, I found out there were exceptions to this rule. When I began doing commercials for a small toy company, the sponsor was just starting up in business. He himself directed the recording sessions. This went on for quite some time. I did all of his commercials and earned about $2,000 a year from them. Since I rarely watch television, and certainly not children's shows, I had never seen them on the air.

One day, I happened to be in a waiting room, thumbing through a copy of *Fortune* magazine. Lo and behold, there was a big story about Topper Toys, the little company that was paying me $2,000 a year—only they were no longer a little company. They were the second-largest toy company in the world, with an annual advertising budget of $30 million. I realized that something was rotten—not in Denmark but in the ad business. I went to my union, the Screen Actors Guild, and asked them to go into the company's books to see what the company should have paid me. They came up with a figure of $35,000 plus a late-payment penalty of 20 percent.

The following day, the sponsor phoned me. He was quite a character, and he said, "Allen, what is this they tell me? It sounds awfully fishy to me, but I like you, so I'll trust you."

I broke up laughing and answered him, "Henry, you are something. You cheat me out of thousands of dollars, and you tell me you are going to trust me?"

What I did not know then was that his ad agency was Dancer Fitzgerald and Sample, a major agency. I did a great deal of work for DFS. After the call from Henry, I received another call from the law firm representing DFS. They wanted a meeting with me at, of all places, the casting director's office. If Henry had smelled something fishy, I smelled a rat. This was an obvious attempt to intimidate me. It was subtle blackmail. Now on my guard, I determined to nip it in the bud.

After introductions and small talk about the weather, I said to the two lawyers, "Gentlemen, before we get into the reason I was called here, let me say that I am a very fortunate actor who earns his living from six hundred different sources. Not one of them accounts for more than two percent of my income. I am a firm believer that no one hires me unless they need me. I don't believe we are meeting in this office because you are casting a commercial, so let's get to the point."

The anger seething inside me had to be obvious, and they fell all over themselves denying that our meeting place had to do with anything other than the fact that it was a convenient place to meet. DFS had at least six floors and hundreds of offices. *Sure, that was the most convenient place!* Whatever their strategy was, it was derailed, but they were not giving up. They asked me all sorts of questions, but the big one was "You're not out for blood, right?"

"That's right," I answered. "I only want what is coming to me."

"And you certainly are entitled to it, but you don't want blood, do you?"

It was amazing how many times they asked the blood question and how many times I said, "No, I just want what's coming to me!"

They then handed me a check for $35,000. I said, "Where is the twenty percent for late payments?"

They seemed hurt. "We thought you didn't want blood."

"That is not blood, gentlemen. There is a reason why that is in the union contract. That money is mine. I could have earned that amount on the money I should have been paid over the last few years."

They then suggested some monkey business about my endorsing the check, which was from Topper Toys, and said they would replace it with a check from DFS. They assured me that I would get another check from DFS for the 20 percent later. The check had a legend on the back, where it was to be signed, stating that it was payment in full. I pointed it out to them and refused my endorsement.

"Well, what would you wish to have on the check?" they asked. "What would make you happy?"

I said, "I want it to include the phrase 'This does not include the twenty percent late payment.'"

They then asked me to write it out the way I wanted the endorsement to read. This I did, and one of them left the room to have a new check drawn with my words typed in. When he came back with the new check, it looked fine to me, so I signed it.

While I was endorsing the new check, one of the lawyers asked me, "Tell me, Allen, where did you go to law school?"

Bells went off in my head—alarm bells. *He knows I didn't go to law school. Why did he say that? He feels like a winner, and it is a form of gloating. In a subtle way, he is making fun of me, so I must be doing something wrong.*

They were in total shock as I folded the signed check and, instead of handing it to them, placed it in my pocket. That lawyer had gone too far. He didn't know when to shut up.

In my days as a shingle bum, I would have said, "He fucked the sale." I said, "That did it. Sorry, gentlemen. You know I didn't go to law school, so I will take this to someone who did." I picked up my things, walked out, and went directly to see the attorney for the union.

The Screen Actors Guild lawyer listened to my tale, tore up the check, called DFS, and told them to get down to his office in half an hour with the correct total on the check and to have it certified. He then told me that if I had signed that check and given it to them, the only way we would have gotten the late-payment money would have been to take them to court and sue them. Beware of flattery from an adversary or a salesman.

∞ ∞ ∞ ∞ ∞ ∞   ∞ ∞ ∞ ∞ ∞ ∞

Doing voice-overs on commercials has many silly sides to it, most having to do with the lack of confidence of the advertising people. I was auditioning for a coffee commercial once, and in reading the script, I noticed something missing in the writing that made it incomprehensible.

When I showed it to the producer, he said, "We know. We can't do anything about it. The sponsor wrote the copy."

The next day, I was in the studio to do the actual recording with the sponsor present. I started to read it and stopped. It was just plain stupid to read it that way when a simple change was needed. I said, "Excuse me—the copy doesn't make sense the way it's written. I think there must be a typo error," and I suggested the change that would correct it. I thought the producer was going to make in his pants. He feverishly motioned me to be quiet.

The sponsor, on the other hand, asked to see the script, and after reading it, he said, "You are absolutely right. Thank you. Let's make that change."

As long as I'm discussing coffee commercials—the last one was for Savarin—I would like to describe the time I was a coffee bean. This one, I believe, was for Tasters' Choice. I auditioned for this bean in New York. But the other bean I was to work with was in Los Angeles, and he was on a TV sitcom and unavailable to make the trip east. So the producer flew me out there, at great expense, for one thirty-second spot. When I met the other actor, it was obvious that he could easily have done the voices of both beans in LA, as I could have in New York. Think of the money they could have saved!

The producer, however, was not about to take any chances with his opus. We should have been finished with this recording session in a half hour at the most. Six hours

310

later, we were still recording. The poor man could not make a decision. I suggested to the other actor, out of earshot of the producer, that he tell the man he had another recording session. "Help the man. Tell him you have to leave. I can't do it, because he knows he has me for the day. You live here—it's easy."

He was afraid, so I had to stay overnight in LA.

I met this same producer a year later in Chicago, when I was to address the Advertising Age Convention. We were both registering at the same time, and I asked him what he was doing there.

"I'm on a panel lecturing on producing voice-over commercials," he told me.

I almost said, "What are you lecturing on—incompetence?" but I held my tongue. I have no experience of other industries, but I imagine incompetence is rampant everywhere. I assume so because I'm frequently sold the wrong item, or workmen screw up what I've hired them to do for me.

What differentiates the advertising business is the fact that they deal in intangibles. If a frame maker constructs a crooked frame that doesn't fit the picture, it's easy to say, "That's wrong. It's no good." But how do you judge copy for a commercial? Who is the judge? The best commercials I have ever done, in my opinion, have never seen the light of day. They were killed before they ever went on the air. Who was right in rejecting them, or was my opinion wrong? One of the problems is that advertisers are afraid of including comedy in commercials. If I've heard this once, I've heard it a hundred times: "Allen, that's too funny. Can you tone it down?"

"What is wrong with being too funny?" I ask.

"Funny commercials don't work," they say. "It detracts from the message."

I know why they say this. Usually, when an agency tries to make a funny commercial, it's not funny. The reason is that everyone is too uptight and unsure of his or her ability to tell if it's funny or not. It is much easier to deliver a straight message. The actor Edmond Kean, on his deathbed, reputedly answered, when asked if he was in pain, "Dying is easy; comedy is hard."

It is difficult to analyze a joke. Either it makes you laugh or it doesn't. If you have to think about it, forget it.

I devised a test years ago to disabuse advertisers of their mistaken notion about funny commercials. I did this in order to sell them on Swift Spots, which were always funny. I would name a series of motion pictures and ask them who starred in them. "There are no right or wrong answers," I said. "If you remember, simply call out the name; if not, it's of no importance."

The outcome was that they remembered the stars in all the comedies and few in the straight films. The capper was that all the straight films had won Academy Awards, while none of the comedies had.

I asked them, "What comes to mind when I say 'Jell-O'?"

Invariably, they answered, "Jack Benny."

"And you think comedy commercials don't work? Jack Benny has been off the air for years, but so indelible is the memory of that association of Benny with his sponsor that you remember it to this day."

It worked in selling the commercials I produced, but with others, it was the same old song. Marty Solow, the head of Solow-Wexton Advertising, was a rare exception. He created the campaign for Vita Herring that had people laughing, raving about the spots, and buying the herring. Of course, it didn't hurt that I played the Beloved Herring Maven!*

*Ed. Note: The radio spots ran from 1965-1969 and won awards from the Hollywood Advertising Club and the Advertising Writers Association of New York, among others. The endurance of the commercials, according to The New York Times, helped establish "maven," a Yiddish word, as an accepted synonym for expert or connoisseur. Typical of the Beloved Herring Maven's advice was "Fish is a brain food and if you feed your child herring he'll probably grow up to be an adult. Or some other kind of tall person."

Allen Swift as "The Beloved Herring Maven"
for Vita Herring, Solow-Wexton Advertising,
Marty Solow, President & Creative Director.

Quite often, I was called in to do a voice-over on a commercial that they claimed was a funny one. Who thought it was funny, I had no idea. The copy read as though it were a straight announcer pitch.

"This is a funny one, Allen, but don't make it too funny," they cautioned.

"I got you," I answered. "Tell you what I'm going to do. I am going to start way out and slowly bring it in. When you hear what you feel is right, say, 'Woof.' Okay?" I would then give them an outrageous voice and slowly change into a less silly one and finally modulate into a straight announcer, as straight as straight could be. Then, and only then, would I hear "woof."

"You're sure that is not too funny?" I'd ask with my tongue bulging my cheek.

"No, no, Allen, that's perfect!"

Once, I was auditioning for one of these supposedly funny commercials with one of the greatest comic actors on the Broadway stage, David Burns. We were with the "creative" group of men and women, when they handed us the script and told us it was funny. My technique, as you have read, is not to comment. I am a whore who wants to get the job. Davy Burns, on the other hand, was irate.

"This is funny?" he asked angrily. "You call this funny? I'll show you what's funny!" He unzipped his fly, pulled his shirttail out, and said, "This is funny!" It shocked them, and they laughed with relief that the shirt was all he pulled out, but he didn't get the job.

David Burns and I were a mutual envy society. Whenever we met, he would ask how he could get those "goddamn commercials." He felt I had it made, while he had to suffer through learning too many sides in all the shows he was doing. I would have given up all my commercials to play some of the parts he did on Broadway. Unfortunately, not too many people know or remember who he was, in spite of all the Tony Awards he accumulated. He was always the second banana, without whose brilliant support the top banana might well not have thrived.

Another characteristic I observed at ad agencies was the age of the so-called creative staff. My wife once asked me how a particular audition went. I said, "Well, I read for the producer. Then his mother came and took him to the bathroom."

That was a bit of an exaggeration, but they were young—
and getting younger all the time. I was called in for a commercial
where the casting girl asked me if I could do Teddy Roosevelt. I
said yes. Then she showed me a picture of the president I was
to do, and it was FDR. I said, "That is not Teddy Roosevelt."

"Oh yes—yes, it is," she answered confidently.

"No, dear, believe me—it's not. He was a cousin of Teddy's,
but it is not Teddy. That is Franklin Delano Roosevelt."

Without batting an eye, she asked, "Well, can you do him?"

"Yes, even better," I said.

∞ ∞ ∞ ∞ ∞ ∞   ∞ ∞ ∞ ∞ ∞ ∞ ∞

Every time an actor does a commercial, whether it's a
voice-over or on camera, he signs a contract that includes
an exclusivity clause in which he agrees not to do another
commercial for a competing product. I always crossed out that
clause and initialed it, the reason being that I can do many
different voices, and I don't want to be exclusive to any one
product. I just wouldn't do the same voice for a competing
product. Only once, in all the contracts that I've signed, did
anyone object. It was at Grey Advertising. Claudia Walden, the
casting director and a lovely lady, called me up after perusing
my signed contract. "Allen, you crossed out the exclusivity
clause."

"Yes, Claudia, I always do. I do many competing products."

"But that's against Grey's policy. You can't do that."

"But signing exclusivity clauses is against my policy, Claudia.
I have already done competing products to the commercial I
just did for you."

"Oh my, but what if Grey came up with an entirely new
product?"

"I would do it. And if someone else came up with the same
kind of product, I'd do that, too."

"But that's against Grey's policy, Allen. What am I going to do?"

Interestingly, up to that point, I had done little work for Grey.
In fact, I believe that was the first job I'd done for the agency.
"I tell you what, Claudia," I suggested, "why don't you send

around an interoffice memo saying that Allen Swift is off limits to Grey Advertising?"

"Allen, be serious!"

"I am serious, Claudia. We are at an impasse. Grey and I have different needs and different requirements. Send that memo. It will get you off the hook."

I remember that conversation because it was so silly and about as far as I could go with negative selling. It marked the beginning of a long and lucrative association with Grey Advertising.

∞ ∞ ∞ ∞ ∞ ∞   ∞ ∞ ∞ ∞ ∞ ∞

ALLEN SWIFT, INC.
110 WEST 57 STREET • NEW YORK, N.Y. 10019 • 582-8925

February 9, 1979

Dear Mary,

Now that the strike is over, I envy you because once again you will be able to use me in your commercials.

Perhaps the strike served a purpose. Management learned what you already knew...talent, comedy timing, versatility and an ability to understand and interpret copy isn't learned in a crash course at Weist-Baron's or any other commercial acting school. There really isn't any substitute for experience. There are differences between PROS and amateurs. Let's face it...there are differences between PROS and pros and once again, the pros' PRO is available to you...relax, breath easier...Allen Swift is only a phone call away.

I only wish I were you so that I could know the sheer joy and security of working with me.

In all humility, I remain,

Cordially,

Allen

Allen Swift

SWIFT SPOTS

Letter to a Casting Director 1979

∞ ∞ ∞ ∞ ∞ ∞   ∞ ∞ ∞ ∞ ∞ ∞ ∞

Maybe the advertising people I worked with didn't believe comedy worked in commercials, but they certainly found me funny. I made them laugh, and it worked for me. I was booked for a recording session in Studio F at National Recording Studios when they were on Fifth Avenue and Fifty-Seventh Street. It was for a Revlon product. Studio F was locked. I knocked on the door, and the engineer opened it a crack and whispered conspiratorially, "Allen, we're running late. Can you wait?"

"Yeah, no problem." Although the studio behind him was dark, I had the feeling quite a few people were in there. Obviously, something hush-hush and important was going on. I had encountered this type of top-secret recording session every so often when a new product was coming to market. There was always an air of conspiracy.

Since I had three hours before my next recording session, I sat in the waiting room and read. An hour later, I went back and knocked on the locked door, and again, apologetically, I was asked to wait. After the second hour, the same exchange took place. This time, I informed the engineer that I had another session in an hour across town.

"Yeah, yeah, I'm sorry," he whispered. "I think we may be coming to the end—bear with me."

Twenty minutes before my next session, I was summoned. The room was still in darkness. William B. Williams came out of the announcer's booth as I went in. He obviously had been given quite a workout.

I had the script and decided I could give them just five minutes and then I would be out of there. I hate to arrive late and never do. Individuals always said they could set their watches by my arrivals at sessions. I finished in two takes and was out of the booth and hurriedly signing my contract.

The engineer was in discussion quietly with someone at the back of the darkened room. He came up to me and said, "Allen, they'd like you to stay and do another spot."

I realized then that they wanted me to redo the one William B. had just done. "I'm sorry—I'm out of time. I have to run. I have another session."

"Allen, it's important."

"I can't. Look, call my office, and make another session. Maybe there is something open for tomorrow. I don't have my schedule with me."

I was heading toward the door, when a loud, gravelly voice boomed out from the back of the darkened room.

"You'll stay and do this commercial, or you will never work in this industry again!"

The secret was out. That had to be Charlie Revson, the owner of Revlon. That was why the air was so thick and the engineer was so shaky. That man had the reputation of being one of the worst SOBs in the business.

I was at the door. I turned, pointed my finger in the direction of the voice, and said, "That, sir, is a threat. You are threatening me, and I warn you—if I never work in this industry again, never, never will my wife use any of your products. And I warn you—she uses a lot of makeup."

I walked out as the room erupted in laughter. The next day, I did the commercial he wanted me to do.

∞ ∞ ∞ ∞ ∞ ∞   ∞ ∞ ∞ ∞ ∞ ∞

I was at the top of my power and career. I could kid anyone without the worry of losing a job or a client, no matter who they were. I was so busy that I rode around town to the studios on a moped. It was one session after another, every day of the week. It became, simply, a routine. It lost its challenge. I had accomplished what I'd started out to do: make a living as an actor. In the midst of it all, I had an epiphany.

I suddenly remembered an art history teacher of my youth. She was a sweet old lady with a crackly voice whom I used to impersonate, to the laughter of all my classmates. The words she spoke at that time meant nothing to me. I just repeated them in her voice. One day, shortly after my run-in with Charlie Revson, I was telling a friend about her, and I repeated my impersonation for him. This time, however, the meaning of her words reverberated in my head: "'If I had two loaves of bread,' Mohammad said, 'I would sell one of them and buy sweet hyacinths to satisfy my hungry soul.'"

I decided right then that I didn't need more than one loaf. I had enough money, and I could do something for my soul. I could venture onto the boards and become a real actor, even a poor theater actor.

So bye-bye, commercials, and bye-bye, chutzpah! I didn't care where I worked. It could be out in the hinterlands—and it was. It was also on Broadway and off. It was in regional theaters, too. I played a slew of roles I'd always dreamed of playing, with some of the greatest actors in the theater and on film and some wonderful actors who were totally unknown.

This was a whole new life, where every role was a challenge. I would have to build a character from the ground up and have him grow through the play. I worked on plays by O'Neill, Chekhov, Arthur Miller, Emily Mann, Neil Simon, and Thornton Wilder—and even one Broadway play by Allen Swift.

Perhaps I shall write another book one day about my life in the theater. It was all made possible by my crazy ability to do voices and, to no less a degree, by my chutzpah!

As Morris Applebaum in *Checking Out*
by Allen Swift at The Longacre Theatre,
September 1976. Photo by Martha
Swope/©The New York Public Library.

Cast of The Iceman Cometh by Eugene O'Neill
1985-1986. Premiered at The Kennedy Center,
Washington, DC, then played The Lunt-Fontanne
on Broadway and The Doolittle in Los Angeles. l. to
r., 1st row: Carolyn Aarons, Director Jose Quintero,
Barnard Hughes, Donald Moffat, Leonardo Cimino,
Roger Robinson 2nd row: Kristine Nielson, Allen
Swift, James Greene, Jason Robards, Jr., John
Christopher Jones
3rd row: John Handy, ASM, Frank Askin, Bill Moor,
Walter Flanagan, Harris Laskwy, John Panko, Paul
McCrane,
Frederick Neumann, Paul Austin Back
row: Pat McNamara Photo by Martha
Swope/©The New York Public Library

As Shelly Levene in *Glengarry Glen Ross* by
David Mamet, Capital Rep Theatre, Albany
NY, & Philadephia Theatre Company, 1989.

As Ferapont in Chekov's *The Three Sisters,*
directed by Emily Mann, The McCarter Playhouse,
Princeton, NJ, January 10, 1992. Front row,
l-r:Laura San Giacomo, Frances McDormand, John
Christopher Jones, Mary Stuart Masterson, Robert
Baumgardner, Alexander Draper,
Allen Swift, Linda Hunt. Back row, l-r: Kurt
W. Coble, Paul McCrane, Edward Herrmann,
Josef Somer, Peter Francis James, Mark
Nelson, Mark Feuerstein, Jeff Glasse,
Gregory Wagner, Sandra Coulbourne, Myra
Carter. Photo © T. Charles Erickson.

As Malachi Stack in "The Matchmaker"
by Thornton Wilder, directed by Emily
Mann, The McCarter Theatre, Princeton
NJ, 1994. Photo ©T. Charles Erickson

Allen Swift and Michael Marcus as *The Sunshine Boys* by Neil Simon, George St. Playhouse & Syracuse Stage, 1997.

From left: Jim Bracchitta, Allen Swift, Marie Lillo, Heather Raffo, Joan Copeland, and Val Avery.

OVER THE RIVER
AND THROUGH THE WOODS

with

VAL AVERY   JIM BRACCHITTA   JOAN COPELAND
MARIE LILLO   HEATHER RAFFO   ALLEN SWIFT

THE JOHN HOUSEMAN THEATRE

As Nunzio *in Over the River and Through the Woods* by Joe DiPietro, Berkshire Theatre Festival 1997 & the John Houston Theatre, Theatre Row, NYC 1999.

Allen Swift

The real Ira Stadlen aka Allen
Swift. Photo by Leah Cohen

Afterword

For those readers who have only just discovered Allen Swift, I'm sorry to have to tell you that he is no longer with us. After a number of hospitalizations he chose to come home with hospice and he died peacefully, surrounded by his family, on April 18, 2010. He was 86.

Allen intended the cover of this memoir to feature Al Hirschfeld's caricature of him as Morris Applebaum in his play, *Checking Out*. He only mentioned the play in the book and I feel readers would want to know more.

An 83 year old widower and former star of the Yiddish theatre, Morris determines to skip the period of decline, loss of independence and suffering that commonly precedes dying. He invites his children and grandchildren to a farewell party, planning to end his life afterward at his own chosen time. His children, appalled, quickly travel from their distant homes to Morris' New York apartment, a skylit studio adorned with paintings of his wife's derriere by well-known artists of the ash-can school. They conclude that he is depressed and set out to cure him, to his increasing distress.

The subject-of-end of life choices was rarely discussed in 1976. In fact, in September, 1976, California became the first state to legally sanction living wills; it wasn't until 1992 that all fifty states had legalized advance directives. The play was not a treatise but the theme was serious, the conflict life-and-death, and the struggle between the ageing, Bohemian, unconventional parent and his adult children was touching and funny. The premiere at the Westport Playhouse in Westport, CT brought rave reviews, including in *MD, the Medical Newsmagazine*, and enthusiastic audiences. Produced by Philip Mathias and Ken Myers, it opened at the Longacre Theatre on Broadway on September 14, 1976. Audiences in New York were also wildly responsive, giving the play and Allen's performance standing ovations. But the New York critics were not as appreciative and it had a limited run. Al

Hirschfeld's wonderful drawing accompanied an article by John Corry in *The New York Times* on September 24, 1976.

The play has occasionally been produced in small theatres around the country. A rewritten version titled *The Endgame Kazotzky* came close to a production but Allen refused to honor the female star's request to enlarge her part. A film version of *Checking Out* starring Peter Falk was produced; Allen did not write the screenplay and it was radically changed from his script.

Among Allen's many rewarding theatre experiences besides those in the photos, he played several roles in Emily Mann's adaptation of Isaac Bathshevis Singer's *Meshuga,* which premiered at the Sundance Theatre Festival, and in Chekov's *The Cherry Orchard*, both at the McCarter Theatre in Princeton; Gregory Solomon in Arthur Miller's The Price (coincidentally, his son & my stepson, Lewis J. Stadlen, played the same role at The Abbey Theatre in Dublin in June 2014); Willie Clark in Neil Simon's The Sunshine Boys, and Grandpa in Kaufman and Hart's *You Can't Take It With You.*

In an earlier draft of this memoir Allen wrote, and I believe he intended to include, that magic remained an important part of his life – stage magic, conjuring, not mystical magic. Fascinated by the magic of the mind, he belonged to the Psychic Entertainers Association and to a wild mental think tank known among magicians as *The Legendary 13*. Considered tops in the field of mental magic, they love fooling each other and they have created some of the choice mental tricks of the profession.

Finally, due to the magic of the Internet, readers and fans can still enjoy him, seemingly alive and well, with Ira Gallen on youtube.com/Allen Swift Interviews. A search of Gene Deitch Allen Swift on Google will bring Gene's recounting of the first time he met and auditioned Allen, and their first film together, "Pump Trouble." His voices on other animated films can still be heard.

Lenore Loveman Stadlen
"the girl in the yellow dress"

Acknowledgements

If Allen could write this himself I know that he would thank, first, his dear friend, Mike Broun, for his creative encouragement and early edit of *Chutzpah!* He'd also acknowledge Audrey Lord-Hausman, I'm sure, as do I, most heartily, for her first edit of the complete book. As Allen's widow, and as a labor of love, I assumed responsibility for further editing and bringing the book to publication. Maxime and Clare Stadlen, our daughters, each gave me invaluable editorial comments and support. Lewis Stadlen, Allen's son and my stepson, suggested that I contact Chris Jerome whose generous advice was challenging and meaningful.

Allen had arranged with iUniverse to publish the book; Editorial Consultant Krista Hill and her associates provided enthusiasm and valid suggestions. For me, the process has been rewarding. I was able to relish Allen's stories yet again and relive many of our joyous and funny adventures. I take responsibility for those chapter titles I added, at the publisher's urging, for the choice of photos, and for any errors or oversights.

The cover design was drafted by Allen to feature Al Hirschfeld's drawing of him as Morris Applebaum in his play, *Checking Out.* I'm most grateful to Arline Meyer for creating the final design of the cover. John Handy, Chris Jones, Vicki Waddell Riggsbee, Mark and Dan Wingate, and Tom Miller of the McCarter Theatre in Princeton have my warm appreciation for their help identifying some of the actors in the photos.

Lenore Loveman Stadlen

Printed in the United States
By Bookmasters